Counseling
Military Families

Counseling Military Families

What Mental Health Professionals Need to Know

Lynn K. Hall

Foreword by Mary Edwards Wertsch

Routledge
Taylor & Francis Group
New York   London

Routledge
Taylor & Francis Group
270 Madison Avenue
New York, NY 10016

Routledge
Taylor & Francis Group
2 Park Square
Milton Park, Abingdon
Oxon OX14 4RN

© 2008 by Taylor & Francis Group, LLC
Routledge is an imprint of Taylor & Francis Group, an Informa business

Printed in the United States of America on acid-free paper
10 9 8 7 6 5 4 3 2 1

International Standard Book Number-13: 978-0-415-95688-8 (Softcover) 978-0-415-95687-1 (Hardcover)

Library of Congress Cataloging-in-Publication Data

Hall, Lynn K. (Lynn Karen), 1946-
    Counseling military families: what mental health professionals need to know / by Lynn K. Hall.
        p. ; cm.
    Includes bibliographical references and index.
    ISBN 978-0-415-95687-1 (hardbound : alk. paper)
    ISBN 978-0-415-95688-8 (paperback)
    1. Families of military personnel--Services for--United States. 2. Soldiers--United States--Psychology. 3. Family psychotherapy. I. Title.
    [DNLM: 1. Counseling--methods. 2. Military Personnel--psychology. 3. Attitude of Health Personnel. 4. Family--psychology. 5. Mental Health Services. WM 55 H177c 2008]

UB403.H35 2008
355.1'2--dc22   2008001571

Visit the Taylor & Francis Web site at
http://www.taylorandfrancis.com

and the Routledge Web site at
http://www.routledge.com

Contents

Foreword, by Mary Edwards Wertsch

Back in the mid-1980s, while doing research at a conference about military families, I heard one of the highest-ranking admirals in the Navy make a remark that had me grinding my teeth in fury.

He was the keynote speaker, and he clearly *thought* he was saying exactly what his audience largely composed of social workers, counselors, and spouses wanted to hear.

"I'm here to tell you," he thundered proudly, "that the *number one priority* of the United States Navy is the *military family!*"

My blood boiled. Was this supposed to be believable? Anyone who has any passing acquaintance with the military knows that the number one priority of the military is never going to be the military family. It is, and must by definition be, the military mission. Everything falls in line behind that. He would have been a better speaker, and a better leader, if he had grounded his talk on that simple acknowledgment of the reality we all know.

That reality is both the glory and the crucible of military families. It tests them to the limit. It is the source of their pride and, for many, their undoing. Nearly all military families, no matter how well informed, find themselves confronting challenges they had never imagined. They need all the support they can get.

Oh, how this book is needed.

Could there possibly be another set of American families as stressed on so many fronts as those in the military?

Even in peacetime, such families must cope with the extraordinary pressures of a very stringent and demanding way of life: a tightly controlled authoritarian system, with its lack of autonomy and limited privacy; financial stress; tours of duty that take father, mother, or both away from the family for long periods; frequent uprootings; and the ever-present possibility of injury or death. In addition, the youthfulness of service members, most of whom are married, means they may lack the wisdom and maturity to sort out the difficult problems they face—and this is only exacerbated by the extreme mobility of military life, which cuts them off from the emotional sustenance of relatives and friends that might otherwise see them through. If someone were asked to design an environment that would be as tough as possible on family systems, it would probably look a lot like the military.

Wartime, of course, is a thousand times harder. Death, injury, brain trauma, post-traumatic stress disorder (PTSD)—the list is long, and the tragedy is compounded by such factors as shortcomings in postcombat care, marriages that founder and crack, and increased alcohol abuse. Not only that, dual-career couples can be sent to combat zones simultaneously, throwing the family into maximum emotional stress. The children of those couples and of single parents could be orphaned at any time—and even if they escape such disaster, the stress of separation and worry takes its toll on all concerned.

Families that survive such challenges intact and functional are living testimony to the adaptability of the human spirit and the power of a purposeful life. It is unquestionable that the inherent nobility of service to one's country helps all military people justify the difficulties and sacrifice. That may strike some civilians as quaint, foolish, or irrelevant—but military families generally do not have to cast about for the meaningfulness of what they do day in, day out. That rock-bottom conviction is reinforced daily through interactions with others who live the same life of duty and service and carry the same sense of dedication.

People will put up with a lot if they believe it serves a noble cause.

But this book is not about military families that are the picture of resilience and psychological health. This book is about military families that are under tremendous pressure and near the breaking point—families struggling with loss and separation, social isolation, financial hardship, divorce and remarriage, substance abuse, family violence, and so on. It is the job of mental health professionals to help these families sort out their problems and address them constructively.

Could there possibly be another set of therapists faced with such overwhelming need, under such difficult conditions?

Mental health professionals working with military families must be broadly trained, extremely well informed, and tremendously adaptable. But even the most gifted and insightful therapists can be thwarted by the sudden transfer of clients long before therapeutic goals are reached or by the sheer enormity of the issues they are asked to address.

It is fortunate for all, however, with the publication of this book, Lynn K. Hall provides an essential tool for everyone giving aid and counsel to service members and their loved ones. She sets out the major mental health challenges faced by military families, gathers and organizes the accumulated wisdom of the past 20 years, and offers insights and techniques grounded in her many years as a school counselor. It is a great service. I believe that the two things therapists working with the military most need are a clear understanding of the military as a unique culture and an up-to-date knowledge base of recent studies, therapeutic approaches, changing conditions, and new resources. Lynn K. Hall provides both.

It is of critical importance that books such as this one emerge every few years to present current therapeutic approaches to the problems of a changing military. Nothing stays the same—and therapists badly need resources that keep up with realities.

One of the things I am most grateful for in this book is Lynn K. Hall's attention to the concept of "military as culture." And by "culture" I mean culture in the anthropological sense, not in the corporate sense or in the sense of a community's artistic capital. Although I was raised in a career Army family, I did not understand the extent to which I was the product of a particular culture, radically different from civilian America, until I embarked on the research for my book *Military Brats: Legacies of Childhood Inside the Fortress*, first published in 1991. The patterns of behavior, thinking, and lived experience among the adult military brats I interviewed were so similar and so powerful that it took my breath away. Every interview was an epiphany. I came to understand that all of us who were reared in career military families possessed something we never imagined could be ours: *roots*. Roots in a particular and very intense culture. Roots that shaped us as decidedly as any culture anywhere has ever shaped its children. Roots that were not geographically defined but that are the equal of any other in the training of minds and hearts. How strange that there could be a culture like this—impossible to define by race, religion, ethnicity, language, or location, yet every bit the architect of its children's cultural identity.

The discovery of my cultural roots inside the Fortress—my shorthand term for military culture—has made a tremendous difference in my own life. It put everything in perspective. It gave me a way to understand my Army family and myself. It opened the door to compassion for my relatives, for all military families, for all military brats. If I had been asked before I wrote the book if I had compassion for all these, I would have said yes, no question. But there is a big difference when compassion is grounded in understanding. It's stronger, deeper, and wiser, and it encompasses far more.

I believe that therapists who develop a thorough understanding of the military as culture put themselves well ahead of the game. Armed with a wider perspective, they are more likely to divine the hidden cultural factors playing into a situation, even if those are not apparent to the clients. It goes without saying that the next steps they suggest are more likely to take those embedded cultural factors into account. Although many therapists do this instinctively, and to good effect, it helps enormously if a therapist brings it all to the conscious level, where it can be examined, questioned, and enlarged. In fact, I would say that a key part of embracing the cultural perspective in working with military families is to adopt a sense of humility in the face of a culture as complex as the Fortress. It's simply a rock-bottom truth that there is always, always more to learn about the ways people are affected by this unique and intense way of life.

What do I mean by hidden cultural factors? To cite just one, in most cases there is an enormous experiential difference between the childhood of the career military parent and that of his or her child. Only a small percentage of career military members are military brats. The great majority comes from rural and small-town America—in other words, from rooted backgrounds. The attitudes and perspectives of a geographically rooted person are vastly different from those of someone who grew up moving, adapting, moving again, *and always knowing this move is not the last*. The mobile child does not identify with the parent's hometown, is not grounded in the stories of a single community over time, and almost certainly has a different concept of time (in which past, present, and future are not a smooth continuum but separate worlds with different casts of characters). He may have trouble focusing on distant goals. He is driven, once arrived in the new place, to set up a new social identity in the shortest time possible, which may have the effect of driving him toward out-groups, always the most permeable. He has certainly incorporated a sometimes contradictory assortment of behaviors and attitudes from the patchwork of places he's lived, which confuse and baffle those around him. If he's lived overseas, he may acquire a worldly demeanor as though he were mature beyond his years. At the same time, he may shockingly mishandle peer relationships—to the dismay of parents and teachers—simply because in moving around so much, he's missed some fundamental lessons about dealing with people over time. The frictions that arise between parent and child are often based in cultural difference and exacerbated by the fact that this difference is not perceived by either one. The therapist with a cultural perspective can illuminate the situation, feeding both parties talking points that help build understanding of themselves and one another as they work toward resolution.

A hidden cultural factor, sure—but like all such factors, it's hiding in plain sight. If those living that culture every day fail to notice, it's simply because, as the saying goes, they "can't see the forest for the trees."

Lynn K. Hall sheds light on another hidden cultural factor in her chapter "The Transition Journey," and I suspect counselors will find it especially helpful. What she does here, in pulling back to look at the forest, is identify "the overwhelming and constant issue of change and transitions, as well as grief and loss, experienced by virtually all military families." That military families undergo a lot of change is not news—but the *cultural* perspective on it is. As she has seen, this is a kind of loss that is not openly recognized by the military culture, where people learn to pave over their feelings and go on. She helped develop a technique, elaborated in this fine chapter, that is an important model of healing. "After almost 10 years in Department of Defense schools," she writes, "I believe that the greatest gift I left most of my students was a better understanding of the process and benefit of grieving, of the importance of understanding transitions."

Although the principal things that characterize the Fortress will never change—authoritarianism, mobility, officer–enlisted class difference, and the all-encompassing warrior mission of continual preparation for war—there are many things that do shift and evolve over time.

After 1973—when the draft was lifted and the all-volunteer force came into being—there were enormous changes in military families. Within a few years, the force became, for the first time in its history, majority married. In the years since, women have come to serve alongside men, including in combat. There are dual-career couples, and single parents. There are many blended families—Hall has an excellent section about stepfamilies in this book—and extended families that include other relatives.

One of the huge challenges facing mental health providers serving the military today is the extraordinary reliance on the Reserves and the National Guard to supplement regular active duty forces in the war effort. These activated members of the Reserves and Guard, many of them deployed to the combat zone multiple times, are older and married, and their civilian spouses and children are reeling from the stress. It's the mental health professionals, inside and outside the Fortress, who are on the front lines helping these families and their uniformed loved ones who are sick with worry.

One positive sign in the current situation is that there appears to be a gradual weakening of the age-old Fortress stigma against seeking help for mental health problems. But no culture in the world undergoes attitudinal change without a rocky period of transition in which, simultaneously, there are clear steps forward and steps backward. Lynn Hall, to her credit, paints a realistic portrait: A soldier fighting in Iraq now has the benefit of embedded mental health professionals in combat units—but upon return, that same soldier may turn to the Veterans Administration for help only to find that it ignores, underrates, or completely disavows mental health issues such as PTSD or depression. And the attitude of the soldier's superior toward such issues could be anywhere on the continuum, from outright contempt to compassionate support. There still are powerful pressures not to reach out for help—especially because therapists in the employ of the military cannot protect their clients' confidentiality; if the commander calls to inquire, they must reveal. Military people and the professionals there to help them are living in a time of confusion and mixed messages.

It remains to be seen if the Department of Defense will do what is necessary to completely eliminate the stigma. It will have to institute or revise policies and regulations, because that is the only way authoritarian societies change. In the military, more than anywhere else, it's the rules that shape the attitudes.

To its credit, the Department of Defense now spends much more money on family services, the result of surveys in the 1990s showing that family dissatisfaction was the primary reason expensively trained members were leaving the service early.

As Lynn K. Hall writes, the guiding dictum of Department of Defense thinking today is, "Family readiness is essential to unit readiness." What a contrast to the reigning dictum of the Fortress in which my baby boomer peers and I grew up: "If the military had wanted you to have a family, it would have issued you one."

That new dictum is one that military families can bank on, unlike the self-serving misrepresentations of that top-brass speaker 20 years ago. I believe that, because that sentence articulates an institutional realization firmly based on survey findings, backed by statistics, and underpinned by the crucial need to improve retention.

Families will always find the military an extremely challenging life. They will always encounter the unexpected. They will always be tested. And they will always need up-to-snuff mental health professionals to help them navigate rough waters and arrive at a calmer place.

That's why we can all be grateful for this book.

Preface

Right up front, I need to say that I am not, nor have I ever been, in the military or a member of a military family. So to some readers, I might appear suspect in that I am attempting to describe "them"—a culture that I have not personally lived in. I hope that my attempts to do so, for others like me to be most effective, are done with respect, care, and a sense of honor for the military establishment and the people who give their lives to it.

I spent over 9 years working as a school counselor for the Department of Defense Dependent Schools System (DoDDS) in Germany, working on a daily basis with the children and families of the military. I have also watched and experienced my son in his life as an enlisted noncommissioned officer (NCO) and career airman, go through the levels of training and advancement while married with three children. But it was probably reading the actual accounts of service members and their families that helped me most understand the devotion, the sacrifice, and the dilemmas that make these remarkable people and their families who they are.

My purpose in writing this book is not to outline the one right counseling technique, theory, or methodology for working with military families. As with any area of counseling, there is such diversity among our clients that there is never one approach that will fit all clientele. It is a little misleading to even think that any one person or one style could, in fact, be the only approach for all military families, because there is not *one* military family. Military families are as diverse as civilian families, so it was my challenge in writing this book to draw the readers' attention to the unique culture of the military and also the multitude of variables within military families.

This is also not an attempt to write everything there is to know about military families; that would be like someone attempting to include in one small volume everything there is to know about any other unique population—Hispanic families, Anglo families, southern families, rural families, Norwegian American families. It just can't happen. So I will say, as an early disclaimer, this is just a beginning; a place to start thinking about this amazing group of Americans who serve our country and, in so doing, serve the world. I hope that no one reading this book will rely solely on this work for their learning; let this be a start for more questions, more inquiries, and more interest and concerns for the families that make up the military.

Rather than write as the expert, I have instead attempted to bring together the writing and research of numerous individuals whose knowledge, training, and insights will be valuable to counselors who find themselves working with military families. Early in my quest to write this book, I found a Web-based search for counseling military families in which there were only three books listed, so it became apparent that not a lot has been written about working with military families for the civilian counselor. The information in this book comes from resources as diverse as Mary Wertsch's information on military culture and military kids; John and Emily Vishers' seminal work on stepfamilies; the research done by the Military Research Institute at Purdue University; the work done at the Center for Posttraumatic Stress Disorder through the Veterans Administration; the resources available from the Military Child Education Coalition; the National Coalition Against Domestic Violence, the RAND Corporation, the National Institute on Alcohol Abuse; the Department of Defense; and a plethora of Web sites directed to and for military families.

In particular I am grateful for one of the first works done in the area of working with military families back in 1984 by Kaslow and Ridenour, as well as for Kaslow's later work, a more recent edited work by Martin, Rosen, and Sparacino, and the very new work edited by Figley and Nash. I have also shared information from the numerous interviews I did during the past year with a number of experts in the field and with civilian counselors who are now working with military families. In addition I also included two areas of particular interest to me that I have spent a great deal of time on in the past 20 years and I hope to have developed some expertise in: the area of the transitions we all experience in life and the grief and loss that go along with them, and the area of divorce and stepfamilies. My goal is to bring these varied sources of information together so that, as much as possible, one resource can include the basic information needed for civilian counselors to get started working with military families.

I have not attempted to create a body of knowledge that will inform psychiatrists and other professionals who work with severely injured or stressed individuals in an in-patient facility. Rather I am hoping to provide basic information for the civilian mental health professional working with service members and their families who need the caring concern and safe environment to process their distress, take care of their transitional and life cycle issues, and make positive decisions for their future.

I mentioned how much I have relied on a few edited scholarly works, but I couldn't have done this without the personal reflections of Kate Blaise, Kristin Henderson, and Mary Wertsch, as well as the work of journalist Karen Houppert, who interviewed many military spouses for her book. It was the personal stories in these books, as well as many news articles and military Web sites, that kept me going.

As time has gone by, while I was writing this book, the war in Iraq and Afghanistan has continued and daily newscasts have reported the future of that war and the impact that war is having and will continue to have on the families of the military serving there. It won't be over by the time this book is published, so I cannot begin to predict the future or write about what military families might have to face in the future. Therefore, I have attempted to touch on the consistent and more general issues that all military families face, regardless of the time in history.

It is imperative that civilian services and programs that target military populations begin to have additional information to better prepare to meet the needs of the families of service members in their communities. To get you started in your journey, I definitely recommend that, while reading this book, you find one of the books listed in the reference section written by or about military families. If you can't experience the military first-hand, reading about someone who has experienced it is a very good way to understand what life really is like for those in the military. I hope this will help you better understand the "heart of a soldier" and the heart of the military family.

Acknowledgments

I probably would never have even considered writing this book if it had not been for the students and their families who allowed me into their lives for the nearly 10 years I was a school counselor in the military dependent school system in Germany. It was from their sharing, their experiences, and their openness that I started to appreciate and understand the uniqueness of families in the military. So my first acknowledgment is to all of those families who taught me so much; I only wish I could reach them all to thank them personally, but, being military brats, they are probably scattered to all parts of the globe by now.

I also can't imagine how I could have completed this without the support of those counselors, psychologists, psychiatrists, and social workers who were willing to spend time with me to share their personal experiences and expertise in the area of counseling military families. I have tried to keep the information they shared as confidential as possible so that none of their clients would be harmed in any way, but I want to list them here as a special thanks, not just for the time they spent with me but for the love and care they give to all of the military service members and families who come to them for support, guidance, safety, and direction. Thanks so much to the following people:

Beth Banks, MA, LPC, LISAC, Tucson, Arizona
JoLynne Buehring, LCSW, Sierra Vista, Arizona
Harry Butler, PhD, LCSW, San Diego, California
Jan Comer, MA, LPC, Tucson, Arizona
Gerald Evans, MD, Honolulu, Hawaii

Michael Hand, PhD, El Paso, Texas
Susan Hansen, MA, MFCC, San Diego, California
Lynne Harrison, PhD, Tucson, Arizona
Toni Leo, PhD, Sierra Vista, Arizona
Catherine Ohrin-Greipp, MSW, LCSW, BCD, Sierra Vista, Arizona
Barbara G. Palmer, PhD, Tucson, Arizona
Chris Pinhey, PhD, Tucson, Arizona
Kay E. Towers, LCSW, La Jolla, California

In addition, a few other people were willing to share their personal stories with me about their experiences with and in the military. John Bourdette, PhD, Silver City, New Mexico, grew up as a military brat, served 8 years in the Army Medical Corps counseling Vietnam veterans, and has spent the past 17 years teaching at and directing the chemical dependency program at Western New Mexico University. Suzanne Thomas, MPT, is a physical therapist in Silver City, New Mexico, and a captain in the U.S. Army Reserve. She spent 13 months on active duty in Ft. Sill, Oklahoma, as a physical therapist so that an active duty therapist there could be deployed to Iraq. To fulfill her commitment to the Army Reserve, she gave up her practice, let her four employees go, and shut her doors. Wanda Hall is the former director of the Hospice Program in Silver City, New Mexico, and knows more than anyone I can imagine about grief and loss, but more important she is the guardian of her two small grandchildren while her daughter is deployed in Iraq.

Of course I mostly want to thank my family, especially my husband, Court Hall, who so painstakingly drove me to all my interviews, put up with my late nights on the computer, and read the entire manuscript before I completed the final draft. I also want to thank my three stepdaughters, who are always cheering me on, and all seven of our grandkids (ages 3 to 10), who didn't help at all in the writing of the book but who someday will be able to read a book by their Oma. And finally a special thank-you to my sons: Chris O'Hern, who always challenges me to think outside the box, and Jeff O'Hern, my Air Force son, who has taught me more about what it takes to be in a military family than I could have ever learned from any other source.

PART 1
Setting the Stage

CHAPTER 1

Introduction

Rationale and Purpose

A staff sergeant (SSgt), John, and his wife, Paula, are self-referred for counseling for acute marital distress following John's return from his second tour in Iraq. The SSgt has filed for divorce. The couple has been married for 10 years and has two children. Before he joined the service, they had struggled with marital issues around how she spent money and the amount and frequency of his drinking. This conflict had abated until after his first deployment and has now escalated over the past 3 years, getting worse after his second tour in Iraq. They separated briefly after his first deployment following an argument that became physically aggressive on both their parts, but they later reconciled.

During the second deployment, Paula had an affair with an officer in the medical corps. Although John is very angry with his wife, he says he loves her and does not want to lose her or break up the family. Paula is feeling guilty and sorry for the affair, but she is also angry with him for his emotional distance, anger, and drinking. The SSgt had experienced intense combat and survived two improvised explosive devise (IED) attacks where others under his command were killed, and he was slightly wounded. He downplays any lingering emotional or physical symptoms, but his wife reports that he has frequent nightmares, is drinking more, is emotionally distant, and has volatile and unpredictable moods. She is also having difficulty sleeping, has gained weight, and generally feels hopeless and lethargic.

What do we need to know to work with this family? Where do we start? How do we intervene? As Paul Harvey questioned in so many of his news broadcasts, what is "the rest of the story"? It is hoped that in the following chapters you will learn about the military, military families, and the ways that have been shown to work in a therapeutic setting with the military. As you do that, keep this family in mind, as the complete case study, or the rest of the story, is available in chapter 10, with a set of discussion questions for you to ponder.

The Need for Services

When I began to envision writing a book in late 2004 about counseling military families, I never imagined the enormity of the need that existed. After concluding the writing, I still have no idea of what the future will bring for our military families. This first section was to be a rationale for the book, but the rationale is being established instead by global events. More and more civilian counselors are working with military families and couples, both because military families are going off base for assistance and because the military is now employing, through employment-assistant–type programs (EAP), civilian counselors to help with the enormity of the task.

The National Military Family Association's (NMFA) *Report on the Cycles of Deployment* (Jumper et al., 2006) confirms that there is a profound need for more professional counselors. The counselors interviewed for this book, who are currently working with military families, all agree that the need exists and will continue to grow. Houppert (2005b) reported that there has been a 300% increase in overseas deployments in the past decade in a military force that has been cut by more than one third. Families are stressed, sometimes beyond the breaking point. We know the need is there and growing, so the question becomes how do we meet the need. The NMFA's report (Jumper et al., 2006) pointed out that the need for counselors who are assigned to unit family readiness groups, as well as on-call professionals, is huge.

Troubled families or emergency situations are currently being thrust on often inadequately trained volunteer family members, because professionals who should be available are often few and far between. More professional support must be directed to the unit level to assist families in meeting these challenges. The study also pointed out that integrating the "suddenly military" families, families of the National Guard and Reserves, into the support system needs to begin prior to the activation of the service member and continue through reintegration of the service member back into the community. A recently formed program called Military OneSource (http://www.militaryonesource.com) remains the best example of a joint family readiness program that is not dependent on a family's service or geographic location. It is, in essence, an EAP that is provided by civilian counselors.

Often military families need assistance in developing realistic expectations about what they can and cannot do, but they do not feel their need is of such a crisis or long-term concern that they need the services of a psychiatrist or a psychologist. They also may believe they have to handle everything on their own, because asking for help would reflect badly on the service member. As Jumper et al. (2006) pointed out, counselors and volunteers should never assume families know what they need to know. Even experienced family members may find new challenges during a subsequent deployment or find that the accumulated stress from multiple deployments can become overwhelming. "A consistent level of resources is crucial in giving them the flexibility to create the comprehensive, responsive support system families need in order to succeed in the face of repeated deployments" (p. 9).

Rotter and Boveja actually debated in their 1999 article if there was sufficient interest in this population to even warrant a journal article, but even then they decided that it was "clear that a substantial portion of our population is affected by what happens to families in the military" (p. 379). They noted at the time there were 2.3 million active duty and reserve U.S. military personnel, and when spouses, children, and living former members of the military and their families were added to the mix, the total figure accounted for close to one third of the U.S. population. Indeed, they stated, "A significant portion of the citizenry is either presently functioning under potentially threatening, stressful situations or have experienced such in the past" (p. 379).

Why Civilian Counselors

Civilian counselors can be trained to help military families meet their needs, but it is essential that we understand the worldview, mind-set, and culture of the military before attempting to intervene and work with these families. My primary goal in this endeavor is to bring together researched and documented information to assist civilian counselors in working with military families. I am not the expert, even though I have years of experience working with military families and their dependents; those who are currently working with and researching the concerns of the military families are the experts, and it is my goal to bring their voices together in one document to assist those who might be interested and empower them to better work with this segment of our population.

David Crary (2007) quoted a mother from Georgia who states that when families talk to counselors, nobody understands them, particularly with the huge losses the families of the military have to deal with. Even though the military has made great strides by improving schools, health programs, and child care (Crary, 2007), they have never before been faced with the toughest problem of all, which is doing right by the ever-growing ranks of the bereaved.

> There is no greater need than for Congress to ensure access to quality mental health services and programs for service members, returning war veterans, their families, and survivors ... as well as easily-accessible and responsive mental health services, from stress management programs and preventative mental health counseling through therapeutic mental health care. (Raezer, 2007, p. 1)

Both the Army Mental Health Advisory Team III (MHAT-III, 2006) and IV (MHAT-IV, 2007) reports further link the need to address family issues as a means of reducing stress on deployed service members. The teams from both years found that the top noncombat stressors were deployment length and family separation. Soldiers serving a repeat deployment reported greater acute stress than those on their first deployment. Although service members who had deployed more than once said they were better prepared because of improved predeployment training, they said their families were experiencing more stress. The reports also determined the leading suicide risk factors were relationship issues at home and "in theatre" (see glossary in Appendix F).

The most recent MHAT-IV (2007) findings added that marital concerns relating to deployment length were rated higher than in previous surveys. As service members and families experience numerous lengthy and dangerous deployments, the NMFA (Raezer, 2007) believes the need for confidential, preventative mental health services will continue to rise and remain high even after military operations scale down in Iraq and Afghanistan. They continue to hear from families that more must be done to link service members and families with the services they require and find ways for the families to get the information they need about post-traumatic stress disorder (PTSD) and other mental health issues. Families want to know mental health services are available when they or their service member needs them. They want to know how to recognize the danger signs for themselves, their children, and the service member, and they want to know that seeking care will result in improved health at no danger to their service member's career (Raezer, 2007).

The Increasing Need

Navy Commander Mark Russell, in an article for *USA Today* ("Military Faces Mental Crisis," 2007), stated, "Mental health trauma is on the rise. Army studies show that more than a third of combat-deployed troops seek mental health care when they return home" (¶ 9). In a survey done by Commander Russell from 2003 to 2005, 90% of psychiatrists, psychologists, and social workers report that they received no formal training or supervision in PTSD therapies.

In addition, more of those mental health workers who are actually in the military are being deployed overseas, thereby depleting the resources at home, as well as increasing the burnout and making it difficult to keep skilled therapists. The Army has contracted with civilian mental health professionals to help meet this huge need. The *Statement Before the Department of Defense Task Force on Mental Health* (NMFA, 2006) pointed out, "The military fuels the shortage of deploying some of its child and adolescent psychology providers to the combat zones. Providers remaining at home stations report they are frequently too busy treating active duty members who have either returned from deployment or are preparing to deploy to fit family members into their schedules" (p. 8).

Despite the well-known stigma about seeking mental health services, addressed later in this chapter, many families actually report that they seek counseling either during the deployment or after the reunion (Raezer, 2007). Both the 2006 and 2007 MHAT reports indicate that the stigma is being reduced, and more service members are seeking counseling and mental health support, even though families remain concerned their service members are not seeking the care they need. Certainly with the current global situation, families are also concerned (Raezer, 2007) that they and their service members do not have enough time to adjust before the service member must deploy again. They worry the service member will not have access to the mental health services they need to monitor medication and continue their care.

In many service communities, just as in many civilian communities, there is a shortage of child and adolescent mental health providers. According to the NMFA (Raezer, 2007), the Department of Defense and Congress have worked to increase the resources available to enhance mental health care for service members and families, but the challenges are increasing at a faster pace than resources. "Ensuring the strong mental health of service members and their families is a readiness issue and the cost of ensuring that health is a cost of war" (p. 1).

Family Preparedness

In the NMFA's *Statement Before the Department of Defense Task Force on Mental Health* (2006), family readiness is imperative for service member readiness; therefore the emotional well-being and mental health of service members are linked to those of their families. Family well-being affects a service member's entire career from recruitment to retention to retirement. The NMFA calls for the Department of Defense to refine and improve the mental health support for families and service members to retain highly trained and qualified service members. The report stated, "No need is greater for military family readiness than a robust continuum of easily-accessible and responsive mental health services, from stress management programs and preventative mental health counseling through therapeutic mental health care" (p. 4).

The authors of the NMFA statement shared that there is a need to expand services and support the program already in existence, called Military OneSource. Military OneSource is available for active duty service members and their families, as well as for Guard and Reserves members and their families, regardless of whether they are activated. This program enables service members and families to receive up to six free face-to-face mental health visits with a professional outside the chain of command. The counseling through Military OneSource is not what the military terms "medical mental health counseling" but rather assistance for family members in dealing with the stresses of deployment or reunion—or the kind of service that most professionally licensed mental health counselors are trained to provide. This kind of service "can be an important preventative to forestall more serious problems down the road" (p. 5). It is certainly unclear how civilian counselors will be called on in the future to contribute to the mental health needs of the military, so it is imperative that we be ready to aid in the prevention and initial intervention stages to support our troops and their families.

> The world is a dangerous place and American military forces can be called on at any time to deploy to hostile locations around the globe. Meanwhile, today's military family members, like those who came before, continue to share a disproportionate burden for family life while experiencing the universal tradition of waiting, worrying, and, for some, grieving. Civilian human service providers engaged in roles that involve service and support to military families can take pride in knowing that their efforts contribute to the well-being of these families and therefore our nation's military readiness. (Martin & McClure, 2000, p. 4)

Continuum of Care

It is important for civilian counselors to understand and recognize that a number of services already exist for military members and families, such as the Military and Family Life Consultant program (see the resource list in the Appendix A), which is preventative in nature and designed to reach out proactively to service personnel and their families with assistance as they cope with the stressors of deployment and reunion. However, numerous studies show that "families continue to raise concerns that more providers who can do long-term counseling and treatment are needed" (NMFA, 2006, p. 7). As recent as April 2007, the Department of Defense Task Force on Mental Health (2007b) met to make recommendations to the Department of Defense regarding their findings after visiting 38 military installations worldwide.

Even more chilling are the stories we are hearing (Ephron & Childress, 2007), such as the story about the young soldier who returned after 16 men in his unit had died in 2 days. After leaving the military and after almost a year of flashbacks and panic attacks, he finally decided to seek help at the local Veterans Administration hospital, only to be put on hold over and over, even though he clearly stated he felt suicidal. He was told that he was number 26 on a waiting list and encouraged to call back periodically. He got drunk and hanged himself.

"How well do we care for our wounded and impaired when they come home?" (Ephron & Childress, 2007, ¶ 4). The question has profound moral implications. "We send young Americans to the world's most unruly places to execute our national policies. About 50,000 service members so far have been banged up or burned, suffered disease, lost limbs or sacrificed something less tangible inside them" (¶ 5). The authors of the *Newsweek* investigation (Ephron & Childress, 2007) focused on the Department of Veterans Affairs bureaucracy that provides medical care to service members from the time they are released from the military. Although it is not my purpose here to jump on the bandwagon and point out all the problems with the Veterans Administration, the report paints a grim portrait of

> an overloaded bureaucracy cluttered with red tape; veterans having to wait weeks or months for mental-health care and other appointments; families sliding into debt as VA case managers study disability claims over many months, and the seriously wounded requiring help from outside experts just to understand the VA's arcane system of rights and benefits. (¶ 8)

These kinds of concerns in the future can be partially alleviated by the presence of trained and informed civilian counselors who can step up and provide the much-needed services. The long-term cost of caring for veterans projects that at least 700,000 veterans from the global war on terror will flood the system in the coming years. Ephron and Childress (2007) stated that it is clear that the Veterans Administration does not have the capacity to process a large number of disability claims at the same time. One spokesman from the Veterans Administration confirmed that it is coping with a backlog of 400,000 applications and appeals—most of those filed by veterans of previous wars. As more service members return from Iraq, the backlog will only increase.

Taking Its Toll

What distinguishes this conflict from previous wars is the number of service members who don't die but suffer appalling injuries. In Vietnam and Korea, about three Americans were wounded for every one who died; the ratio in World War II was about two wounded for each death. In Iraq, 16 soldiers are wounded or get sick for every one who dies (Ephron & Childress, 2007). In addition, those who do return injured are often amputees or injured in such grievous fashion that it will take years of treatment, both psychological and physical, for them to heal. The young veteran who hanged himself was twice turned away from the Veterans Administration, the second time because he was told alcoholics must dry out before being accepted into an inpatient program. A spokesperson for the Veterans Administration who wanted to remain anonymous was quoted in the article as saying, "The system does not treat mental health with the same urgency it treats general health care" (Ephron & Childress, 2007, ¶ 21). It is hoped that civilian counselors who understand and are interested in working with military service members and their families can begin to take up some of the slack.

John Clark (2006), in a letter to the editor of the American Counseling Association's *Counseling Today* newspaper, stated, "We have been recognizing and honoring the correlation between a soldier's home life and job performance" (p. 4) since 1965. It was called the "X Factor" for years, because it was understood that the stress and strain on relationships is real and traumatic. "I would suggest the focus be on support; normalizing the anger, fear and sadness; and working to accept the major changes in the relationship. War and war games change the person; new roles change the spouse. Counseling can help to move the partners to acceptance and embracement of the new 'other' " (p. 4).

I could not say it any better. Although we might believe that the military would have the capacity to care for its members, as well as for their families, the fact is that they don't, and the military is very aware of the problems and needs that are being created for the future. As the number of families that need services increases, civilian counselors are being called on to work with military families, either during active duty or later. In many cases, these civilian counselors, although well trained in therapeutic theory and techniques, do not have an understanding of the military culture. Numerous reasons why these services are not available and what is causing the increased need for these services are pointed out in chapter 2 when we explore the difference between the military in the days of the draft versus the all-volunteer military. Although the military has taken major steps in the past two decades to meet the needs of military families, there will be greater and greater need for families and service members to find civilian counselors who understand their unique needs and can work with them to reach their personal and emotional goals.

> When the approximately 300,000 U.S. service members deployed overseas finally head home … they won't be ready for the emotional reality of their homecoming—and America won't be equipped to support them.… The need for this counseling is only going to increase the longer this conflict goes on. (Marshall, 2006, p. 32)

This book is for those counselors—counselors who are working in the civilian sector with a unique population that they might not yet truly understand. As civilian counselors, we must be equipped to deal with the issues unique to the military. Martin and McClure (2000) contended that civilian human service providers will play an increasingly important role in the delivery of health and social services to military members and their families. "Contracted civilian employees, contracted services, other forms of privatization, fee-for-service arrangements, and even military–civilian community partnerships in the delivery of services will continue to evolve" (p. 20), and in most cases these services will come from professionals who typically will not have any personal experience in the military and, more than likely, will have little professional preparation for working with military families. It is hoped that this information can enhance the exchange of knowledge between military and civilian communities on issues related to morale, health, and well-being of military service members and their families. Developing better knowledge about these families' experiences is vital to the military mission.

The Stigma Against Seeking Help

"The whole culture of the military is that you don't talk about feelings or emotions" (Marshall, 2006, p. 32). One of the long-held beliefs about the military is that service members are hesitant to seek psychological help and are especially concerned about the risk of seeking support from civilian providers. Pryce, Ogilvy-Lee, and Pryce (2000) stated that this stigma is influenced by the pervasive philosophy of the "right stuff," which implies that those who have it (the right stuff) do not need assistance to cope with the demands and stress of the military. In addition, another inhibitor in the use of human service programs, especially counseling, by the military and their families is a belief that the use of such services is widely perceived as having an adverse impact on the military member's career. According to a retired psychiatrist, this stigma is still pervasive, but currently the level is more conditional and often based on the particular branch of the service, a particular unit and commander, or even rank and grade. He explained that the Marines and the Army still seem much less accepting of seeking mental health services, whereas the Air Force is more likely to see it as a way of maintaining personal health and wellness to complete the mission. A major reason for this concern is the lack of confidentiality, which is often limited in the military human service setting, compared to the civilian mental health setting, because all actions are subject to review by the military member's commander. The consequence, as a therapist in San Diego pointed out, is that the military often distrusts military counselors. He gave the example of a naval officer client who stated, "You can be depressed while in command of an aircraft carrier but you will be relieved of command if you seek treatment for the depression" (Butler, personal communication, October 6, 2006).

There are many reasons for this stigma, which will be addressed a number of times throughout the book, but the most important thing is to understand that it is real and has to be explicitly acknowledged in counseling. Kennedy (2004) pointed out that service members are concerned that they will be stigmatized by seeking any type of counseling, so counselors must be able to assure the family of confidentiality. In addition, it is helpful for counselors to point out that rather than demonstrating weakness, seeking counseling is both a sign of strength and an act of valuing the family unit. Also, the family must be assured that the "command" will not be made aware of the request for treatment, as the stigma does exist and has, on some occasions, affected the progress of service members in the military. Whether this concern is valid often depends on factors such as the value a particular commander puts on counseling, the tradition of a certain branch of the military and even of the particular unit the service member is a part of.

The assumption of the military, at least in the past, was that if a lapse in competence is the only time that one might get killed, then it follows "that if they need professional mothering, as offered by any psychotherapist, it must mean they allowed a lapse in their competence" (Keith & Whitaker, 1984, p. 153). When family members seek available assistance, they will be concerned about the impact that acknowledging distress may have on career advancement and therefore believe it is necessary to seek assistance from the private sector. It is because of this that civilian counselors and family therapists need to make their services known to the local military community so that referrals can be made to accommodate these concerns. Civilian counselors in communities where military establishments exist may find it helpful to network with those entities in the military community that offer services and provide some collaborative activities.

Embedding Mental Health Professionals

Despite this history, one of the practices in some current combat zones is the embedding of mental health professionals into the units; a retired psychiatrist explained that mental health services have increased exponentially in the past decade more because of what he called "the possibility of disaster" than because of a current need. In reality, he said, many are sitting around without much to do, but they are there in case they are needed. By having mental health professionals available within the military unit, the regular practice of talking to a professional may inadvertently lower the stigma of seeking help.

In the analysis of the survey completed by the NMFA (Jumper et al., 2006), it was reported that a great number of respondents did recognize counseling as an option for them, and that families believe counseling is especially helpful if it is confidential and professional. Often the respondents requested anger management classes and family counseling for the service member, spouse, and children. In addition, almost half of the respondents commented that they have used or would use counseling. This percentage was even greater among families who had dealt with multiple deployments. Three quarters of the respondents stated they were better able to deal with subsequent deployments after counseling.

Overcoming the Stigma

When a congressional task force determined what factors must be addressed to enhance the mental health of service members, a major issue reported in the *Proceedings of the Task Force on Mental Health Care* (Department of Defense Task Force on Mental Health, 2007b) was the awareness and willingness to access services by the service member. Task force members pointed out that family involvement is critical in raising awareness of the service member regarding mental health services and in reducing the still-present stigma that discourages some members from seeking these services. An article in the *Arizona Daily Star* (Alaimo, 2006b) stated, "Getting soldiers to seek help can be tricky in a macho environment where troops tend to fear negative career impact if they're seen as weak or unable to cope" (p. B1). Personnel from Ft. Huachuca, Arizona, stated that the army has "done a lot to overcome the stigma. Soldiers are starting to figure out that it's smart to get help.... The smart people do something about it. They don't want to be one of the statistics" (Alaimo, 2006b, p. B2).

A civilian counselor, who lives near a major military installation and primarily works with military clients, stated that the commander always knew, in the past, if a service member or family member went to counseling because the referral had to come from the on-base behavioral health unit. However, because of recent funding cuts of on-post services, and, in some cases, the elimination of behavioral and mental health positions, a new policy in 2006 at that installation required all dependent care must come from private or civilian sources. As more and more families became aware that services existed off post, they began to contact the civilian counselor directly rather than go through the referral service, thereby eliminating the need for the commander to know about the service.

Another civilian counselor often heard from his military clients that they came to him because of a negative bias about on-base professionals, feeling that the care they received on base was often inferior. This counselor mostly works with lower-ranking enlisted service members and has not felt from his clients the fear of being weak or being seen as incompetent because they were going to counseling. He did, however, believe that fear might be greater for officers or even career enlisted. A civilian psychologist who does work with officers explained that military members, particularly officers, often want to pay in cash to eliminate any possibility of having their visits recorded. Most of the issues faced by the clients that this therapist worked with had to do with relationship problems, including anxiety and fear most often related to divorce and separation issues, rather than with anything related to their military careers. However, as members of the Department of Defense Task Force on Mental Health reiterated in their hearing in April 2007, relationship issues should be resolved before sending service members into combat, as it is often the unsolved problems at home that produce concerns in theatre.

A psychologist who often worked with naval officers confirmed this fear by stating that the officers he saw believed that if they go to services on base, they will not be confidential, for instance in the case of a navy officer who had an affair with the wife of his commander. Attempting to have some anonymity in situations like this would be virtually impossible if seeking help from a counseling service within the military community. It is unfortunate that situations exist where service members are not allowed to get the service they need, even when counseling is working and has a commander's blessing. One male single-parent service member who had been deployed three times had worked with a civilian counselor for six sessions but, because of cutbacks, the commander would not sign off for additional sessions. This young man had significant, ongoing family issues for which he was getting much needed and appreciated assistance, particularly in light of his three deployments, when he had to leave his children with grandparents. In another situation, a young airman with marital problems believed there was no stigma attached to seeing a counselor and didn't believe that it would affect his career, but because counselors were hired on a contract basis to provide on-base service for 3 to 6 months only, he and his wife were forced to see three different therapists within a time span of fewer than 6 months.

None of the civilian counselors I interviewed for this book had heard of actual cases where seeking mental health care actually affected a service member's record, but virtually every military client they saw mentioned that concern. Civilian counselors are used to a world where a group of people who feels that something is unjust often join together to force the powers that be to change; but in the military, there is often a belief that one cannot fight the system. As we will see in chapter 3, the military is, and must be, an authoritarian system, and therefore the level of vulnerability is high, because the families and service members have relatively few options. Although the military community can be, and usually is, very supportive, it is up to the individuals to get involved and seek out that support. We know that some do, and others tend to isolate themselves, which, in the long run, creates additional problems.

The statement made by the NMFA (2006) reported, "Some service members and families feel the stigma against seeking mental health care and choose to try to 'ride out' the rough spots on their own" (p. 10). However, on the basis of its survey data and conversations with family members, the NMFA reported that the increased stress caused by multiple deployments is, in fact, causing more families to seek help. And, as the report pointed out, although the increased stress is bad news, the good news is that many now recognize counseling as an acceptable and necessary option for them. The MHAT-III's report, made public in December 2006 (Harben, 2006) stated that soldiers reported that they have better access to behavioral health care when it is needed, and more soldiers report receiving care. The concerted effort on the part of the military to reduce the stigma attached to receiving behavioral health services is evidently paying off. The number of soldiers reporting items such as "avoiding care" to "avoid being seen as weak" on the advisory team survey has decreased significantly since the last report in 2004.

It appears that for the first time in combat history, the embedding of psychological support (Department of Defense Task Force on Mental Health, 2007b) within combat units in the Iraq and Afghanistan theatre may play a large role in the categories of "avoiding care" and "avoiding being seen as weak." One of the suggestions made to the task force by the soldiers was that if all military members were required to get mental health assessment and evaluations, just like they do medical care, the stigma might soon fade away. The MHAT-III report (2006) did point out that even though 80% of those who suffered from serious mental disorders acknowledged that they had a problem, only 44% were interested in receiving assistance, and just 35% actually got formal help. The Department of Defense Task Force (2007b) members found that up to 50% say they believe that seeking help would be damaging to their career. So although there was some improvement in the attitudes toward seeking assistance, many soldiers are still clearly concerned that they will be stigmatized as having a weakness, which could hurt their military careers.

It also needs to be considered that the stigma issue may be greater than what is reported here or by most of the surveys. Suffice it to say that it is a major issue in the military and will probably continue to be, as "seeking help implies a personal weakness, a moral weakness as measured against the macho code" (Keith & Whitaker, 1984, p. 150). To actually understand this stigma at a much deeper level, we must understand the issues, which are discussed in more detail in chapter 3, regarding the military culture and the major psychological component of honor and sacrifice and the shame that exists if these cannot be fulfilled. The concern of all warriors, regardless of the time in history, that they may not be good enough to fulfill the mission and support their comrades or that they may be seen as a failure and not able to hold up their end of the bargain, or any combination of these, is far greater than just a surface look at why military members have traditionally avoided seeking mental health services.

The Need for Culturally Competent Counselors

As this book evolved, it became not so much a book about what to do as a counselor in working with the great variety and diverse aspects of military families but instead a book about discovering the unique culture of the military and what happens in the life of military families. We must, as counselors and human beings, first become aware of our own boundaries, biases, and perhaps prejudices regarding the clientele we serve and then also discover the unique issues, concerns, and strengths that the military families bring with them to our counseling offices.

Certain personal issues must always be considered when attempting to work with a new population; this is certainly true when working with military family systems. A key component of working with anyone in the midst of change, regardless of the framework we work within, is being cognizant of the culturally diverse populations we work with. Certainly the unique culture of the military is definitely one that is indeed foreign to most civilian mental health professionals. As we know, "All experiences originate from a particular cultural context; the counselor must be attentive to this context and the role that cultural identity plays in a client's life" (Dass-Brailsford, 2007, p. 78). Regardless, then, of whether we are working with an ethnic, religious, military, or any other diverse population, we have to consider and be well versed in the three recognized areas of multicultural competencies (Engels, 2004; Sue, Arredondo, & McDavis, 1992) of (a) becoming aware of our own behavior, values, biases, preconceived notions, and personal limitations; (b) understanding the worldview of our culturally different clients without negative judgment; and (c) actively developing and practicing appropriate, relevant, and sensitive strategies in working with our culturally diverse clients.

A culturally competent counselor will consider the dimensions of (a) beliefs and attitudes; (b) knowledge; and (c) skills (Sue et al., 1992) for each of the three areas of competencies just noted. Engels (2004) listed 24 different competencies that fall under these characteristics and dimensions, but it is my purpose here to point out that working with military families requires us to use our multicultural skills, and be cognizant of the competencies necessary to work with any diverse population is essential. I included in this chapter information regarding the first two characteristics of culturally competent counselors and left the third characteristic of developing appropriate skills for the third section of the book.

Understanding Ourselves and Our Biases

The first characteristic of a culturally competent counselor is the ability to understand our own behavior, values, biases, preconceived notions, and personal limitations. In working with military clients, we need to be aware of our own values and beliefs concerning the military, including our beliefs about who joins, why they join, and why they stay. We might also have unexplored beliefs or biases from World War II or Vietnam, based on our own or our family experiences. We might need to examine if our political or religious beliefs have biased our view of the military and, certainly, if the experience of Vietnam, whether military or not, has biased our view of the military in general. Questions to consider include the following:

1. What is our own experience with the military: as a military brat, as a family member, as a casual observer? Do we have an "us versus them" mentality?
2. What other special populations have we worked with, and how have we been successful with or challenged by them?
3. What do we need to know to round out our knowledge of military service members and their families?

4. Do we believe some of the common misunderstandings and stereotypes about the military, including (a) military members believe that war, or killing, is the answer to all conflict; (b) people join the military because they can't do anything else and just want to be taken care of; (c) the military is full of people interested only in control, and those who are control freaks join the military; (d) they join because they believe in and want U.S. domination; or (e) the military provides all the required needs for those in the military so they are financially well off and any need is automatically granted?
5. How do our political views affect our beliefs about the military, and can we stay neutral when working with the military? On the other hand, can we work within the paradigm that not all military families support the current conflict, while wholeheartedly supporting their service members?
6. Can we be compassionate to those whose worldview might be different from ours? And can we be compassionate for those who have made a commitment to the military but might still have a sense of being used or of not getting what they bargained for—but will continue to honor their commitment?
7. How well do we understand the concept of honor, a sense of mission, or the belief in doing something for the greater good, or a belief in sacrificing for others?
8. Can we work with people who have a heightened sense of duty and responsibility for life-and-death issues and who might be emotionally and/or physically harmed by both watching their buddies and civilians being killed and sometimes being responsible for those deaths?

Concept of Honor

It is to these last two points that Dr. Butler (personal communication, October 6, 2006) from San Diego warned female counselors that women may not understand the concept that getting killed is an honorable choice if it is in the carrying out of the mission. It might be compared to the mentality of the athlete that getting hurt is honorable if it is in the winning of the game. It might even be comparable to a mother risking her life for her children. But it is worth noting that the majority of counselors are women, and it might be more difficult for some female therapists to understand.

Keith and Whitaker (1984) believe that a therapist who "belittles or disregards this side of the man will have problems helping the family" (p. 150). Perhaps a more understandable comparison that Dr. Butler makes is that honor in the military is much like the concept of money, or accumulating wealth, in our U.S. civilian culture. For some in our much commercialized world, money does determine the self worth of many civilians. Dr. Butler shared the extreme example of a former pilot who eventually became a politician. He was later disgraced because of his behavior in politics and was eventually even jailed, but many in the military believed he should not have been prosecuted because he had behaved with honor in the military. Counselors must learn how to respect and possibly even use the concept of military honor as a way to generalize honoring family, women, and children. Perhaps the most powerful point for civilian counselors who work with military families is that "the military family does not come to the clinic to learn how to become a civilian family, but rather it needs help to live inside the military system" (Keith & Whitaker, 1984, p. 150).

Us Versus Them

The following additional thoughts for civilian counselors who choose to work with military families come from other current counselors working with the military. The first is that there is almost always, at least for service members who are beyond the first three or four pay grades, a mentality of "us versus them," or a sense that civilians can't possibly understand the military world. Civilian counselors will have to go the extra mile to get the training and, it is hoped, obtain experience in working with the military to come across as unbiased in their work. One therapist, who holds PTSD support groups for veterans, shared that it took a few sessions for the vets to believe in her and begin to trust her, but that came only when they learned she had some experience working with and understanding military life, and she was there to listen and learn from them.

Another point came from a therapist who found that when she first started working with the military, she continually pointed out how much support was available to them until she realized that just the concept of "finding support" suggests that they are incapable of handling their life. The military culture has a very self-sufficient mentality, and most service members want to believe that they can make it on their own. It is often important to point out how courageous it was for them to seek help rather than point out what they did not do. This is not to say that knowing what is available both on and off the military installation is unimportant; in fact, it is crucial. These resources can be used to support our work, and as the family begins to make positive movement, it may be more open to other ongoing support from the military community.

Engaging the Entire Family

In much the same light, most therapists believe it is important to establish rapport early in the therapeutic process. Because families have so much hesitancy in seeking help, if there is any reason for them to not return, they will usually end the counseling. In addition, it is important that we, while clearly being the professionals, help the family understand that our role is to work with them as a team. It is much more acceptable if they believe their input will be valued and trusted rather than the therapist appearing to have all the answers for the family. Another concern raised by a retired military professional is the possibility of colluding with the family or service member against the military on a specific issue with the military. As in all counseling, there is usually more to the story than the client tells us. Depending on the filter through which we work, we may be too willing to believe the service member's account of what happens in his or her job without the ability to determine the role he or she played in creating the situation. This is true with any counseling, but many civilian counselors may not have the ability to balance a service member's perceptions with a perspective gained from our own background or experience.

Understanding the Worldview of Others

The second characteristic of a multiculturally competent counselor is the ability to understand the worldview of the populations we work with, which in this case means we must obtain the necessary knowledge to feel competent in working with military families. Some of the challenges for civilian counselors as we begin to work with military families includes understanding the acronyms, the rank and grade system, the culture of the military, the mores and unspoken beliefs within this lifestyle, the difficulties with long absences of one parent (or two in some cases), and the impact of the required frequent moves.

In some cases it might be important to assume ignorance, while keeping an open and accepting mind, and ask for help from the families to understand issues that seem foreign to us. Asking questions about areas we are not familiar with actually shows our interest, and the simple act of asking can give them confidence that we do indeed care and are interested in learning.

We need to be aware of what is not being said and understand the restricted nature of the military with its many boundaries, rules, regulations, and habits and understand that the military members might even have a love–hate relationship with the military. Some may feel trapped, particularly those who are from multigenerational career families who joined the military because of a family tradition rather than a passion for the military. Even acknowledging emotionality may not be acceptable, even in the context of counseling, and the simplest question of "How do you feel about that?" might be initially off limits.

Recommendations

Some of the more practical concerns to be considered (Williams, 2005) include the fact that military clients may not be able to wait days or weeks for an appointment and that their high level of stress and dealing with short time frames are part and parcel of their daily existence. Also, during the initial interview, civilian counselors might want to speak in the language of the military while gathering information about their home of record, deployment and redeployment history, pay grade, permanent change of station history, temporary duty history, rotation possibility, unit, chain of command (see Appendix F for definitions), e-mail address, and all other contact information including cell phone numbers.

John Moore suggested that the initial interview should be precise, concise, timely, and highly informative, keeping in mind the importance of building rapport quickly (Marshall, 2006). It is also important to understand that many military families have financial difficulties, so expecting them to be full-paying clients might not work. It might be a way of giving something back to our community by advertising a sliding rate to military personnel and relatives. Moore, who has counseled over 1,000 members of the military and their families, offered the following succinct advice: (a) be open to learning from your military clients; (b) treat the entire family; (c) try group work; (d) always think about giving the family members a safe place to work and help them understand that they are not alone; (e) be patient, as it may take them more time to open up and share feelings; and (f) leave your political opinions outside the door (Marshall, 2006).

Pryce et al. (2000) pointed out the following recommendations for civilian human service providers:

1. Strive to understand military hierarchical culture and its requirements, as rank is one of the defining features and may reflect education, income, access to resources, and level of responsibility.
2. Understand norms and beliefs in relation to families and how they may affect delivery of services and how they fit into the military setting.
3. Individualize the "citizen solder" and family (Guard and Reserves), as they have varying commitments to the military depending on the importance of the service member's job to the family.
4. Respect the limits of military confidentiality, and acknowledge that sensitive issues such as sexual orientation must remain confidential.
5. Establish a safe environment for communication; understand that rank can be an inhibitor to open and honest communication, so leaving rank outside the door may be ideal, but it is often very

difficult for individuals with high attachment to position. We must know how to talk about rank before it becomes a problem.

6. Understand the developmental issues and conflicts and that normal separations of the military often disrupt normal developmental processes and may leave conflicts unresolved. Help families anticipate the absence of military members on special occasions and recognize when communications are failing or strained.

7. Support the limits of self-determination that is inherent to the military. Understand that the ability to adjust and cope may depend on the family developmental stage and the level of commitment to the military.

8. Advocate for prevention and intervention without the stigma by normalizing and facilitating the use of social services as a form of self-reliance and self-sufficiency. Know and use the military resources that are available.

Advocate for Change

Although I chose to address the third characteristic of developing appropriate, relevant, and sensitive strategies for working with culturally diverse clients in the third section of this book, I have included an additional recommendation here, which I believe is also the responsibility of a culturally competent counselor. The NMFA (2006) has recently supported efforts by the National Board for Certified Counselors and the American Counseling Association to urge Congress to add licensed mental health counselors to the list of other mental health service providers to the military TRICARE insurance plan. Currently, psychiatrists, psychologists, clinical social workers, and licensed marriage and family therapists can independently treat TRICARE beneficiaries for TRICARE-covered mental health conditions. Licensed mental health counselors with master's or doctoral degrees in counseling or related disciplines with training similar to that of clinical social workers and marriage and family therapists cannot (TRICARE Beneficiaries, 2005). They may see TRICARE patients only under the supervision of and referral from a physician. This requirement obviously increases the difficulty for military families in accessing care, limits their choice of provider, and, by requiring an additional step in the process of obtaining care, often discourages families from seeking care.

Recently there was a report stating that TRICARE is actually cutting reimbursements to therapists, so there are waiting lists for service members to see their primary physician to get a referral, and then they have to wait weeks to find a therapist ("Soldiers Struggle to Find Therapists," 2007). Some therapists are opting to provide an hour of therapy a week free to veterans. The article indicates that as many as one third of returning soldiers are seeking counseling in their first year home. "Counselors need to fight for the right to provide services to our veterans and their families in all needed areas. Our veterans and their families deserve nothing less" (Wakefield, 2007, p. 23).

CHAPTER 2

Military Service Members

Despite the fact that America is once again engaged in major combat operations overseas, most Americans have only a limited grasp of what it means to go to war.... Only these warriors and their families are experiencing the day-to-day sacrifices, small and large, that war requires.... Yet, in our American democracy, the warriors themselves don't get to decide when those sacrifices are to be made.... It is up to our civilian Congress to declare war. (Henderson, 2006, p. 4)

Active Duty

As of 2005, there were 1,373,534 active duty military and 1,113,427 Reservists and Guard members. The Department of Defense's *2005 Demographics Report* (Military Family Research Institute, 2006) of military personnel stated that there were almost 3.5 million military personnel when the 811,873 civilian personnel funded by congressional appropriations and by revenue-generating activities are added to the active duty, Reserves, and Guard members mentioned previously. Data as late as March 2007 show roughly the same number of active duty military members, just over 1,370,000.

The current military force is just under one-third smaller than it was in 1990, with the decline ranging from as small as 8.4% in the Marines to just over 34% in the Navy. About 26% of the military active duty is Air Force, almost 35% is Army, just over 12% is Marine Corps, and almost 27% is Navy, with the Coast Guard having slightly over 1%. According to the 2005 report, there was a total of 200,470 women in the military, which is just over 14% of the total force, with 34,821 women officers and 165,649 enlisted women. This number increased slightly by the end of September 2006.

Over one third of the total active duty military are minority (492,735), an increase from 9% in the officer rank in 1990 to over 22% in 2005 and an increase from just over 28% of the enlisted military in 1990 to over 38% in 2005. Almost one half of active duty service members are younger than 25 years old; as expected, the average age of officers is older, at 34.6 years. The average age of the enlisted ranks is 27.1 years. Over 86% of the officers have at least a bachelor's degree; fewer than 5% of enlisted have a college degree, even though almost 95% have at least a high school education.

The *2005 Demographics Report* (Military Family Research Institute, 2006) shows that over 54% of the military force is married, 70% of officers and almost 52% of enlisted. At that time there were 1,865,058 family members (including spouses, children, and adult dependents) of active duty military; when added to the active duty service members, we are talking about 3,238,592, just over 1% of the U.S. population. As noted, over half of the active duty force has family responsibilities, with over 37% married with children, 5.4% single parents, and almost 7% dual-career military couples. There are almost 470,000 military dependent children between the ages of 1 and 5, approximately 375,000 children between the ages of 6 and 11, and over 285,000 children between the ages of 12 and 18. In addition, there are over 8,000 adult dependents of active duty military.

Almost half of the spouses of active duty members are 30 years of age or younger, but 75% of the spouses of officers, who tend to be older, are 31 or older. Just less than half of the active duty officer spouses are either employed or seeking employment in the civilian labor force, and 11% are employed by the Armed Forces. Over half of the enlisted spouses are either employed or looking for employment in the civilian labor force, and 14% are working for the Armed Forces. The average age of a military spouse at the birth of the first child is 24.5, but over one half give birth before the age of 24. It is obvious that lots of babies are being born to very young people in the midst of major changes, stresses, and transitions in their lives.

Although service members come from all 50 states, the states that have the most active duty military are California, Virginia, Texas, and North Carolina, with over 100,000 each, followed by Georgia, Florida, Washington, and Hawaii, with between 40,000 and 70,000 each.

Citizen Soldiers

In addition to active duty personnel, there were 1,141,735 Reserves and Guard family members reported in the *2005 Demographics Report* (Military Family Research Institute, 2006). These citizen soldiers are also often referred to as "suddenly military." These military families include over 338,000 children between the ages of 6 and 14, almost 180,000 children younger than the age of 5, and over 125,000 children between the ages of 15 and 18. Over half of the Reserves and Guard members are married, with almost 35% married with children and just over 8% single parents; 2.6% are dual-career military couples. Approximately 17% of the Reserves and Guard members are women, roughly even in the officer and enlisted ranks. Almost half of the spouses are 35 years of age or younger, while 8% of the spouses are male.

The Reserves and Guard force is, in general, a little older and, to some extent, more educated, with fewer than 25% younger than the age of 31 and over 25% older than the age of 40. Almost 85% of the officers and almost 8% of the enlisted have a bachelor's degree. Approximately 30% of these citizen soldiers are minority (251,692); the number of minority officers increased from just over 12% in 1990 to over 20% in 2005, and the number of minority enlisted members increased from 24% in 1990 to just over 32% in 2005.

Representativeness of the Military

The Department of Defense (Garamone, 2005) tracks what it calls "representativeness," which examines everything from race, education, social status, income, and region of the country. Curt Gilroy, director of the Department of Defense's accessions policy at the Pentagon, stated, "When you look at all of those [factors], you find that the force is really quite representative of the country. ... And where it doesn't mirror America, it exceeds America" (Garamone, 2005, ¶ 2). The data actually show that our military force is more educated than the population at large, as more service members between the ages of 18 and 24 have more college experience than typical 18- to 24-year-olds. In addition, the military is a leader in equal opportunity and only in recent years has begun to show some concern because of a slight drop in the number of African American men and women. Even though Hispanics are the largest minority group in the United States, and young Hispanic men and women have a strong tendency to serve in the military, so far only the Marine Corps has been able to continue to recruit significant numbers in the recent years (Garamone, 2005).

On the socioeconomic side, according to the Armed Service Press Service, the military is strongly middle class, with recruits from poorer families actually underrepresented and trends showing the number of recruits from wealthier families and suburban areas increasing (Garamone, 2005). However, urban areas provide far fewer recruits as a percentage of the total population than small towns and rural areas do.

Unlike the years of Vietnam, during the days of the draft (Henderson, 2006), today's enlisted ranks do not include the extremely disadvantaged. Instead, the ranks are filled with the upwardly mobile working class, 96% of whom have graduated from high school, compared to only 84% of the rest of Americans. Service members are more likely to describe themselves as conservative, but like civilians, they are relatively evenly divided among Republicans, Democrats, and Independents. That is not true, however, in the officer corps, where trends over the past 30 years have resulted in Republican officers outnumbering Democrats 8 to 1.

Compared to the average American, those in the military are more likely to be following in the footsteps of a close relative who also served, and they are more likely to have been raised in a hierarchical religion such as Catholicism, by a single parent, and in the Old South, with nearly half of all service members listing their home of record one of the southern states (Houppert, 2005b). Kate Blaise (2006) shared, "When world leaders send soldiers to war, [her husband] is the kind of person they gamble with: a good man, a patriotic man, a country boy with nice manners who says please and thank you and loves to work on his old Chevy. The kind of man America is made of" (p. 14).

Military members come from across America, from small rural towns, decaying urban cores, and close-in suburbs past their prime, as well as minority and immigrant communities (Henderson, 2006). Two years into the Iraq war, the state with the most war zone deaths per capita was rural Vermont, whereas the state with the highest rate of National Guard mobilization was multiethnic Hawaii. In some ways, "the U.S. military is thrillingly American.... The military is the one institution in America that has come the closest to achieving Martin Luther King Jr.'s dream of rewarding people for the content of their characters, not the color of their skin" (Henderson, 2006, p. 23). More and more people of all colors and both genders are rising through the ranks to positions of leadership and at a higher rate than in the civilian world. Today's all-volunteer, professional military is a uniquely modern tribute to the egalitarian ideal of the American dream.

Although the military prides itself in being quite representative of the nation, virtually none of those who serve come from America's elite classes: business executives, politicians, academics, and celebrities. Until the 1960s, America's elite saw military service as a duty of citizenship for themselves and their children (Henderson, 2006). Vietnam changed all that, and as opposition to the war grew among the elite classes, college deferments enabled the children of the elite and the educated middle class to escape the draft. "Vietnam created an entire generation among the privileged that still mistrusts anything to do with the military" (p. 24).

The All-Volunteer Service

There are major changes just in terms of numbers in the modern all-volunteer service since the days of the draft, which ended in 1970. On the whole, the Reserve force is 24% smaller today than in 1990. In the active duty numbers for the four major branches of the military (Army, Air Force, Marines, and Navy), the highest numbers were during Vietnam in 1969, when there was a total of 3,458,072. That number fell by 1990 to 2,043,705. By 2000 the total active duty number in the four major branches was 1,384,344. Ephron and Childress (2007) noted, "Iraq marks the first drawn-out campaign we've fought with an all-volunteer military. ... That means far fewer Americans are taking part in the war: 12 percent of the total population participated in WWII, two percent in Vietnam and less than half of one percent in Iraq and Afghanistan" (¶ 6).

There are other major differences since the days of the draft. Rotter and Boveja (1999) outlined dramatic reforms in the military since Vietnam, including the fact that there are more women in the military, more dual-career military couples, more married service members, more service members with children, and more military wives working outside of the home. These changes that resulted from the all-volunteer military created many issues that the Department of Defense had to address. Martin and McClure (2000) mentioned that the change in the size of the force, the percentage of married personnel, and the early entry into parenthood are major changes for the military. Most recruits are single when they join, but many marry prior to the end of their first enlistment and start having children earlier than civilian peers, who take more time to pursue education and employment opportunities prior to marriage and family. "These families are at the bottom of the pay scale, and they are typically inexperienced in dealing with the stresses of marriage, parenthood, and military life" (p. 7).

Having more women in the military means there are more male spouses, an increase from just over 1.5% in 1973 to 8.5% in 1980 to almost 12% in 1993 to just less than 14% in 1998. Almost half of the female military members are married, and more than half are in dual-career military marriages. So far "anecdotal evidence indicates that civilian husbands tend to be socially isolated, and as military spouses the military community often overlooks them" (Martin & McClure, 2000, p. 8). The social role of a man who stays home or who follows a woman "is suspect, especially in the military which continues to emphasize traditional masculinity to such a large degree" (Martin & McClure, 2000, p. 8).

For those in dual-career families, the military must consider the needs of the working spouse to retain their career military personnel. As noted earlier, at least half of military spouses are either employed or are interested in working. Martin and McClure (2000) pointed out,

> Underemployment is a significant problem for civilian spouses of military members ... [and] even though the military has outperformed many civilian employers in providing affordable, quality childcare, the costs are still prohibitive for many military families, and the demand for childcare in military communities far exceeds the current supply. (p. 9)

In addition, the military has to consider the changes in family structure, with the increasing divorce rates that no longer carries a stigma in the military that it used to when a divorce may have ruined an officer's career. Also, the increase of active duty single parents creates additional concerns, as does the high percentage of military who remarry after a divorce, as "early research indicates that when children are involved, stress in these blended families is high, as is the likelihood that the second marriage will fail" (Martin & McClure, 2000, p. 9).

Philosophical Differences

Some of the philosophical differences (Martin & McClure, 2000) that the all-volunteer service carries with it include a change from the days of the draft when married service members were treated simply as if they were single, versus the current primarily married force. Also, the all-volunteer service values diversity as the norm, versus a time when there was limited ethnic, racial, and gender diversity. The same authors also pointed out that this change in the military marked the differences from (a) guarding the U.S. coasts and exploring frontiers versus the current level of operations around the globe; (b) lengthy and frequent postings to remote areas of the world versus the current level of rapid deployment from a home station and the constant focus on readiness; and (c) a life where the duty and personal worlds were viewed simultaneously, with considerable tolerance for professional mistakes and personal misconduct versus a perception of a zero-defect in both the duty and personal life environments.

In the past, rank had its privilege, and earning benefits was the norm, compared to a more current growing concern over equity and fairness, together with a focus on entitlements for service. In the past there was a limited recognition of families compared to the current focus on profamily values and family well-being. In the past the military provided basic life needs, whereas the current approach is to provide multiple programs and services to enhance recruitment, retention, and readiness and the emphasis on privatization of programs and services rather than the military having to provide for all needs. A retired Army psychiatrist explained that one of the major differences relates to the responsibility of the commander; in the past the unit commander was responsible for those in his command 24/7, which means he was accountable for what his soldiers did after work, on the weekends, and with their families. Today the commander is responsible for the service member only during duty hours, unless, of course, there is any infraction of the law or behavior "unbecoming to the military." This does have an impact on whether a service member might seek mental health services, as he or she is not required to report to the commander if her or his family sees a therapist after duty hours, whereas in the past that was all recorded.

Even the military communities have changed from frontier posts, or the concept of "company towns" where social control required that single service members remain inside the gates, to a concept of a "military hometown" that includes both barracks or dorms and on-base and off-base apartment living. In the past, rank provided for on-base family housing and corresponding economic advantage, which included access to the military community facilities; contrast that with the newer concept of the right to own property being an important economic advantage, which has resulted in real concerns about the deterioration of on-base housing and the prevalence of privatization of community functions (Martin & McClure, 2000).

Back in 1984, when many of the concerns that created these changes were being raised, one of the editors of perhaps the first book written for mental health professionals concluded, "This country's move to an all volunteer force and the increased recognition of the effect of family members' attitudes upon military retention rates necessitate attention and answers to be found to the questions raised by these issues" (Ridenour, 1984, p. 1). We can see now that the military is significantly different as a result of the all-volunteer force, because these issues have been, and continue to be, addressed; the inclusion of the needs of the family has made a major impact on the structure and organization of the military.

Titles, Rank, and Hierarchy

What do we call or how do we address our military service members? In the Army, they are soldiers; in the Air Force, they are airmen; in the Navy, they are seamen; in the Marines, they are marines; in the Coast Guard, they are usually referred to as their rank or as members of the Coast Guard; and in the Reserves or National Guard, they are referred to as either members of the Guard and the Reserve or Guard and Reserve personnel. The Reservists can be called reservists or soldiers or airmen, depending on the branch of the Reserves they are attached to.

For the purpose of the book, even though there will be times when I point out something unique to one particular branch of the military or quote sources that specifically address members of one branch or the other, all members of the military service will be referred to as *service members*. As we will see, the position, rank, and title of service members are important issues for civilians to understand, and I hope I have addressed the issue with respect and understanding.

As noted in chapter 1, a strong recommendation for civilian therapists is to strive to understand the military hierarchical culture, as this often reflects education, income, access to resources, and level of responsibility. Enlisted service members usually do not have a college degree prior to joining the military, whereas commissioned officers either have a college Reserved Officer Training Corps (ROTC) commission, have attended Officer Training School (OTS) usually with a college degree, or have a degree from one of the three federally funded military academies: the Air Force Academy in Colorado Springs, Colorado, the U.S. Military Academy at West Point, New York, the U.S. Naval Academy in Annapolis, Maryland, or the state-supported Virginia Military Institute (VMI) in Lexington, Virginia. This distinction is important to understand, as there are two clear subcultures in the military, that of the enlisted and that of the officers.

A noncommissioned officer (NCO) is someone who has risen from the lower ranks of the enlisted to enlisted officer status, but an NCO is still a member of the enlisted culture, not the commissioned officer culture. This has an impact not only on the service member but also on the family. Rank status in the military community is always visibly present and manifested by differentials in quality of housing and some social–recreational facilities, as an officer's club or other facility (Rodriguez, 1984), even though these are generally on their way out on most installations. The distinction in facilities and services has been greatly reduced since the all-volunteer service has come into place for many of the reasons previously discussed in this chapter.

Three terms are important in the discussion of "authority and responsibility in the military: rank, rate, and grade" (Powers, n.d., p. 1). *Rank* determines a service member's status and authority in comparison to others; the Navy and Coast Guard use the word *rate*, whereas all other services use *rank*. *Grade* is used for personnel and pay functions, as all military personnel across the services receive the same pay based on their rank and time-in service, but because the *ranks* have different names in the different branches of the military, the word *grade* is used to define pay functions.

It is also important to know that there are three categories of rank or rate: enlisted personnel, warrant officers, and commissioned officers. All commissioned officers outrank all warrant officers and enlisted members, and all warrant officers outrank all enlisted members. Blaise (2006) explained that a warrant officer floats between enlisted and commissioned officers; often they are former enlisted soldiers who are highly respected, perform all kinds of jobs from maintenance to aviation to supply, and are generally considered experts in a chosen field.

The pay grade and rank are indicated by the stripes and bars, called insignia, worn on the shoulders, arms, and collars. It is not always easy to learn the meaning of every insignia, but those within the particular branch of the service that a counselor primarily deals with are valuable to know. These insignia indicate who has authority and responsibility and who has more power and status. One of the fundamental principles of the military is respect, not just respect for status or rank but true appreciation and honor for those who have done more, seen more, experienced more, and learned more. Rank is a time-honored tradition that goes beyond the U.S. military and has been an inherent part of the military structure worldwide for centuries.

Addressing the Military

In her book *The Heart of a Soldier,* Kate Blaise (2006) wrote that she was only 24 years old and a second lieutenant, and her husband was 26 and a chief warrant officer, but because she was a commissioned officer, Army regulations dictated that her husband salute her and call her "ma'am." When ribbed by his buddies, he proudly stated that she worked hard to become an officer, and he saluted her out of respect for the effort she put into getting there. Although we might have a tendency to overlook or find this hierarchy unimportant or irrelevant from a more democratic and egalitarian civilian worldview, we must understand and respect it when working with the military.

As a school counselor with a doctorate, I did not think it was so important for me to be referred to as Dr. Hall, but it was very important to the military service members that their children use my title when referring to me. Even though it is true in most public school systems that adults, whether they are teachers, counselors, administrators, or janitors, are not called by their first names, it was also expected that I be referred to as Dr. Hall, as a sign of both personal respect and respect for the tradition of hierarchy in a military environment. When, out of naïveté, I first suggested that the teachers or other members of the community could call me Lynn or Ms. Hall, they were aghast that I would not insist on using my earned title. Although it may seem too formal, it was indeed a sign of respect for this level of education, experience, and, in the end, titles. It was a continuation of the importance of respect for those with more education or a unique set of skills and experience.

To ask a service member to refer to us by our first name can often be interpreted as a lack of courtesy and respect for who we are, as well as the education we have attained. It could even signify that they should not take us seriously. At the same time, to be high and mighty about it could also be harmful. It was mentioned earlier that many service members come from the southeastern United States, and I often found that southern families in the military felt particularly comfortable in an environment where this kind of respect, use of titles, and deference to education, age, and experience was encouraged, because, perhaps in more than any other region of the country, this is still the norm.

I found the advice in an article (Williams, 2005) written for lawyers who work with the military also appropriate for mental health professionals. For instance, the author pointed out that when military clients make appointments, ensure that the intake staff is instructed to get their rank, because not only it is a sign of respect to address military personnel by rank but it may also give us insight into the relevant complexity of the concerns and the client's ability to pay. The author also noted that it is disrespectful to call a commissioned officer "Mr.," as the title "Mr." is reserved for warrant officers, which is a subordinate rank to a commissioned officer. There are a number of examples of possible confusion, one being that an eagle insignia can be the enlisted rank of "specialist" (E-4) or the officer rank of "colonel" (O-6). These are not good to confuse (Williams, 2005).

Understanding Rank and Insignia

It is, on the other hand, not always essential for civilians to understand or know the names of every rank or insignia for all services; it can be quite confusing, and remembering each insignia would not be expected if a counselor is seeing only a few military service families in counseling. Most counselors who work near a military installation will see members from mostly one branch of the service, and they will want to become familiar with the ranks of the service branch of the military they see most often. In that case, it is valuable to understand at least the names and insignia of the different ranks within the service most commonly seen. These are listed in Appendix G of this book.

It is, at first, acceptable to simply call all service members either "sir" or "ma'am" (Williams, 2005), even though the enlisted are not always comfortable with these terms, particularly the lower ranks of the enlisted. In counseling, a simple question such as "How would you like me to address you?" solves the problem up front and shows them the kind of respect they deserve. One more tidbit is to maintain the respect for the spouse as well as for the service member. If referring to the service member as Staff Sgt. Hall, then call his wife Mrs. Hall. Refrain from using first names with the spouses while addressing the service members by their rank or title.

Why They Join and the Reasons They Stay

Mary Wertsch, the author of a book called *Military Brats: Legacies of Childhood Inside the Fortress* (1991), outlined a number of reasons that people choose to join the military. These reasons, from Wertsch's work, are presented here to help us understand why people join the military, as well as help us understand their commitment level to the military, how they decide how long to stay in the military, and if they decide to make the military a career.

Family Tradition

In November 2006, I was sitting next to a young airman on a flight to Arizona. In a typical airline-friendly conversation, I asked him what he did, and he said he was an analyst in the Air Force, which, at that time, was the same occupation, or Military Occupational Specialty (MOS), as my son. So I asked what drew him into the military. He said he grew up as a military brat because his dad was enlisted career military. He was born in Japan; had lived in Spain, Panama, and England; and eventually graduated from high school in Delaware. He said being in the military was just a "family thing," and even though his father had actually discouraged him from carrying on the military tradition, it was "all he knew." One of the therapists I interviewed shared a story of a female seaman who complained about being stuck in clerical positions in the military and was quite bothered by her inability to move ahead. When asked why she stayed in the military, she said she came from a military family, so she understood the culture and didn't want to get out, as she was quite anxious about living in the civilian world.

This is the story often told: young people who grew up in the military later join the military because it is more comfortable than civilian life. That is not to say, however, that the majority of young people who grow up in the military eventually join. An Air Force veteran being interviewed by the 2006 president of American Counseling Association (Wakefield, 2007) stated that his father retired from the Navy, his brother retired from the Army, and his father-in-law retired from the Air Force. "I think it is important to note that many families have numerous members who have served our country proudly and have provided them the emotional support to complete their tasks" (Wakefield, 2007, p. 23). My Air Force son had a grandfather, on his father's side, who was a West Point graduate and retired as a colonel in the Air Force, an uncle who was a VMI graduate and retired from the Pentagon as a colonel in the Air Force, and another uncle who was an Air Force Academy graduate and retired as a colonel in the Air Force.

Even for women, there are stories of wanting to follow in their father's footsteps. Kate Blaise (2006), who was mentioned earlier, in writing her touching story of her life as a member of a dual-military couple, said that she can lay her interest in the military at the feet of her father, whose story of service to God and country began with his ancestors during the Civil War. Even though Blaise kept her dreams of being a soldier to herself during her early years, she could never forget her father's message that it is the duty of all citizens to give something back to their country. She shares that he never imagined he would eventually have not one but two daughters leading soldiers in a war zone in the Middle East.

Between 10% and 15% of seniors in the Department of Defense school where I worked as a high school counselor were planning to go into the military right out of high school or go to college with the goal of going into the military as an officer. These military-minded students were representative of the entire student body, from the best academic student to the worst student, from the best athlete to the nonathlete. Undoubtedly that percentage is higher in a school of mostly military dependent students, but when students tell us they are planning a military career, they often have some history of a family member or members who served in the military. One young man told me he joined the military at age 18 because he wanted to bring that tradition back into the family; his dad had not gone into the military after college graduation in the late 1960s, but up until that time there had been numerous family members in the military. He somehow felt that it was his duty to not let that family tradition die, so by joining the military he was able to "live out the legacy of the family."

The pressure may be stronger in higher ranking officer families, as Gegax and Thomas (2005) reported that about one third of the Army generals in the U.S. military have sons or daughters who have served or are serving in Iraq or Afghanistan. "It is not unusual in military families for children to follow their parents into service. History is full of heroic examples.... The father–son tradition of inherited sacrifice and honor goes on and on and now includes some mothers and daughters as well" (p. 26). Officers will often reveal that there is a special poignancy to the stories of fathers and sons in the military, as they know their decisions may put their own sons in harm's way.

Benefits: Financial Support, Education, and Equality

Henderson (2006) suggested that the number one reason young people join the military is money. In 2003 the average brand-new recruit made just over $15,000 a year, plus housing, health care, and, if they serve out their enlistment period of usually 3 or 4 years of active duty, a little money for college. Although this might seem low, when housing and other benefits are considered, it is probably higher than what an average 18- to 20-year-old makes in the civilian world. "The military is one option young people have after high school. Military service offers money for college—money a large segment of the population doesn't have" (Garamone, 2005, ¶ 6). Henderson (2006) pointed out that people who join the military for the kind of money they will receive "tend to come from places that lack other economic opportunities" (p. 22).

The military is an attractive option for many young people who don't yet know what they want to do. It is seen often as a transition for young people who will use the military as a place of service, as well as a time to decide what they want to do for the rest of their lives. Often, at least initially, these are the young people who do not see themselves college bound but realize that working in a fast-food restaurant or on a road crew isn't going to provide them what they want and need in life. One young soldier shared with me that he had been a mediocre high school student and that after high school he didn't really have a career goal. After starting at a junior college, he realized he was bored and restless in school. He had never been a great student, but he knew he needed a direction and believed some kind of structure would help him decide on a career. He decided the military would open a lot of possibilities and take the financial strain off of him and his family, who were attempting to finance his college education. By joining the military, this young man was able to meet his educational and financial needs, as well as find a direction and structure to help him mature.

The military has been what someone called the "great equalizer" for many in our society. Historically a high percentage of lower income youth have correctly seen the military as a chance for upward mobility, education, respect, and prestige that they believe would be impossible if they remained in the civilian world. In addition, the military has indeed set a standard for the civilian world for the integration of ethnic groups and gender. It is a relatively safe world for the families of lower income service members and their families (Schouten, 2004). The sense of community felt while spending time in a military housing area where children often have the ability to explore the world around them, as many of us did who grew up in the mid-20th century, does not always exist in the civilian world.

The military's nondiscriminatory promotion practices encourage minorities; whereas minorities are only 20% to 25% of the general population, they make up more than one third of the military. African American men and women have traditionally seen the military as on-the-job training opportunities, as they often gravitate to specialties such as communication, medical corps, and administration at a rate 2.5 times more than Caucasians, which equips them with marketable skills later in the civilian world (Henderson, 2006). In her interviews with adults who had grown up in military families, Wertsch (1991) shared that many of the Black military brats told of experiencing racism for the first time in the civilian communities and often "grew up acutely conscious of the contrast between their safe, secure life in the military and the tenuous existence of their civilian relatives in small rural towns or big city ghettos" (p. 338).

A teacher referred a young seventh grader to me in my first school in Germany who was chronically late for class and consistently unwilling to do the assigned work. When I talked to him, he explained that his mother had just married a military service member, and he didn't feel comfortable in this new school. When I asked for more detail about his reluctance to do his work, he shared that he had, prior to becoming part of a military family, witnessed the shooting of an uncle and a brother on the streets of his hometown. He stated simply, "Why should I study, I will be dead by the time I am 20." He could not yet believe that by moving away from his world of violence and by becoming a member of a military family, he just might have a different legacy.

Identity of the Warrior

On a deeper perhaps more psychological level, many who join the military feel a need to "merge their identity with that of the warrior" (Wertsch, 1991, p. 17). The structure, the expectations, the rules, and even the penalties and overriding identity are reassuring while providing them with security, identity, and a sense of purpose. A therapist from San Diego (Butler, personal communication, October 6, 2006) who has worked with the military since the time of the draft, stated that during the draft, everyone went in and had to survive. Those whose personality and needs fit with the military culture stayed in. He noted that the profile of the service member who stayed in during the time of the draft is often similar to those who now volunteer, as the military offers a reenforcement of a belief system and a personal sense of who they are.

Defense analyst James Hosek, the key author of a 2006 RAND study on enlistment, stated, "Many military service members are eager to go to war, and say the experience is exciting and meaningful, and allows them to use their training" (¶ 6). Money was also found to be a key factor in the positive feelings, including higher combat pay, bonuses, and tax-free salaries while deployed to war zones. The RAND study (Hosek, 2006) pointed out that those who were not deployed often felt left out. Previous work on the topic of war (Nash, 2007) has explored the "psychology of war as a test of manhood and a rite of initiation among males in many cultures" (p. 17), so it is not uncommon to find this need to merge their identity by being a part of something meaningful is a motivation to join the military.

Gegax and Thomas (2005) suggested that although military sons tend to talk about duty, when asked why they followed their fathers to war, their more personal motivations are more difficult to understand. They suggest that combat may have been a test, and certainly in some cultures *the* test, of manhood throughout the history of warfare. "There is no better way to win a father's respect than to defy death just the way he did. Indeed, the effort to surpass one's father or brother's bravery has gotten more than a few men killed" (p. 26). Henderson (2006) pointed out that young White men often view a stint in the military as an adventure and are 50% more likely to choose infantry and other frontline combat units, with the most elite combat units historically being almost all White.

A therapist in Arizona who primarily works with adolescents and their families finds that the military often provides the needed structure to life for many adolescents who seem the most lost as teenagers but who, upon entering the military, find that the warrior mentality works for them. He finds this is true especially for the 18-year-olds who are not college material or those who seem to need a source of external discipline even to hold down a regular job. It is ironic that some kids who seem to actually resist structure as they grow up often do well in the military structure, because for the first time they have something meaningful to do while not having to think independently. A retired military man told a therapist that what he didn't like about civilian life was that nobody was in charge. This therapist pointed out that military members often are not free thinkers; in fact, they value the structure and often function better within clear boundaries where they don't have to make too many decisions.

An Escape

There are also young people who seem to need a way of separating from the world they grew up in; for whatever reason, they need to get away. In doing so, the military also satisfies "a need for dependence ... [drawing them] to the predictable, sheltered life … that they did not have growing up" (Wertsch, 1991, p. 17). Ridenour (1984) reported that from a systems perspective, military service often is an alternative or extended family system and that sometimes young married couples come into the military "possibly as a result of escape from their respective families [only to] unconsciously run toward becoming part of a third extended family system" (p. 4). As one returning soldier stated, "There's no place in the world where you can have a job like that. It's a brotherhood that's deeper than your own family" (Hull & Priest, 2007, ¶ 45).

Often the recruitment techniques beckon many into the military to provide solutions to personal problems (Schwabe & Kaslow, 1984), including those who cannot find work, are tired of their parents' nagging them, or have just ended a significant relationship. The recruiter is there to provide "friendly fatherly attention, a ticket to leave town, a job, money and a promise of a new life" (p. 130). It is unfortunate that it often places these recruits in a highly structured, slowly responding system with little opportunity for privacy or independence where "impulsive young men and women find themselves trapped in a system best suited for those with considerable patience and a compliant nature" (Schwabe & Kaslow, 1984, p. 130). Wertsch (1991) pointed out, "Joining the military in order to put one's self in the care of a good surrogate parent is hardly the sort of thing one is likely to advertise; in fact, it is a secret so deep-seated that those who act upon it rarely admit it, and guard the secret carefully" (p. 17). In so doing, however, the military eases a lot of anxiety by providing a solid job, a route to adulthood, and the separation from the family of origin. One injured veteran told a journalist that, even though his father, uncle, and both grandfathers were in the military, he was mostly attracted to the idea because he wanted some discipline in his life, as he had grown up without his father in the home and he "needed the stabilization where I had no choice but to go do what they told me" (Houppert, 2005b, p. 183).

As so often happens in the civilian world, however, this attempt to flee from problems does not mean the problems end; so instead of dealing with or facing the effects of childhood violence, gangs, addictions, or abandonment, these people bring their problems into the military, just like they are brought into other segments of American society. For many growing up in difficult families, perhaps with violent pasts or uncertain futures, this lifestyle offers a glimmer of hope, but if these issues go unresolved, it can be a "potentially ominous shadow" (Wertsch, 1991, p. 17) for the future of that military service member and possibly his or her future family. That shadow was certainly true in 2005 when a young Special Forces trainee (Houppert, 2005b) wounded his wife and another soldier and then shot and killed himself. The young man had been indicted for rape 6 years earlier at the age of 19, which "should have kept him out of the Army in the first place" (¶ 2), but because the victim's parents had decided it was not in the best interest of their daughter to pursue the trial, the case was dropped.

Although there are probably as many reasons to join the military as there are military service members, these seem to be the most overarching reasons and are those that civilian counselors might want to consider when working with families. Exploring the reason for joining will be important for military families in most of the decisions they have to make during their family life cycle, including those who are considering staying in or getting out. Ridenour (1984) pointed out that it is true that therapy with military families may free some to leave the military, but it may help others to become individuated enough to choose to remain a part of the military and its extended family system. It is also important that the mental health professional not become "a controlling foster parent and try to influence the family's choice while it is making it. [We] should respect the family members' right to make and live out their own choices" (Ridenour, 1984, p. 15). Our goals of therapy must be to recognize the struggle over these difficult choices, help the families establish increasing comfort with the ambiguity, and foster diversity of methods to deal with it.

PART 2
The Military Family

CHAPTER **3**

The Unique Culture of the Military

The Warrior Society

> You sacrifice a lot of personal liberties when you put on an Army uniform; you go where you are told, do what you're ordered to do, fight an enemy you're ordered to fight. But that lack of freedom also makes things easier in a way. Many of your big, life-altering decisions are made for you. (Blaise, 2006, p. 5)

Mary Wertsch (1991) shared assumptions and generalizations she came to after surveying a large number of teachers, psychologists, physicians, and social workers who grew up as military brats in the 1950s and 1960s, prior to the all-volunteer service. Her explanation and insights regarding the culture of the military, which she described as a Fortress, offer a depth and understanding that I did not find in any other single resource. I had the occasion to hear Mary speak a number of years ago at a Military Child Education Coalition conference in Florida, and I was overwhelmed at how suddenly I had a much deeper understanding of the world of the kids I was then working with on a daily basis in a military-dependent school in Germany. She readily agreed to allow me to use the following character- istics of the Fortress to describe this warrior society. Wertsch defined this warrior society as a Fortress to differentiate it from the democratic society of most U.S. citizens. "The great paradox of the military is that its mem- bers, the self-appointed front-line guardians of our cherished American democratic values, do not live in democracy themselves" (Wertsch, 2001, p. 5). Even though Lyons (2007) suggested that perhaps the term *warrior* is controversial or even politically incorrect, it is being used more and more in the current media as, what appears to be, an appropriate description of the culture of the military.

Authoritarian Structure

A military officer being interviewed for a television news show virtually quoted Wertsch when he stated that the military members are fighting for democracy in Iraq, even though they don't practice it. The first characteristic of the warrior society is that it is maintained by a rigid authoritarian structure. In many cases, this rigidity extends from the world of the service member into the structure of the home, as the household is often run as a military unit. Although the concept of the authoritarian military family is frequently referred to, and about 80% of the military brats Wertsch (1991) interviewed described their families as authoritarian, "there are warriors who thrive in the authoritarian work environment without becoming authoritarian at home" (p. 5), so it is important to understand that authoritarianism is not the only model of military family life. However, within the authoritarian families, some of the common characteristics were military parents who would not tolerate questions or disagreements, frequent violations of privacy, and children who were forbidden to engage in any activity that smacked of individuation. There are clear rules for behavior and speech in this authoritarian structure ("yes, ma'am," "no, ma'am") for both children and spouses.

Until the late 1980s a service member's wife's behavior (women service members were still few and far between) was a part of the service member's efficiency report. In the past, wives of the military member were even told what to wear. This history and tradition in which the expectation was that the service member would have the ability to "run a tight ship at home" was very much an advantage to his career in the military. A therapist who works near a military installation in Arizona shared that for her clients, many of whom were military spouses, it was clear that any protest was not OK. The spouses were not allowed to object to any condition or problem on the installation; in fact they were specifically told they could not participate in any kind of demonstration. Keith and Whitaker (1984) shared the insight that "the military family lives in a community in which no one dies from old age, only violently … lead[ing] to an illusion of eternal youth and vigor" (p. 156) and that the father (who is military) outranks his wife because he has a closer affiliation with the base commander. These authors contended that this imbalance in authority and permeability of the family boundaries cause problems, as the families are often organized like a miniature army.

For those families where the authoritarian military structure extends into the home, this parenting style can work, at least while the children are in elementary school or in schools on military installations. A therapist in Arizona, however, pointed out that when families live "on the economy" (in a civilian community), the children, particularly once they reach adolescence, often rebel against this authoritarian parenting style because they see kids in other families with very different family structures. Many times in these families, the children may respect the military parent as a fearless leader, but often it is a charade played out only when the parent is present (Keith & Whitaker, 1984). Within the military community, this can be both comforting and suffocating. It is, in some ways, much like a "company town" mentality, where, as one therapist said, there is always some drama and everyone knows everyone else's business. Perhaps a better way to define it is as a culture that is not necessarily closed but more inward focused, with consistent structure and hierarchy and a constant sense that someone else calls the shots.

Another therapist, who does pro bono work with military families, says that her military dependent clients who have major problems in their adolescent years often come from almost tyrannical and sometimes abusive families. The children then blame the military for all their problems, as they see no way out and realize that even their extended family cannot step in to help. They have a "sense of betrayal" by the military, because they do not have the right to make the choices they see other young people making, but they realize their parents are not in a position to make many personal choices either. Often the soldier's office at home is a shrine; a shrine to what is, indeed, an honorable profession but perhaps, in some cases, coming before or instead of the needs of the family. As Keith and Whitaker (1984) pointed out, the family will always have a subsidiary role in the military environment.

Isolation and Alienation

The warrior society is also characterized by extreme mobility, resulting in isolation and alienation from civilian communities as well as from the extended family. An average tour of duty may be 3 years, but the moves can be much more frequent. There were quite a few students in my high school in Germany who had never lived in the States or anywhere near their extended family or home of record. An adult military brat recently told me that he had gone to six schools between 7th grade and 12th grade. Some of the kids in my schools had never visited their grandparents' homes and had no idea what having contact with kids they knew in elementary school was like. Although the ability to stay in touch with friends from elementary school through high school is certainly less prevalent in the United States today than in the past, it was virtually unheard of in military families until recently, with the explosion of the Internet. The irony is that every time the family moves, it is called a Permanent Change of Station (PCS); permanent, that is, until the next move.

This isolation can often be seen when military families live on the economy by a lack of concern for the wider community in which they live. There is often a sense that this is temporary, so the focus is inward, as noted previously, to the military world rather than outward to the local community. For those families who spend some time on foreign soils, the isolation can seem overwhelming, as most housing areas in foreign countries are walled off from the outside culture, so it becomes "an oddly isolated life, one in which it is possible to delude oneself that one is still on American soil" (Wertsch, 1991, p. 30). For those families who see living in a foreign country as an adventure, they find themselves learning the language and experience aspects of the culture that they begin to appreciate; those who are more skeptical or anxious may spend their entire tour of duty within the fences of the military installation. Although it was not the norm, it certainly was not uncommon for students who were leaving my school to tell me that they had never left the base, as their parents were either too anxious or not interested in traveling in a foreign country.

During the first Gulf War, as the on-base security was heightened, it took almost 2 hours every morning to get just from the installation gate to the school where I worked, and it was only two blocks away. Years later after the events of September 11, 2001, as the high school tennis coach in the school where I was also a counselor, I was faced with the difficulty of taking the tennis team off base every day to practice at a German tennis facility. It didn't take long to realize that our practice time would be cut almost in half, because we had to compete for a U.S. military bus to transport us each day and then wait for the high level of security checks required upon returning to the base after practice. All of a sudden the sense that we, the Americans, were different became very clear, and it was easy to understand why families might choose not to leave base very often.

Even when children attend public schools in the United States, as virtually all military children do, there is a sense of "us versus them," as it is "next to impossible to grow up in the warrior society without absorbing the notion that civilians are very different and sometimes incomprehensible" (Wertsch, 1991, p. 315). A psychiatrist Wertsch quoted wrote that military people are "seen by the nearby community as transients and are often targets of mistrust and hostility" (p. 16). Underscoring (Gegax & Thomas, 2005) the isolation of the military from the rest of society is the fact that America is divided between the vast majority who do not have military service experience and the tiny minority who do. During World War II, 6% of Americans were in uniform. Even those military members who don't feel superior or even always isolated from the civilian world often report that they are unimpressed by the civilian work ethic (Gegax & Thomas, 2005), keeping them psychologically isolated, even after leaving the military.

While working with military families in Connecticut, O'Beirne (1983) developed what she termed an "Isolation Matrix," where she pointed out that military families are part of five families: (a) the nuclear family, consisting of one's spouse and children, if married, or one's parents and siblings; (b) the extended family, consisting of one's relatives and sometimes a network of very close friends from one's hometown or previous duty stations; (c) the military unit family, made up of the personnel in the specific unit to which one is attached and their families; (d) the immediate neighborhood family, which is made up of the friends in the community where one is currently living; and (e) the service family, which incorporates the particular branch of service that provides official and unofficial support services.

Along with these types of groups, O'Beirne stated that families often experience four types of isolation: (a) geographic isolation, where the family is separated physically from its support system; (b) social isolation, where support might be available only at the level of acquaintances or surface recognition; (c) emotional isolation, where the support of deep friendships and lasting ties and the recognition of one's abilities and thoughts by others are not available; and (d) cultural isolation, which includes everything from ethnic issues, such as having a foreign-born spouse, living overseas, or moving to an unfamiliar section of the country, to aesthetic issues, such as the availability of visual and performing arts, education, or intellectual endeavors, to spiritual or philosophical issues, such as the pursuits of religious or spiritual practices. The author suggested then that we could put these dimensions on a matrix (see Table 3.1), with the five family types on the horizontal axis and the four types of isolation along the vertical axes.

This may help us assess and understand how and when families either have the support to function well or experience greater stress than normal. If families can identify on this Isolation Matrix where and how they get their support, they can begin to make decisions that might minimize their isolation and engage in activities that will lower their sense of alienation.

Opportunities for meeting challenges above and beyond the commonplace do exist for military family members. Their awareness of the noble dimensions that are possible in their lives can be an important coping skill. Knowledge of their strengths and weaknesses enables military families and their care providers to deal with the omnipresent challenge: isolation. (O'Beirne, 1983, p. 4)

Table 3.1 O'Beirne's Isolation Matrix (1983)

Isolation Type	Nuclear Family	Extended Family	Military Unit	Immediate Neighborhood	Service Family
Geographic isolation					
Social isolation					
Emotional isolation					
Cultural isolation					

Class System

Nowhere in America is the dichotomy so omnipresent as on a military base; nowhere do the classes live and work in such close proximity; nowhere is every social interaction so freighted with class significance.... The thousands of people on a military base live together, have the same employer, dedicate their lives to the same purpose—yet they cannot, must not, socialize outside their class. (Wertsch, 1991, p. 285)

Within the warrior society there are the two subcultures of the officer and enlisted ranks, as noted in chapter 2, with very different lifestyles. The noncommissioned officers (noncoms), who are usually the top five of the nine enlisted ranks, seem sometimes caught in the middle, as one person Wertsch interviewed said, "They don't have enough power, but they have enough so that they have the appearance of having it" (1991, p. 99). But if you ask noncommissioned officers where they live and whom they socialize with, they will say with the enlisted, absolutely not the officers.

The rank structure affects families and creates a distance, not just between the military and the civilian world but among the military itself. Although service members socialize with their buddies within the officer or enlisted ranks, the spouses can also be isolated from each other. Often the officers' wives on an installation become a close-knit group, almost like a sorority where they have a strong sense of belonging. As Wertsch said, the military has its reasons to make these distinctions and perhaps would be dysfunctional without them, but it seems that "the only equality among officers and enlisted is in dying on the battlefield" (1991, p. 288).

Over the years in the United States, there has been an attempt to affirm and equalize the differences in society, but the assumption in the military, in any country, is that it is essential to the life and purpose of the organization to maintain a rigid hierarchical system based on dominance and subordination. Although the children go to the same school, the children of both the enlisted and the officers almost always are uncomfortable associating outside of school with the children of the other rank. Housing on most installations is separated, with single military in one area, enlisted family housing in another, and officers' quarters in another. It is obvious, just by driving through a military community, which is which.

When the students associate with each other at school extracurricular events, such as sports or drama, the unease with which they work together, at least initially, is often quite obvious. There is also often a distinction, for instance in sports, as those students who play football are, more than likely, the children of the enlisted whereas the tennis players are mostly children of officers. The officers' kids who want to play football often end up as the quarterbacks, and the enlisted kids who want to play tennis better have a very high level of self-confidence, as well as talent as a tennis player. Military brats seem to be able at a distance to distinguish between themselves and civilians, but they very early also intuitively detect whether another student's military parent is enlisted or officer rank. "This ability to tell rank ... is critical ... because their social world is so thoroughly stratified" (Wertsch, 1991, p. 260).

Parent Absence

This is a society with a great deal of parent absence, and, as a result of the world events since the early 1990s, sometimes both parents are absent at the same time. I was brought to tears when I was told that the graduation ceremonies from Wiesbaden High School the year after I left were held with a transcommunication system between the ceremonies in Germany and a location in Baghdad, Iraq, where nearly 40% of the almost 100 graduating seniors had a parent deployed. The students were able to speak to their parents, and the parents could see their children earning their diplomas. This has now expanded to include 18 high school graduations in Europe, and the ceremonies are transmitted to Iraq, Afghanistan, Africa, and other locations around the world (Department of Defense Education Activity, 2007). Despite very emotional examples such as these, parent absence during important events can be crushing for young people, but they are nothing new for these families. A parent is often absent for the prom, big football game, drama production, or graduation. The families must make the adjustment. The son of a career naval officer told a therapist that it took about a month each way, his father leaving and returning, to make the adjustment.

These transitions often work against deep and lasting attachments to friends and community. As Martin and McClure (2000) stated, the conditions of military family life, "including long and often unpredictable duty hours, relatively low pay and limited benefits, frequent separations, and periodic relocations … remain the major stressors of military family life" (p. 3). The issue of deployment of at least one parent is covered in great detail in chapter 7, but it is mentioned here as a major characteristic of the warrior society. Even in peacetime the absence of the military parent is a condition of military life; these military parents are continually leaving, returning, leaving again, or working such long hours that their children cannot count on their presence. Research dating back to World War II documents that schoolwork suffers, more for boys than girls, that visits to the health clinics for both the spouse and children increase, and that reports of depression and behavior problems go up when a parent is deployed (Wertsch, 1991). "Part of the training every military child receives is that one is expected to handle this disturbing fact of life in true stoic warrior style" (p. 66).

Sometimes this constant coming and going results in either the military parents protecting themselves from the pain of separation or the family forming a kind of cohesive unit that keeps the military parent out. This can be seen by the military parent's distancing from the family, both physically by working long hours or spending time away from home and emotionally through alcohol or other ways of soothing the self. The family, on the other hand, becomes so conditioned to the loss that when the service member returns, it sometimes wears a mask of happiness, all the while knowing that it won't be long before the parent leaves again.

Rosen and Durand (2000) reported that in their survey of marital adjustment of couples 1 year after the first Gulf War in the early 1990s, only 17% of the respondents shared that they felt more distance from one another than prior to the deployment, and only 14% of the soldiers felt left out of the family. We can then assume, at least from this one study, that the negative effects of parent separation are not causes for concern for military spouses. Apparent in their study is that 78% of the returning soldiers were pleased with the spouse's running of the household, and 68% of the respondents reported having greater feelings of closeness after the deployment. On the other hand, when somewhere between 14% and 17% of couples experience a high level of stress as a result of a deployment, it means there are a lot of families in the military living in stressful situations.

The military parent may also expect major adjustments when he or she is home, adjustments that may be resented by the other parent or children, resulting often in a sense of relief when the next set of orders to leave arrive. Frequently students in my school become more nervous and anxious when their military parent was expected to return than prior to their leaving;

after making the adjustments in their family that were necessary upon the departure of the service member, the students sometimes became angry and resentful that their family patterns had to change again.

Importance of Mission

The conditions and demands of the military have "historically been perceived as requiring a total commitment to the military—typically a commitment to one's unit, the unit's mission and its members. This is the very essence of the concept of military unit cohesion" (Martin & McClure, 2000, p. 15). This deeply felt sense of mission and a commitment to a better world is, after all, the purpose of the military; for each service member, the commitment is not just about having a better education or training for a job but, in fact, a felt sense of mission to make the world a better and safer place. The recruiting ads are "mini coming of age stories focusing on the challenges that make a boy a man" (Houppert, 2005b, p. 3). Basic training is designed not to bring an adolescent into independence but rather to shift the recruit from dependence on his family to dependence on the team; "the soldier must learn that he can trust no one but his buddies" (Houppert, 2005b, p. 4). Thankfully, today military members, unlike during the Vietnam War, are widely honored (Gegax & Thomas, 2005), and "incongruous as it may seem for the millions whose closest brush with battle is on cable [TV], Soldiers and Marines on the front line are proud to be there and willing to serve again. The overall effect is to heighten the sense that the military is becoming a proud cult that fewer and fewer outsiders want to join" (p. 26).

This dedication to the country and fellow soldiers (Fenell & Weinhold, 2003) sometimes creates serious issues for the family. Service members are often required to spend long hours on the job and frequently are part of a tight team, almost a second family. If this military second family is perceived to be more important than the family left at home, serious conflicts can emerge. Shifting alliances from the family to the military is the very foundation of modern warfare or combat capability (Houppert, 2005b). Fenell and Weinhold (2003) pointed out that although research has shown that military service members who have solid families perform better on the job, it is still a difficult balancing act for service members to be a part of both of these families who are so integral to the success of the mission and to their personal career. A therapist, who not only had been a career military officer's spouse but is now the mother of a career officer, called it a form of brainwashing; the family must take on this stance of the military that demands loyalty, dedication, dependency, and a sense of mission.

Career service members often see themselves as a breed apart (Gegax & Thomas, 2005, p. 27), and as one general was quoted as saying, "It's good people, its very rewarding, you feel a great sense of service, duty, personal discipline" (p. 27). Of the 100 or so generals who have children serving, one is a mother. Her son was proud to have a general for a mother, as he was able to get not only motherly advice but also ideas and strategies for his military service. Her advice to him as he went to Iraq was, "No matter what, you are there for your buddies" (Gegax & Thomas, 2005, p. 29). Mary Wertsch (1991) wrote that the real determining factor in most military families was not their parents but something outside the family. It was the all-powerful presence that was often unacknowledged by the family called the Military Mission; it was this presence that went with them everywhere and without which their lives would have no meaning. "From the viewpoint of the military's extended family style and demands, the mission takes precedence, and therefore, often the service member's relationship with his peers is found to take precedence over [the relationship] between himself and his spouse, children, or parents" (Ridenour, 1984, p. 7).

Preparation for Disaster: War

A large sign at the front gate of the Ft. Campbell, Kentucky, military installation tracks the number of fatalities each year along with the number of days the post has gone without an accident (Blaise, 2006). The warrior society is a world set apart from the civilian world because of its constant preparation for disaster. That upfront reality may not have been as obvious for the first two decades after the all-volunteer military came into existence, but it has definitely become a reality since then. From the beginning of the all-volunteer service until the early 1990s, those going into the military seemed to have less of a sense that they were going into harm's way. During the high rates of deployment from Europe in 1991 during the Gulf War, there were many who very vocally said, "But I didn't join the military to shoot people." That obviously has changed dramatically, returning to the mentality of the military prior to the all-volunteer service.

Virtually no one now joins the military believing they are not going into harm's way. Even in peacetime, being an infantryman is a dangerous job. Soldiers get injured or killed in training accidents or, more often, while driving too fast or drunk off post (Blaise, 2006). The men and women who go to war believe that the loved ones they leave behind have a profound effect on their ability to hold up under fire (Henderson, 2006). "Military readiness is like a three-legged stool. The first leg is training, the second equipment. The third leg is the family. If any of these three legs snaps, the stool tips over and America is unprepared to defend herself" (Henderson,

2006, p. 5). Martin and McClure (2000) wrote that military service has an unlimited commitment, and the possibility that service members could conceivably be asked to sacrifice their lives for their country is deeply rooted in the military tradition and is accepted as a condition of service.

> Civilians often seem to blithely overlook a central truth military people can never afford to forget: that at any moment they may be called upon to give their lives—or lose a loved one—to serve the ends of government. Even if it never comes to that, [they] sacrifice a great deal in the course of doing a job that most civilians on some level understand is necessary to the country as a whole. (Wertsch, 1991, p. 16)

The Fortress

The contribution of thinking of the military as a Fortress by Wertsch (1991) is extremely valuable. This Fortress encompasses the way of life and the physical communities in which the military members live, as well as their mental and psychological world. It is a combination of characteristics and self-perceptions that sets the military world apart from civilian societies. It is perhaps the greatest of paradoxes that the military's purpose is to defend and protect American democracy, while at the same time those in the military live in one of the most undemocratic systems where individuality is discouraged and freedom of speech and assembly is not allowed. Those who join the Armed Forces give up a lot of freedom to ensure that other people can continue to enjoy them, including their freedom of speech and, sometimes, their right to live. "No other institution in America wields so much power over the lives of its members. And even though their families haven't joined the military, it controls the families' lives, too" (Henderson, 2006, p. 5). The following concepts of secrecy, stoicism, and denial, which Wertsch (1991) defined as Masks of the Fortress, further describe the psychological world of the Fortress.

Secrecy

The first Mask of the Fortress is the need for secrecy, or, as the saying goes, "what goes on in the family, stays in the family." The one imperative for family members is to not get the service member in trouble or do anything that will reflect badly on him or her. Incidents of child abuse, domestic violence, alcoholism, and drug use (before mandatory testing) were rampant but often beneath the surface, where they were difficult to detect. Recent reports are showing spikes in the use of alcohol and family violence (Alaimo, 2006b; Ames & Cunradi, n.d.; Houppert, 2005a) resulting from the conflicts in Iraq and Afghanistan. A client of one of the counselors I spoke with shared that after reporting her husband's violent behavior to the military police (MP), his commanding officer said to her, "We aren't going to be hearing about any more reports to MP, will we?" As a school counselor I found that because the methods of questioning a student who reported abuse, usually by a male MP "who are inadequately trained to investigate … violence" (Houppert, 2005b, p. 119), armed and in full uniform, were so intimidating that the student would end up denying the story during questioning. In some cases, even when it was substantiated, the process often somehow got derailed because of the "importance of the mission" or "he's a good soldier."

As noted in chapter 1, in the discussion of the stigma against seeking help, the latest report on the mental health status of the military (Mental Health Advisory Team, 2007), stated that, although the stigma may be decreasing, it has by no means been eliminated. Usually if a service member and his or her spouse have marital problems and decide to go to counseling, they will make sure the spouse is the patient or client, and the spouse carries the diagnosis for insurance purposes, believing this will protect the service member. A retired Army psychiatrist stated that while he was on active duty it was his responsibility, when working with a soldier, to report it to the commander. That is happening less and less because of the move by the military to outsource many services, including new employment assistant-type programs such as Military OneSource, which provides free counseling by civilian counselors with no requirement for reporting.

This is a culture in which the standard operating procedure is that information is shared on a need-to-know basis and secrecy is second nature (Wertsch, 1991). The secrecy extends into the home because service members are advised not to speak freely to their spouses about the harsh realities of war, and the spouses are told to watch how much they tell their military husbands. "You only have to hear once that a distracted soldier is a dead soldier to start weighing your words and re-crafting the email narrative that goes out to your spouse" (Houppert, 2005b, p. 146). In addition, some military members have jobs that involve classified information, creating a situation in which open communication about work is impossible, leading to an even wider gap at home. A therapist who works with service members outside of the Army Military Intelligence base in Arizona pointed out that if one works in a culture of classified information, then everything becomes secretive, including one's personal life. As an Air Force sergeant in Military Intelligence jokingly said, "If I tell you what I do, then I would have to kill you."

Stoicism

A second Mask of the Fortress is stoicism, where the unexpressed goes unshared and leads to more isolation. Often a lot is left hidden, buried for many years. In counseling kids in my high school who were considered to have anger and behavior problems, I would often uncover years of buried grief and pain, as well as a great deal of difficulty in finally being able to express their fears, hurt, and even hopes. The stoicism is carried over into the families, and the family members become part of the system, part of the mission. A major issue during deployment is helping the family understand that readiness means family readiness, also. "Warriors believe in the mask of stoicism.... They expect stoic behavior from one another ... [and] expect it of their children" (Wertsch, 1991, p. 1). Stoic behavior is rewarded, whereas emotionality is not only discouraged but often punished; often the first casualties are family relationships. It is ironic that, because of the stressors inherent in combat and the preparation for combat, service members may know one another better than they know their family; "the bonding of warriors in war is the kind of communion of the spirit that military families pretend to but rarely achieve" (Wertsch, 1991, p. 41). Along with understanding the stressors inherent in combat, and equally important, is "an appreciation of the shared attitudes, beliefs, and expectations that prevail within military units as part of their shared culture and traditions. These culturally shaped attitudes and beliefs form a lens through which combat and operational stressors can be either filtered or magnified for individual warriors" (Nash, 2007, p.11).

Denial

Military families often also live under a mask of denial; they have to! The service member parent may eventually pay the ultimate price; particularly in the current global situation, everyone knows so many who already have. If these families had to constantly be conscious of these fears, it would be unbearable, so the possibility of disaster is repressed; in the process, most other feelings are denied also. Warriors cannot do their duty without denial, and the spouses and families need the denial to not feel so vulnerable. To not understand this as a therapist is to not understand the military culture and, thus, the military client or family. Yet it is often in direct conflict with generally accepted norms in counseling, where we champion openness, honesty, and expression of feelings. In the arena of war,

> tendencies for sympathy and compassion are often used as lures to entrap the unwary.... Losses are often inevitable.... The warrior must build a wall around tender emotions to be able to function in a calculated, all-about-business manner to stay alive and not jeopardize

other comrades. A quiet moment to fully mourn a lost friend or the opportunity to stop to aid a wounded civilian are luxuries that are often not available.... To keep alive and perform combat duties successfully the individual may have to remain in this combat mode 24/7.... [It] becomes second nature. The pattern does not fully shut off even after the person is home and safe. (Lyons, 2007, p. 312)

All three characteristics of the Fortress—secrecy, stoicism, and denial—are crucial for success of the warrior, success of the mission, and ultimately success of the military. In understanding the effects of trauma (National Institute for Trauma and Loss in Children, n.d.), we can differentiate between Type I and Type II trauma. Type I is the one-time incident, such as what happened on September 11, 2001, school shootings such as the recent Virginia Tech incident, or any horrendous accident. But Type II trauma is the trauma that occurs over and over again, often in small increments; for instance, domestic violence, alcoholism, military relocations, or numerous deployments. I believe that many families in the military are experiencing Type II trauma as a result of the constant fear and constant planning for disaster, the constant readiness for change, and the constant awareness that even if the disaster has not yet affected us personally, it has happened to those around us. These families are not allowed to grieve, to mourn their losses, and to learn and grow from their losses to move on in a healthy manner. When the culture encourages secrecy, stoicism, and denial and discourages or even punishes the expression of fears and grief, families and service members are often faced with the same kind of consequences we see in clients who suffer from constant levels of Type II trauma.

Parent-Focused Families

Another way of looking at the family within this Fortress is to compare the military family to what Donaldson-Pressman and Pressman (1994) defined as the narcissistic family. I am uncomfortable with this term, because the last thing I want to do is label military families as narcissistic families or in any way suggest that just because families are in the military they are dysfunctional, so I prefer using the concept of parent-focused families. In the early 1990s, the authors (Donaldson-Pressman & Pressman) found that some of the military families they worked with had many of the dynamics of alcoholic or abusive families, but they found no history of alcohol abuse or other forms of dysfunctional parenting such as incest, physical abuse, emotional neglect, or physical absence. Wertsch (1991) found many of the same similarities in her interviews with adult military brats. Donaldson-Pressman and Pressman began to track the traits of families in their practice who fit these dynamics.

The pervasive trait present in these families was that "the needs of the parent system took precedence over the needs of the children" (Donaldson-Pressman & Pressman, 1994, p. 4), which is why I have chosen to use the term *parent-focused families*. Developmentally, parent-focused families, and certainly many military families, have difficulty meeting the fundamental needs of trust and safety for their children, because the family is consumed with dealing with the needs of the parents. In military families, as we have discussed in this chapter, the focus is on not just the functioning of the parental system but how the family system learns to operate within the larger external system of the military. Also, making sure that what happens in the family does not affect the military parent's career is a given, which builds an all-encompassing web around the family. In parent-focused military families, there are similarities with the families Donaldson-Pressman and Pressman wrote about, particularly when there is a child who is exhibiting behavior problems. These similarities are as follows:

1. The belief that the child does not have a problem but instead is the problem.
2. The child does not have a need, such as anxiety, a developmental delay, depression, or academic issues, but rather is given a label, such as lazy, stupid, a class clown, a screwup, or some description that does not fit the model of military families.
3. Children learn that their feelings are of little or negative value, so they begin to detach from feelings, which becomes functional because they learn early that an expression of feelings only adds fuel to the fire.
4. Responsibility for meeting the emotional needs become skewed when the parents, because they are either physically not present or emotionally unable, leave the child to become inappropriately responsible for meeting the parents' needs.
5. Because children discover early that their own feelings are a source of discomfort and may not be validated if they are expressed, they tend not to develop a sense of trust in their own judgments. In so doing, they either become reactive by choosing to go along with whatever is happening, rebel against everything, or become reflective of others by mirroring them, which often is interpreted as inadequacy or failure.
6. Because of the emotional unavailability of the parent, children often learn not to trust others or themselves and may have difficulty letting down the barriers required for intimacy later in life.

Often we can see these characteristics played out in military families. For example, if a mother's primary focus is on the father and anything that "threatened the father's status, ego, or peace of mind was intolerable" (Donaldson-Pressman & Pressman, 1994, p. 7), an emotionally healthy environment is not created for the children. The parent-focused military family can "look great, until you bite into it and discover the worm" (p. 8), which is a reflection of the secrecy, stoicism, and denial pointed out earlier. Instead of providing a supportive, nurturing, reality-based mirror, the parents may present a mirror that reflects only their needs, resulting in children who grow up feeling defective.

As has already been noted, many military children are born to very young, immature couples who tend to be in a society without their own parents or other older adults to rely on. The external needs of the larger military system make parenting education even more difficult to acquire. "When one is raised unable to trust in the stability, safety, and equity of one's world, one is raised to distrust one's own feelings, perceptions and worth" (Donaldson-Pressman & Pressman, 1994, p. 8).

In most cases, the physical needs of military children are indeed met; they are well nurtured and have both their physical and their psychological needs met in healthy ways during childhood. However, when they begin to assert themselves and make emotional demands, the parental system sometimes is unable to tend to the needs, and parents find themselves resentful or threatened by the needs of the children. I frequently found this to be true with many of the students who had emotional or behavioral problems in the schools where I worked. Often when a student was having either behavior or academic problems, the parents couldn't understand why their child couldn't just change or why the school couldn't just "fix it." The parents often simply did not have the maturity or the skills to imagine that they could make a difference and, in some cases, even that it was their responsibility to do so.

The culture of the military, with its demands on the family, "creates a situation similar to the intermittent and unpredictable reinforcement common among narcissistic families" (Donaldson-Pressman & Pressman, 1994, p. 8). Again, it is not my goal here to label military families; labeling never works. But the ability to understand how some families in the military are organized, not just because of who the parents are but, more important, because of who the parents are in the midst of the demands of the Fortress in which they live, can be helpful in working with those family systems that are struggling so we can help them adjust and change rather than quickly apply their own label to their child. We will look at children's issues in chapter 5 and find that children's reactions to living in the Fortress can be extremely varied, so that even within this structure, by no means will all children face life with behavior or emotional difficulties.

The Military and the Male Psyche

It seems appropriate to discuss the military as it relates to the male psyche, because traditionally the military has been a male domain. Obviously that is changing, but much of the culture of the military is still a very male culture. Dr. Harry Butler has worked with military members for over 30 years in San Diego. From his unique perspective as a male therapist, he believes this issue can easily be overlooked, particularly by female therapists working with male service members. There are still almost three women to every man in the field of counseling, at least at the master's degree level. The majority of civilian counselors interviewed who are working with military families are women. Because the military is still predominately composed of men, Dr. Butler's insights about working with men in the military are invaluable.

To work with men in the military, a therapist must understand male psychology and in so doing give due attention to the concept of "honor" that is so central to the psychology of the military and so central to male psychology. Even though I am not making a judgment here that the concept of honor is not important to female service members, Gilligan (1996) did point out that social scientists have discovered that there is a marked difference between men and women in studying the culture of honor. Perhaps the most important point to understand, for civilian therapists or anyone working with military families, is that the military probably couldn't do its job without the strongly held beliefs of service members, both men and women, regarding the importance of honor. The concept of honor is so ingrained that officers have no need to enforce it, because the service members themselves enforce honor.

When discussing the stress of war, Nash (2007) used the example of athletics and stated that the genius of great athletes "lies in the ability to perform as if there is no distance or weight or danger" to overcome and the genius of the warrior is to "fight as if there is no terror, horror, or hardship" (p. 4). Nash suggested, "Helping professionals … must always consider the possibility that they may do more harm than good by asking warriors in an operational theater to become more aware of their own stressors and stress reaction" (p. 5). When the concept of stress enters the awareness of leaders, it becomes a challenge to their leadership, as troop morale is essential for the prevention of stressors. "To the extent that leaders see themselves as personally responsible for the management of combat stress … they may also see themselves as personally to blame for the appearance of disabling combat stress reactions ... and as evidence of a relative failure of leadership in that unit" (Nash, 2007, p. 27).

One of the major tenets of war is generating combat stress in the enemy and thereby mitigating operational stress in their own troops. The concept of honor comes into the picture because, to inflict suffering on an adversary, the warrior must not identify with that adversary or feel remorse for the suffering of the adversary. That type of callousness cannot be turned on and off easily, so it "may be asking too much ... to acknowledge their own or their comrades' vulnerability ... at the same time they are exploiting their adversary's vulnerability to almost the same stressors" (Nash, 2007, p. 14). Through leadership, training, and unit cohesion, stress reactions are managed and honor is maintained; "searching for ways to become more comfortable or safe in war can be not only a distraction from the real business at hand, but also a serious hazard to success and even survival" (p. 15).

Sam Keen (1991) wrote that the "wounds that men endure, and the psychic scar tissue that results from living with the expectation of being a battlefield sacrifice, is every bit as horrible as the suffering women bear from the fear and the reality of rape" (p. 7). He explained that throughout history, men have been assigned the dirty work of killing and

> have therefore had their bodies and spirits forged into the shape of a weapon. ... It is all well and good to point out the folly of war and to lament the use of violence. But short of a utopian world from which greed, scarcity, madness, and ill will have vanished, someone must be prepared to take up arms and do battle with evil. We miss the mark if we do not see that manhood has traditionally required selfless generosity even to the point of sacrifice. (p. 7)

For instance, without this commitment to honor and the possibility of sacrifice, the officers and men at Gettysburg would never have engaged in that well-known historical mission. In most battles of the Civil War, where the chances of being wounded or killed were extraordinarily high, the soldiers continued to enthusiastically march directly into the fire, lest any faltering be seen as dishonorable. The officers didn't need to hold a gun to their backs to get them to do what they did. Thus, given the choice between death and dishonor, many military men would choose death, and quite frequently they do. Thus is the power of honor.

Gary Paulsen, the author of a small book called *A Soldier's Heart* (1998), poignantly shared the story of one young soldier from Minnesota during the Civil War and his ability to be consumed by that sense of honor, even after watching and experiencing horrendous deaths and dismemberment of his fellow soldiers. "But he could not run away. None of the others had and he couldn't.... The training must work, he thought. I'm doing all this without meaning to do it. He felt like a stranger to himself, like another person watching his hands move over the rifle" (p. 33).

Dr. Butler (personal communication, October 6, 2006) shared a story of a client, a former Marine pilot, whose vision of honor for him was "the ability to fall on a grenade to save his buddies." He said that if this could be his epitaph, it would be an honorable death. The concept of honor is extremely valuable but perhaps difficult to understand. Of course, military service men are not the only men driven by honor. As noted by Nash (2007) previously, it can be compared to the professional athlete—the need to go the distance, to work through pain, to be there for the team—but the athlete doesn't have to face the possibility of death. The concept of honor is so central and so prevalent in the military that it is inevitable that a therapist working with military families will encounter this issue, and more often than not it can even present an obstacle to therapy. We are, however, learning over and over now with our returning veterans that honor can also be as much an impediment as a strength. A returning veteran who has been diagnosed with PTSD was recently interviewed on a TV news show, and in describing his experience, he stated, "It would have been more honorable for me not to come home."

Relationships at Home

One of the obstacles that the concept of honor presents in therapy is that many military men often believe that, because of their military commitments, they should be given a pass when it comes to relationship issues with family and children. In some cases the concept of honor doesn't seem to extend to conduct with wives and children at all. With career military men, what may appear as a form of neglect is actually the sense of honor to the military family unit in the name of duty. This neglect or inattention may endure for 20 or more years, just the span of time in which children grow to adulthood, often with an absent and emotionally self-contained father. In these cases, everyone loses—resulting in a wife not having a husband, the children not having a father, and the service member feeling misunderstood, neglected, and somewhat martyred. In a metaphorical way, a military man married his military service, and the real-life male–female marriage is thus an extramarital affair (Keith & Whitaker, 1984).

As already noted, the military service member has two families, the personal family of spouse and children and the members of the military unit; more often than not the military unit comes first, emotionally as well as out of a sense of duty. Dr. Butler said, "It is as though all military men are bigamists with two families and the military unit family takes precedence."

One client told him, "Every formation is a family reunion." Many clients told him that they, and many of their fellow comrades, would rather spend Christmas with each other than with their wives and children. Often he found that even the more educated or sophisticated officers actually felt guilty about not being interested in participating in events with the family, as the draw to the camaraderie of their fellow officers encompassed their whole life.

One of the female therapists I spoke with, who was also a wife of a former military officer, shared that she repeatedly felt left out when the families got together after the return of their officer husbands, because invariably the military members wanted to spend the time together instead of spending time with the families. It took her a long time to understand that when a group of people goes through the experiences that these husbands had, it was understandable that they had difficulty making the transition back into the marital family; each time, however, throughout his military career, she stated it was a difficult time for the whole family. A client, who was a wife of a decorated officer, finally began to understand that the time her husband spent drinking with other officers at the Veterans of Foreign Wars (VFW) post was the only time he believed that those around him would understand the thoughts and memories that were constant in his mind, even if they didn't talk about them. She began to understand that this was how he could cope with the tremendous shame for what he believed he had done and for what he had witnessed. Lyons (2007) pointed out that a reluctance to divulge horrible details might very likely be due to the importance of the relationship rather than an indication of the contrary.

The Power' of Shame

In understanding male psychology, the concept of shame seems to be an important key. Mejia (2005) talked about how the socialization of men requires the adherence to many behaviors and attitudes that are deemed to be masculine. Often the way in which young boys learn these behaviors and attitudes is through shaming.

> The use of shame is one of a number of societal factors that contribute to the toughening-up process by which it is assumed that boys need to be raised. Little boys are made to feel ashamed of their feelings, guilty especially about feelings of weakness, vulnerability, fear, and despair. The use of shame to control boys is pervasive; boys are made to feel shame over and over in the course of growing up. (p. 32)

Mejia pointed out that healthy coping strategies for dealing with shame and trauma are suppressed in the socialization process of boys, so it is not surprising that often boys who were socialized from a shame-based perspective find themselves a natural fit with the military culture. It is a natural extension to the socialization that taught them to "avoid shame at all costs, to wear a mask of coolness, to act as though everything is going all right, as though everything is under control, even if it is not" (Mejia, 2005, p. 33). This is the making of an ideal warrior, who, while serving in the military, can act on his learned tendencies under the code of honor and sacrifice for the greater good. If we put the concept of shame-based socialization on a continuum, we would see that at the extreme end "violence and aggression may also be avenues through which some boys and men compensate for uncomfortable feelings such as shame and hurt" (Mahalik, Good, & Englar-Carlson, 2003, p. 125). James Gilligan (1996), in truly the best work I have read about violence, shared,

> Behind the mask of cool or self-assurance that many violent men clamp on to their faces—with a desperation born of the certain knowledge that they would "lose face" if they ever let it slip—is a person who feels vulnerable not just to the "loss of face" but to the total loss of honor, prestige, respect, and status—the disintegration of identity, especially their adult, masculine, heterosexual identity; their selfhood, personhood, rationality and sanity. (p. 12)

Gilligan wrote that the "most dangerous men on earth are those who are afraid that they are wimps. Wars have been started for less" (1996, p. 6). Sam Keen (1991) outlined the characteristics of the warrior psyche, which includes (a) a heroic stance; (b) willpower, danger, action, and a heightened awareness that comes from living in the presence of death; (c) identification of action with force; (d) a paranoid worldview; (e) black-and-white thinking; (f) repression of fear, compassion, and guilt; (g) an obsession with rank and hierarchy because obedience is required if there is a denying of one's freedom; and (h) the degrading of the feminine. This of course does not mean that every military male fits this description, but there is a history, a tradition, in the military that is carried on by some who would maintain that this is the true description of a warrior, at least by degree. When the recruiter of the soldier described earlier who wounded his wife and another soldier and then killed himself was asked if he knew of the soldier's previous violent history, the recruiter replied, "That's just the kind of boy we want to turn into a man" (Houppert, 2005a, p. 2).

The passion for honor and conformity to tradition so typical of many military men may be at odds with the necessities of therapy for openness and critical examination of a client's assumptions about life. Wives and children have traditionally been seen by the military, both the establishment and individual service members, as support services for the military mission instead of people who have their own needs, values, and life missions. Although this is definitely changing, the historical significance cannot be overlooked. The demands of the wives and children are sometimes seen as interfering with the military man's duty. As the old Marine saying goes, "If the Marines wanted you to have a wife, they would have issued you one."

It happened often enough in my experience as a school counselor that a student might be sent back to the States to live with a grandparent or other relative rather than stay in the country because the child's behavior might have an impact on the military parent's reputation. There were even times, although infrequent, where allocations of abuse were disregarded because the military parent was essential to the military mission. As the institutional military has made necessary accommodations for the family in the past three decades, it is becoming more family friendly, and families and therapists are experiencing fewer situations such as these. At the same time, we need to be constantly cognizant of the fact that the military cannot do its job without the commitment and dedication to honor and sacrifice.

> Thankfully, we have learned as a nation not to blame the warriors for the war as we did when our soldiers came home from Vietnam. This time around, even fervent anti-war protesters support the troops.... And that's good, because one of the best things we can do for these [service members] is to welcome them with open arms. Even more, we need to create opportunities at home for vets to use the skills they learned in the military. (Brothers, 2006, p. 5)

Women in the Military

We know from the statistics that approximately 14% of the military is now made up of female service members. In her beautifully written story of being both the wife of a soldier and an officer in the Army, Kate Blaise (2006) explained, "The military isn't what it used to be, thanks partly to the large number of women who are choosing it as a career. Being a woman in the U.S. Army is far more nuanced than being a man—and in some cases, not necessarily less dangerous" (p. 4). Perhaps the typical civilian has a preconceived notion of what female service members are like, but Blaise stated that the variety of women never ceased to amaze even her; in fact, it was a little microcosm of female types from "girly-girls, tough girls to nerdy girls." "Women in the U.S. military have always had a 'tough row to hoe' and we owe a lot to those women who literally broke ground, opened doors, and made the choice of a military career easier for those who followed" (*Military Women "Firsts,"* 1996, ¶ 1). Military women have a long way to go in overcoming the stereotypes and the generalizations made by their male counterpoints.

For the first 2 months, Blaise (2006) was immersed in the strictly male culture as she struggled to be recognized as a soldier rather than as a woman in a uniform, until she realized for that to happen was "about as likely as Saddam turning himself in to CENTCOM [central command]" (p. 90). She was aware of subtle differences in the way she was treated, for example, a male comrade might say "you look nice this morning" simply because she remembered to comb her hair for a change, or another might say "hey you smell good" because she had run baby wipes over her dusty skin. She finally realized that she would always be seen as a female first and that her "dual identities as officer and woman were fused together like conjoined twins who shared the same brain; separating them was next to impossible" (Blaise, 2006, p. 190). She found her time in the military to be a tender balance; if she acted too masculine, she would be considered butch, and if she acted too girly-girly, she would be considered a lightweight. Blaise explained that her strongest leadership trait was her ability to get along with everyone; however, with one male cadet, her gender continued to be the issue. He often made comments such as "we don't need your kind ... don't know why you think you need to be in the Army." She never knew if he changed his attitude, but as she said, "At the end of the day he was standing in formation and following my orders just like everyone else" (p. 99).

From the first Medal of Honor awarded to Dr. Mary Walker during the Civil War to 1926 when Olive Hoskins became the first woman promoted to warrant officer to 1970 when Brigadier General Elizabeth Holsington became the first woman to attain star rank to 1990 when Commander Darlene Iskra became the first woman to command a U.S. Navy ship to 1994 when Lt. Kara Hultgreen, the first fully qualified female fleet fighter pilot, crashed her Tomcat into the Pacific Ocean and became the first woman combat pilot to die in service (*Military Women "Firsts,"* 1996), women in the military have been serving this country in what one posting on the Military Women Organization Web site said "is not a right to serve, it is an honor and a privilege" (Military Woman Organization, 2003, ¶ 1). Secretary of Defense William S. Cohen was quoted in 1997 in a RAND Corporation study as saying, "Leadership, training and mission determine how well units perform—not the presence or absence of women.... However, more needs to be done to improve career opportunities for women in the military. ... America's sons and daughters deserve no less" (Department of Defense, 1997, ¶ 2). The same study from the RAND Corporation pointed out that the military has opened 80% of the specialties to women, including over 99% in the Air Force and just over 91% in the Navy. The study concluded that "gender integration is perceived to have a relatively small effect on readiness, cohesion, and morale," even though the researchers heard "repeatedly how double standards undermine women's credibility and generate hostility" and they recommended that new policies need to be developed that avoid "establishing double standards for men and women in the same positions, and where possible, eliminate the double standards that exist now" (¶ 3). The Military Woman Organization Web site points out that the major concerns for military women still include issues of sexual harassment, assault, differential treatment and conditions, and being a parent.

Women in Combat

The role of women in combat continues to be a hot topic. Worldwide, even though women are recruited to serve in the military in most countries, only Canada, Denmark, Finland, Germany, Norway, and Switzerland permit women to fill active combat roles (*Contemporary Debate on Women's Roles in the Military*, n.d.). Those who believe women are better suited away from front lines show a lack of understanding of the new face of war (Blaise, 2006). The lines separating the good guys from the bad guys are smudged as the enemy has decided that anyone hailing from a particular country is the enemy, soldier or not, men or not. Blaise told the story of the checkpoint searches in Iraq that frighten the little girls, so the female Marines asked that friends back home send teddy bears to give to the children to calm their fears. The modern military needs that kind of compassion, as the winning over of civilians may be half the battle, and it is a vital attribute that women bring. "I am proud of those soldiers and the job they are doing and the fact that they were doing it from the heart" (Blaise, 2006, p. 38).

An article from Defend America (Dickinson, 2007) pointed out that in a culture where contact with women is forbidden, the necessity of searching female civilians is a challenge; however, in recent operations in securing Baghdad, the women soldiers perform the task that their male counterparts cannot do. "Amid all the controversy of talk of opening combat arms to women, side by side service doesn't seem to be much of an issues in this unit" (¶ 6). Women are now part of combat, and, according to Blaise, they belong there; it would be absurd to assume that the military could fight as effectively by removing women from forward positions, as they would be hard pressed to find male soldiers to fill the slots and do as good a job as they do. Two female Army Guard members recently earned Combat Medical Badges for their work driving armored Humvees to provide medical support for the 3rd Infantry Division of the Afghan National Army in

Afghanistan (Straub, 2007). They say that because they were women, it was hard at first to earn the respect of the Afghan soldiers with whom they worked, but together they have "broken the glass ceiling in the crucible of combat, once considered a domain for men only" (¶ 5).

> As women we have just as much right to defend our country as any male soldier. This means, inevitably, we will die for it as well. Are women suited to be in combat? Some are, but many men aren't fit for combat, either. … The genie is out of the bottle, and no amount of politicking will coax her back in. (Blaise, 2006, p. 338)

The Downsides

One downside (Blaise, 2006) is the fact that because there are still so few women in any given unit, it often means that they are housed together, enlisted with officers rather than officers being with other officers. Blaise found that she missed the necessary time to discuss work with other officers and just kick back with her peers, and the enlisted women weren't too excited about having an officer in their presence. She also wrote that she secretly refused to abandon all her "girly indulgences" just because she was going to war, so instead she adopted a "policy of stealth femininity" by painting her toenails with red nail polish, which she kept in her rucksack next to 10 pairs of cotton panties in bright colors and stripes, but no lace, from Victoria's Secret. Although she didn't wear makeup, style her hair, or wear any color other than brown, she always knew she had bright red toenails.

A number of obviously more serious concerns for women in the military have been written about; as noted earlier, one of the major issues is for those moms who are deployed. A therapist in Tucson, Arizona, talked about how it seemed much more difficult for these women to leave their children, feeling they were abandoning their kids rather than feeling the sense of doing their duty usually felt by men. Although the therapist found that men also struggle to some degree when they leave their kids, they are usually assured that the children have their mothers to care for them. Women, on the other hand, seem to have a deeper connection and feel more guilt about leaving their kids. Almost every posting on the Military Woman Organization Web site reflects how hard it was for these moms to leave their kids, but so often they felt they were contributing to the mission, which would eventually make their children's life easier.

A concern shared by many women on this Web site, many of whom had survived childhood abuse, is the level of sexual assault they experience while in the service. These women often are unwilling to report the abuse because of the possible negative consequences to their military career, even if the perpetrator were to be punished. This obviously leads to additional mental health issues, such as PTSD, that may go untreated.

Another concern is the high level of infidelity. This was verified by Blaise (2006), who said, "Infidelity and fraternization among the troops had become rampant" (p. 37). The world of the military, particularly with the current high rate of deployments, is ripe for infidelity, which obviously affects both men and women and the families left behind. In addition, the *2005 Demographics Report* (Military Family Research Institute, 2006) showed that women in the military experience divorce at a greater rate than men, are more likely to remain divorced, have a higher rate of single parenting, and are less likely to remarry. The report also showed that a substantial number of military women never marry, more than twice the number of women in the general U.S. population.

Regardless of the issues they face and the hardships they endure, as Blaise said, the genie is out of the bottle. Women will always be a part of the military system, and my guess is that almost all of them would agree with the statement that "no one deserves the opportunity to join ... you earn that by proving you are qualified" (Military Woman Organization, 2003, ¶ 1).

CHAPTER 4

The Military Family

Living in the Fortress

So often when writing this book, I would see new stories in the national news. One of these was an article titled "It's Tearing Families Apart," which reported on the families who had been directly affected since the beginning of the war in Iraq in 2003 (Skipp, 2006). Almost daily, I found myself struggling with an attempt to write somewhat general but, I hoped, worthwhile information regarding military families without getting caught up in the current global issues. One of the most interesting questions I read came from a civilian reporter, who asked a military spouse, who had recently published a book titled *While They're at War: The True Story of American Families on the Homefront* (Henderson, 2006), if it ever bothered her husband that she was writing about the wives instead of about the *real* story! What could be more real than the stories about how the families of the military are affected by both their life in the military and the current military situation?

As Marie Wakefield wrote (2007), "From a mental health perspective, it is very important to recognize that veterans do not experience war alone and that the experience of war does not end when a tour is over. Families, maybe for generations to come, are affected in many ways" (p. 5). By early January 2007, 3,350 Americans had lost their lives in Iraq and Afghanistan; over 47% of those were married, leaving behind almost 2,000 children (Crary, 2007). Crary stated, "Compared to the heavily draftee combat troops of the Vietnam War, today's volunteer fighting force is older, more reliant on National Guard and Reserves citizen-soldiers, and more likely to be married" (¶ 7).

Gegax and Thomas (2005) explained that the modern military is demanding on families. They compared the military during the cold war, which they described as a "garrison force" with service members staying on bases for long periods of time, to the war on terror in which the military has increasingly become an "expeditionary force" where service members more and more leave their families for long tours overseas. Back in 1984, Ridenour listed the unique facets of life, both positive and negative, within the military, all of which remain true of the current military family, including (a) frequent separations and reunions; (b) regular geographic household relocations; (c) life under the "mission must come first" dictum; (d) a need for the family to adapt its natural growth and development to rigidity, regimentation, and conformity; (e) early retirement from a career in comparison to civilian counterparts; (f) omnipresent rumors and background threat of loss during a mission; (g) feelings of detachment from the mainstream of nonmilitary life; (h) the security of a vast system that exists to meet the families needs; (i) work that more than likely involves travel and adventure; (j) the social effects of rank on the family; and (k) the lack of personal control over pay, promotion, and other benefits. These are, in summary, the plusses and minuses for the families living in the military Fortress, and although "it is evident … that large segments of our society deal with one or more of these aforementioned concerns and stresses … there may be no other major group that confronts so many or all of them" (Ridenour, 1984, p. 3).

The Warrior Clan

This warrior clan (Gegax & Thomas, 2005) is viewed by the civilian world outside of the Fortress as a mixed bag. For families who live within the Fortress, the boundaries sometimes get blurred between family and work, especially those in career fields such as military intelligence, where they are trained to be interrogators. That is their job, they go to school to be good at grilling people, and they sometimes end up using the same tactics at home. A therapist near a large Army intelligence base talked about the families she works with who feel that they are often being interrogated by their military parent rather than having a parent who is simply interested in who they are as people. Missing in their interrogation training seems to be how *not* to use these techniques in relationships or in families. Military life, according to Rodriguez (1984), inevitably has an impact on the military family, with its attention to regimentation, rules, and standards; authoritarian–authoritative modes of discipline; and tight constraints on individual expression. Although there are undoubtedly few current military fathers right out of Pat Conroy's book *The Great Santini* (1976), military family life can become a caricature of the military unit, depending on how thoroughly the parents adopt the military values and how pervasive the expectation for adherence is to rules in the military community.

> A ubiquitous structure, clearly defined social expectations for conduct, and close quartered opportunities for community camaraderie exist in military communities. To some families these standards and their corollary sanctions may seem intrusive, conflicting with family values, or impeding individual freedom of choice. (Rodriguez, 1984, p. 56)

Families are also being affected by the increased political polarization being seen in the United States over the current issues facing the military. Most military families view the military not as a job but as a lifestyle and are at one with the service member in fulfilling the mission, but they are being faced with a burden to explain or justify to others their entire way of living. This can be a heavy burden and take a heavy toll on families, especially as active duty service members are deployed more often (Bannerman, 2007). Henderson (2007) wrote, "Out of pride, or perhaps from a feeling of vulnerability, those of us who live the homefront life often feel the need to protect ourselves from anyone who has never been left behind during a deployment" (p. 3). Another military wife made the statement that "a lot of military wives take the protests personally ... but I don't see these protests as being against the military, it's the administration they are protesting" (Houppert, 2005b, p. 173).

Family Readiness

A major part of living in the military Fortress is the issue of readiness, as it takes a family to defend a nation. Adler-Baeder and Pittman (2005) wrote that the military brings together a unique system of individuals, families, communities, and work units that must coordinate to function effectively. Given the demand of the military mission and the readiness requirements, the morale and productivity of both the service members and their families are critical to mission effectiveness. Family readiness is essential to unit readiness.

> Family readiness is defined as a family's ability to adapt to and deal with the stressors associated with military danger and a military life style, such as frequent moves, deployments, unaccompanied tours, and overseas assignments. There has been much effort in recent years

to better understand family readiness and its relationship to troop readiness, including a focus on stressors and factors related to family adaptation in the context of stressors. (Adler-Baeder & Pittman, 2005, p. 5)

Research (Adler-Baeder & Pittman, 2005) suggests that the protective factors that promote family adaptation and readiness include spouse support, leader support, and a positive perception of the unit culture by the family. Data also suggest that spouse employment may better prepare families to deal with deployments by providing them with additional financial resources (Russo, Dougherty, & Martin, 2000). Since the late 1980s more programs have been established to help families plan and prepare for deployments, including making the emotional adjustment and learning coping skills. These programs emphasize using human services as a resource, based on the belief that a partnership philosophy of unit readiness is equivalent to family readiness.

Houppert (2005b) wrote, "Every study, every report, every training manual, and every brochure that the Army has produced about deployment and the family in the last ten years emphasizes how family readiness— read maturity, competence, independence—affects a soldier's readiness" (p. 86). Although many of the support programs, such as the family readiness groups, are supposedly there to help the families, the concerns Houppert heard from military spouses is that this attempt to get the spouses on board for the sake of the mission is not so much to support the family but a decision by the military that what "the wives need to properly buck up is their own brand of unit cohesion" (p. 86). Houppert suggested that these support programs are just a shift in language based on the notion that the role of the military isn't really to support the spouses or family but to "teach them to be self reliant" (p. 86).

Family Strengths

Military families are faced with numerous challenges and opportunities that help them develop diverse strengths (Rodriguez, 1984). These strengths include the following: (a) they have a relatively predictable, safe, well-provided-for, and orderly life; (b) they usually have some support built into frequent relocations, compared with many mobile civilian families; (c) the children often exhibit the ability to accept newly arriving children into their neighborhood and school; (d) the conditioned expectations of the constant relocations are considered a social norm that comes along with economic and social security; (e) some reports from the 1980s reported that military children were intellectually brighter and exhibited fewer psychological maladjustments and that there is some evidence of less juvenile delinquency; (f) although studies do not negate the concerns that military families experience, they do indicate that rates of dysfunction are comparatively lower than might be expected, given the challenges the families face; (g) families tend to be resourceful and self-reliant, which might be a contradiction to the belief that they are overly dependent and passive; (h) although they are dependent in some aspects of life, they are often creative in exploring their options and sometimes demonstrate independence not seen in some nonmilitary subcultures; and (i) there are unique positive aspects of the military life, including the awareness of other people and world communities, the participation in and service to a national mission, and a shared personal and family pride of accomplishment that provides special rewards for most military families.

Lyons (2007) suggested that for many, even the horrors of combat can be a learning experience that can be brought home to the family.

> Facing death so much earlier in life than most people can lead to acceptance of mortality or a numbing of reaction that can appear cold and uncaring. Many families are surprised, however, to see how the warrior shines in times of tragedy. Combat mode kicks in and the warrior may gear up quickly in times of crisis, efficiently drawing on the skills ... developed during war.... Many who survive horrors and rigors of war emerge with new clarity of their own abilities and limitations, a strong sense of values and beliefs and an ethical maturity that many others do not develop until old age—if then.... Many warriors are successful in imparting some of these survival skills and values to loved ones, helping them develop these characteristics without having to endure the trauma of combat in the process. (p. 321)

The Military Spouse

The new generation of military families, particularly the military spouse, has been more vocal in pressing for more compassionate and effective support for families, particularly those suffering losses as a result of the current global conflicts (Crary, 2007). This outspoken push for support has resulted in numerous policy changes, including improved benefits for families of fallen service members. One spouse was quoted by Crary (2007) as saying that even though being a good military spouse was accepting that you don't come first, there is a concerted effort being made on the part of the spouses to push for change for those families left behind.

At least two organizations have been formed by people with loved ones in uniform; one is Military Families Speak Out, an organization that is made up of family members who are "breaking the military's traditional code of silence by publicly protesting this war" (Bannerman, 2007, ¶ 7), and the other is Military Families for Peace. In her year of interviewing military spouses, Houppert (2005b) found that there was more opposition to the war among wives than she ever imagined. "The military seems oblivious to the level of opposition among wives to the U.S. war in Iraq.... These women, who straddle the military world—one foot on post, one foot in the civilian sector—were getting their news from civilian sources and they were weighing the 'inevitability' of this war with the potential personal costs" (p. 224) to themselves and their families. Russo et al. (2000) said,

> Today, military spouses are more independent and less likely to view themselves as just an extension of the military members. Spouses are concerned with how they are treated by the military. Many feel that their actions as spouses should be independent of the military member ... [but that the military should still] be supportive of families' needs and provide families with the services and programs necessary to cope with the demands of today's military lifestyle. (p. 89)

Support Services

Since the early 1990s, the military has worked to help spouses and families adapt to military life in a more formal way, with numerous activities, classes, and organizations. For instance, every company is required to have a volunteer network of spouses, usually known as the family readiness group (FRG), that along with other programs provide guidance on how to manage the emotional phases of deployment and teach, among other things, the history of that particular branch of the service (Henderson, 2006). Many spouses, particularly the young and newly enlisted, don't know such orientation programs exist, some don't have time, and others just don't see the point.

As we saw from the statistics in chapter 3, military spouses are generally women and young, often giving birth to their first child in their late teens or early 20s. Most of the military spouses seen by a therapist in Tucson were married to young enlisted airmen who got married young and often were quite immature. The isolation can be monumental for these spouses, who may live on or off base but still feel confined while their husbands goes off to work or are deployed for months at a time. One chapter in Karen Houppert's book *Home Fires Burning* is titled "All That You Can Be: Young, Poor and Alone" (p. 79). That about sums it up. Regardless of where they live, they are in a new community without the resources, family, or friends that they left behind. If they are willing to seek out others, they obviously do much better, but often for the newly enlisted, newly married, and very young, these may be skills they have not yet developed. When she and her husband were new to the military, Henderson (2006) didn't feel it would be important to reach out to others, because she "hadn't yet grasped that the military institution [her husband] had joined now controlled his life. And since my life was intimately bound up in his, it now controlled me, too, and it would be to my benefit to know a little something about it" (p. 35).

Unlike some other communities, Navy families who live in San Diego, California, live all over the community in numerous military housing areas rather than in just one central location; these differing communities offer a variety of services for families. A therapist in San Diego worked with a seaman whose wife was a teacher; this couple constantly struggled with their relationship, as he was gone a lot, which is very typical of the Navy. After discovering the programs available on base, she found the support was very valuable but commented that these programs were really used only by the wives who live close or on the particular base that happened to have the programs. This young teacher could always find substitute teaching positions, but she commented on the concerns she had for those spouses who didn't have the ability to work, and if they did not live on base how isolated they become, particularly those with young children.

Many of the spouses Houppert (2005b) interviewed questioned whether the military created these programs to improve the wives' actual circumstances or to improve their attitudes. "Does the idea that women ought to be paid for the work they do, rather than volunteer for the good of their husband and their husbands' units really mark a decline in 'idealism'?" (p. 225). Durand (2000) told of her former life as a military spouse, or one member of a "two-person career," where she carried out the demands of the military wife, which was to create the right background so that her husband's work reflected his life at home. The term "two-person career" was actually coined in the early 1970s to describe those jobs where only one person is paid but both spouses keep the institute afloat, such as ministers, diplomats, politicians, and military members (Houppert, 2005b). The goals were for the spouse to keep a positive attitude toward the military, to always maintain an interest in his duty, and to be very flexible and adaptable.

Yesterday and Today

In her study of military wives, Durand (2000) discovered key differences between today's Army wives and those of her era. One of the differences is that spouses are no longer members of Wives' Clubs; in fact those clubs often don't exist, which means the wives attend fewer "coffees," do less volunteer work, and participate less in community activities. The major reason for this change is that the majority of spouses are working or going to school, and almost 70% of those surveyed live in civilian communities. A second difference is the attitude has changed from a joint couple focus on the Army as *their* career to a belief that the Army is his job, not hers, which has led to an "egalitarian gender ideology precipitated by the women's movement ... an increase in the labor participation rates of women, a rise in their educational levels, and a shift in fertility patterns" (p. 74). Many women said that they would even forsake living with their husbands if they wanted a career or even insist that their husbands leave the Army on their behalf. Even if today's military spouse is not career minded, there appears to be a limit on how much she is willing to sacrifice for the Army. "Wives, who are not in the Army, need to be released from their Army tasks; wives need real improvements in their circumstances, not attitude adjustments. While women's sacrifices on behalf of their husband's career continue to be glorified in the Army, many wives today believe they have an equal right to an income and job of their own" (Houppert, 2005b, p. 226).

Military wives in Durand's survey still believe the military has expectations about how they should conduct their private lives, including being responsible for the care of their children, cooking for their husbands, and participating in Army activities. The data from her survey led Durand to conclude that the wives "did not appear to be behaviorally committed to the Army, but they were attitudinally committed" (2000, p. 80), with 41% saying they would be sad to leave the Army, compared to 14% who said they would be happy to leave and 44% who were unsure how they would feel. The majority overwhelmingly preferred the military lifestyle to a civilian-based lifestyle, and over 74% were committed to their husbands' career by being willing to attend unit events, make changes to help him advance, and work together as a team to further his career. Durand (2000) made a point to service providers that the old world of the military wives is no longer an accurate reflection of the current world of the military but that our clientele in counseling might still be composed of both the older individual from the earlier era of what was called "two for one" and younger spouses from today's military. The interventions must then be attuned to the possible confusion some of these women feel in this changing environment of military spouses.

Officer Spouses Versus Enlisted Spouses

There has also been information written regarding the differences between the spouses of the enlisted versus spouses of the officers (Durand, 2000; Henderson, 2006). Henderson (2006) wrote that not long after she followed her husband to one of his duty stations, the wife of his commanding officer called to take her to lunch and invite her to the next monthly gathering of the coffee group for the battalion spouses. She shared that officers' wives had a long tradition of organizing themselves. "On the surface these clubs and groups seem to be all about eating and drinking, and occasionally conducting business meetings, raising money for military charities ... but really they're all about making connections. This is how you meet people who can give you advice or step in when you need help" (p. 33). There are clubs for enlisted spouses, too, but officers' spouses benefit from the fact that there are simply far fewer of them. Although the service branches vary, on average there is approximately one officer for every five enlisted service members, and a corresponding difference in the number of spouses (Henderson, 2006). Officers' spouses are likely to have more education and more income, as well as greater life experience, as the largest single age group is older than 41 years old, whereas the largest single age group among enlisted spouses is younger than 25 years old.

The tradition of the military is that officers and enlisted families, and therefore spouses, remain segregated. As noted in chapter 3, the segregation of the traditional military is like nothing we would experience in any other community in the United States. Henderson's (2006) experience was that, even though it is no longer required, the two groups of spouses still frequently segregate themselves. Certainly part of that is attributable to the demographics discussed previously, in terms of age, experience, and education, which will naturally lead to a lack of common interests. However, in the hierarchical world of the military, officers are not supposed to form close friendships with their enlisted subordinates, and although there might be many reasons for this, in the end it all boils down "to the unhappy reality that, as an officer, one day you may have to order your subordinates to go die" (Henderson, 2006, p. 33). They have to be able to make decisions based on the needs of the mission, not on friendship. In the past, officers' wives followed suit, refusing to socialize with the wives of enlisted men, but Henderson (2006) said that things have changed dramatically for military spouses, as they are now free to live their own lives, illustrated by the leaders of an orientation class for spouses who told the participants to use just their first names and not to discuss their spouses' positions, making the point that "we spouses are not in the military, we have no rank, and therefore rank is irrelevant" (p. 34).

Strengths of the Military Spouse

Many of the therapists who were interviewed for this book talked about the incredible resiliency, hope, and strengths of the military spouse, often the result of the sometimes overwhelming challenges they have had to face. Other strengths they found in working with spouses, particularly those who had been a part of the military for a number of years, were (a) an openness to new experiences, new cultures, new ideas, and new adventures; (b) the amazing willingness and skills to make friends easily; (c) a strong and often profound relationship with their spouse, perhaps as a result of the many shared experiences they have had; (d) a high sense of loyalty and commitment to service; (e) a willingness to get involved in their community or other volunteer efforts; (f) adaptability and flexibility in their ability to make change, often quickly; (g) a skill as planners who could take on multiple tasks at the same time; and (h) an amazing competence as parents with real connections to their children, who could move from the role of single parent to dual parent at the drop of a hat.

Concerns of the Military Spouse

At the same time, the challenges for the spouses, and ultimately for the couple, who live within in this military Fortress do cause many concerns. The most common are issues around employment, infidelity, depression, frequent moves, the all too frequent and lengthy deployments, and online addictions, including porn and gambling. Many of these, for instance, infidelity, depression, and addictions, are often the result of the issues faced during deployment or because of the frequent moves.

Frequent Moves

Families have no choice: frequent moves are a part of the marriage contract, so aptly illustrated by the decorated station wagon in a community military parade in Southern California with a sign that read "Navy Wives Moving Again." A southern Arizona therapist explained that when the families move to a new and sometimes strange place, there is no support system, and the spouses' education or career, or both, has to be put on hold. If they need or want to work, they are faced with having to take only lower paying jobs. Marie Wakefield (2007), in an article for *Counseling Today,* told of her military son who, in 14 years, had approximately 40 temporary duty assignments ranging from a week to 6 months long and experienced 10 permanent changes of station in which the family was also required to move. "The many short-term relationships, complications of spousal employment, university transfer issues, escalated misbehavior of the children, day care arrangements, spousal loneliness and increased financial obligations are just some of the issues military personnel face that can lead to frustration" (p. 5). Dr. Bourdette (personal communication, 2007) shared that growing up as a military dependent child in the 1950s and 1960s, he went to 12 schools in the 12 years of public education. This was not 1 year per school; in at least one location, he changed schools three times in 1 year. But he remarked he was quite fortunate because his family made only four major moves.

In the high school where I worked in Germany, I had a sophomore arrive in the community with his family to register in November. While I was attempting to determine his credits and his classes, he shared that he had not yet been in school that year. Incredulous, I asked the reason for his not going to school, and he explained that his parents originally got their orders in late August, so they decided not to put him in school, knowing that they would be leaving soon. By the time they got additional orders that delayed the move by 2 months, their household goods had been packed, so they went to live in a different state with the child's grandparents. The school near his grandparents' house would not register him because he didn't carry any records with him (they were in the household goods), so they decided to wait until they arrived in Germany for him to register for school. The dilemma of placing a student who had not yet been to school in classes in November, halfway through the semester, was only one we faced because of the frequent and sometimes unexplainable moves of our military kids. These kinds of moves are extremely difficult for the military spouse. More than likely the military member will either go ahead or stay behind to begin a new assignment or finish up the old, leaving the spouse to deal with all aspects of the move, as well as with the children. We will deal with the problems this creates for the spouse's employment in a subsequent section.

Some of the adaptive skills that children develop (Wertsch, 1991) are also learned very early by military spouses. The first of these skills is how to take on the characteristics of the military Fortress, described in chapter 3, of maintaining a certain level of secrecy, becoming stoic, and learning to deny the pain associated with the uprooting. Another skill is what Wertsch called "forced extraversion," or the ability to make friends, explore a new community, or be assertive enough to ask for the necessary services for their children or themselves. These may not come easily for many young spouses with young children who are in a strange community or a new country, but to survive they have to learn it.

A third skill is the skill of "traveling light," or being able to move quickly without the burden of years of accumulated possessions that so many civilians have when they stay in one place for most of their lives. But traveling light is not just being able to pack things quickly but also withholding the emotional investments with people and the communities in which they live. Dr. Bourdette (personal communication, 2007) explained that one of the legacies left for him was the psychological perspective that meant "don't get close, you will be leaving soon." Another skill that military spouses and children learn is the ease of saying good-bye. Obviously connected to the previous skill is the ability to make that mental switch from being in the present to being in the future. Somehow it seems that it makes life easier, the pain less conscious; "it's easier to handle the loss—or to trick ourselves into thinking we've handled it—if our first act in a new place is to burn all bridges behind us" (Wertsch, 1991, p. 269).

A number of years ago, my husband and I found ourselves at an auction in Arizona where a large amount of household goods was being auctioned off. We were curious where they came from, as there were boxes of new sets of dishes, knickknacks, and souvenirs from all over the world. Many of the items were in boxes that were from the 1950s and 1960s but were completely intact and had never been opened. The story we were told was of a military career female nurse who spent over 30 years traveling around the world in the military, accumulating not only special things but sundries such as cases of soap from every country she was stationed in, presumably to enjoy upon retirement. Even though we never knew the whole story, what we later learned was that these purchases were shipped back home and kept in storage for all those years, but upon retirement the nurse became ill, went into a care facility, and eventually passed away, never having enjoyed her treasures. It seemed like such a sad legacy to what was a lifetime of service for her not to be able to enjoy the special things she found as she traveled the world, only for them to end up at an auction.

Lengthy Deployments

The topic of the ever-present issue of deployment is discussed in detail in chapter 7, but a short piece is included here because of the profound effects that deployments have on the spouses of the military. Spouses become the sole parent and then have to adjust to being a dual parent over and over again. Being married to a soldier is "a little like riding a roller coaster—a cycle of wrenching separations, honeymoon, reunions and bumpy readjustments" (Alaimo, 2006a, ¶ 16). The most common concerns faced by the families seen by one therapist interviewed are the high stress levels faced by the spouses who have to take on all the challenges of the household while the military parent is deployed. In addition to the concerns of child rearing and employment, one client was a woman who was former military but is now married to a military officer. They have five adopted children, most of whom are developmentally delayed and have special needs. Often families with special needs children are not in one place long enough for a proper diagnosis, let alone proper care for the children, so the concerns can be overwhelming.

A play therapist in Arizona helped a mom who was separated from her deployed husband and was struggling with her children, who were acting out a lot of depression and anger. In play therapy there was often a lot of "war stuff" and anxiety acted out about their dad's deployment. The nonmilitary parent is left to deal with all the issues faced and feared by the children. Although schools can be supportive, the burden is left to the at-home parent to deal with the fears of losing a parent, which often lead to behavior problems, or to the child, usually the oldest and often the boys, who wants to take on the role of the missing parent. According to most therapists who work with the entire family, the boys seem to struggle the most, and although it may no longer be the case where the oldest boy is told that he must now "be the man of the house," often that child takes on the role on his own.

Henderson (2006) told the story of a young couple who, after a number of months with her husband's company redeployed to the heart of Baghdad, felt that they had grown distant, like "two planets spinning farther away from each other" (p. 41), to the point where the phone calls were even getting stale. After months of separation, they were losing sight of the thread that tied them together. The wife spent her days at home with two little ones, and, through the phone conversations with her husband, she began to realize that he did not understand how the children had developed into kids who were different from the ones he knew when he left. She said sometimes she gets so mad she has to get it off her chest with e-mail after e-mail. The first one, she said, is full of messages about how she hates his guts, in the next one, she is still mad, and by the last one, she is telling him how much she loves him. From his perspective, he does his best to stay engaged, but he spends most of his day on perilous duty, just trying to stay alive while completing the mission; he often returns bone tired from the lack of sleep. When he finally gets a chance to log in to the base computers, his patience is short, and he is wrenched emotionally when he reads these messages. Her universe is doctor checkups, parent–teacher meetings, and costumes, whereas his is improvised explosive devices and the ever-present threat of death. He told Henderson (2006),

> The stress on my wife centers around her feelings of waiting to continue her life, our future together. Both of us consistently remind ourselves we are responsible for more than each other and our two children; I am responsible for 168 men and their families; she is

responsible for them indirectly by bearing some responsibility for my well-being. (p. 42)

Henderson (2006) started her book by stating, "Eventually you figure out ways to cope—or not. But they never get easy. A wartime deployment is always a mountain, no matter how you climb it" (p. 1).

Infidelity

Certainly one of the most difficult issues to deal with, often the outcome of deployments and other frequent separations, is the issue of infidelity in the military. The military appears to be taking infidelity (Butler, personal communication, October 6, 2006) more seriously, with the possibility of dismissal or legal action that would greatly affect the chances of promotion. But the environment and the circumstances for both the service member and the spouse are ripe for the possibility of infidelity. The possibilities obviously increase during deployment, when both partners, in their own way, are lonely, scared, and less likely to be caught. A soldier who corresponds to a counselor online wrote about how difficult it was to remain faithful to his wife during deployment, and after 4 months, found himself having an affair with a woman who was recently divorced (Marshall, 2006). The effects of the long deployment and the "very ambiguous and risky situations" make it very difficult to not get involved with others. Marshall (2006) quoted John Moore as saying, "You can't fight an enemy effectively if you're worried your wife is sleeping with someone or if your kid is sick" (p. 32).

Virtually every therapist I interviewed talked about the concerns over infidelity. The circumstances of being away from friends and a supportive community, long separations, dangerous situations, and fearful circumstances on the part of the military members, as well as the spouses, make these young people very susceptible. Fenell and Weinhold (2003) pointed out that when one or both spouses are unfaithful, all other concerns become exacerbated; if they can gain immediate support from a therapist who understands the culture of the military, they can prevent anger and hurt from turning to violence. Fenell and Fenell (2003) also recommended marriage and family enrichment activities, coupled with counseling, to both reduce the incidents of infidelity and, it is hoped, prevent the possible resulting divorce.

Internet

An additional concern brought up in most of my interviews with counselors was the issue of Internet addiction, even to the level of Internet porn addiction by service members who are deployed. If the practice ended when the military spouse returned, it more than likely would not create problems in the family, but when it has reached an addiction level and that addiction comes into the marriage, the couple will inevitably suffer. I have found no studies, research, or writing about this issue; it simply may be too new. However, many of the therapists I spoke with brought it up, and each one finds it a major problem that is now always addressed in marriage counseling, even if the couple does not bring it up. A recent Associated Press article (Baldor, 2007) did point out that the military is making changes in the clearance they are allowing military members by cutting off access to many sites that are currently being used, such as YouTube and MySpace. "Internet use has become a troublesome issue for the military as it struggles to balance security concerns with privacy rights" (¶ 11). Although the powers that be seem to realize the importance of the ability to communicate with those at home, it appears there are misuses of the Internet. At this point I cannot report on the extent of the problem but only recommend that it be brought up when working with couples and families.

Employment

"The challenge of combining a military lifestyle with a family and career can be daunting. Climbing a corporate ladder is difficult when a moving van is backing into your driveway every few years" (Peck, 2007, p. 38). The location of many military bases can also put a crimp on a spouse's career advancement. Frequent moves are only part of the challenge, as deployments create temporary single parents often without a family network of support. In addition, assignments to remote areas mean limited job opportunities or child care services. Many spouses learn to measure career success with a different yardstick, but no matter which path is taken, "a healthy dose of frustration accompanies the journey" (Peck, 2007, p. 42). A long-term military spouse who was interviewed for Peck's article said that if she looks at the financial success of her career in comparison with civilian peers, she would be an abject failure, but if she looks at the success of the work she was able to do and that she loved, along with the experiences she had all around the world, she believes she had a pretty successful life. A less positive reflection came from a spouse who felt that at the end of her husband's military career, her life had been on hold for 20 years, saying she was overeducated and underexperienced.

Peck (2007) pointed out that military spouses tend to withdraw into themselves when just the opposite would be more productive, even if it means volunteering, because "sometimes satisfaction or opportunity comes in a most unexpected place, and by giving, you get back more than you expected" (p. 40). Although we expect seniority in the civilian world to translate into increased pay and benefits, these same rewards of a career are sacrificed in the military with each move. Often the requirements for licensure and certification of some professions can be a problem, as most are determined at the state level. Although teaching and nursing seem to be hailed as two professions that are almost always available, these are only for those who have the education and training required. One of the faster growing fields for military spouses is in the technical computer fields, particularly work that can be done at home. Some corporations will even equip home offices, as most of this work can be done from anywhere, but it takes a lot of resilience and creativity to build a portable career (*Spouse Employment,* n.d.).

A young airman's wife started out working for one of the largest educational publishing companies as a freelance writer and editor on a contract basis. She has since branched out and works for other companies as well, doing everything from writing state educational standardized tests to editing flashcards for an online medical school. She makes anywhere from $20 to $50 per hour, but, of course, it is not always steady work. Obviously someone wanting to get into this field would need experience in teaching and writing, but the great advantage is that the work is completely done at home. Other spouses have done transcription and call center work from home. These women all caution other spouses, however, that there are a lot of work-at-home scams to watch out for.

As more and more women seek employment and career opportunities and are joined by the civilian male spouses of female service members, spouse employment is recognized as an important quality-of-life issue by the Department of Defense (Russo et al., 2000). It is an issue that reflects the changing nature of American society as well as the most diverse military in the world. For those women who do work, they tend to experience more role conflict and interference from work to family and family to work than do men. Many life cycle and personal factors influence employment status, and an attempt to balance work and family life is a particularly difficult challenge for the military spouse, who has the additional task of adapting to the demanding aspects of military life. One spouse told Houppert (2005b) that she had always believed in being independent, but she gave all that up for love, and now she finds herself being "lulled into leading this halfway comfortable life when work was so important to me; I am not independent anymore and that is something I despise" (p. 217).

The unique aspects of being an employed military spouse (Russo et al., 2000) are as follows: (a) the level of commitment and dedication to service; (b) the little personal control over duty requirements; (c) the lack of personal control over when one's spouse comes and goes and the required periods of time spent away from home for training or deployment; (d) the reality that the civilian spouses' work or career comes second; (e) the fact that military spouses must function in their careers almost as if they were single; (f) the more junior the military spouse's rank, the less control one has over many aspects of his or her career; and, finally; (g) family responsibility is likely to fall predominantly on the nonmilitary partner. Russo et al. (2000) also listed a few obvious benefits of employment for military spouses and their families and some barriers they must overcome.

Benefits
1. As in civilian sectors, more families need a dual income; in the military this may be necessary to meet financial obligations or achieve a more comfortable lifestyle. Many face the challenge of beginning a family while quite young. A junior enlisted service member in 1998 earned slightly more than minimum wage, so the additional income is often required to meet the significant financial costs during the early family life cycle stages. The difficulty for many young civilian spouses is the lack of necessary skills or training for employment other than at minimum wage jobs.
2. Additional income can enhance the family's quality of life, so that, in addition to meeting basic needs, it can provide quality-of-life opportunities, whether it is to buy a stereo system, own a home, take a vacation, or pay for the children's college.
3. A second income can also enhance personal well-being on the part of the spouse, whether that is a need for independence, self-esteem, or to continue one's education. Even though balancing work and family can be difficult, it is also a way for spouses to be recognized and appreciated for their efforts.

Barriers
1. It seems that often military spouses either lack necessary training and education or find employment opportunities to be below their education or skill level. Many of the younger spouses have not completed high school, let alone post–high school training or education; therefore, they can enter the job market at only minimum wage, usually in service industry jobs. Although a growing segment of the labor market consists of less intrinsically rewarding service sector jobs, these jobs can be initially satisfying for younger spouses new to the workforce, but obviously less so to the spouse with advanced education or skills.
2. The impact of military duty requirements, including long and unpredictable work hours and frequent relocations and deployments, and the irregularity and unpredictability of a service

member's work make it difficult to plan for child care and other family or household responsibilities.

3. Child care concerns are always a source of stress for young families; the expansion of military child care facilities across the country has helped military families, but the demand for child care is also related to the earnings of the military spouse. So it is not just the availability but also the expense of child care that can be a barrier to employment. For many young spouses who would like to work part-time, child care expenses can sometimes equal or exceed the income. Usually officers' wives are able to pay more for child care than wives of the enlisted are because of their higher income, so they are more likely to use child development centers on base. Enlisted wives are more likely to use family day care homes. Another issue regarding child care then is the quality of the facility and materials available to children, including the training of staff and developmentally appropriate curriculum, with child development centers tending to offer higher quality of care.

4. There are also a number of structural employment barriers, including geographic location, availability of transportation, and attitudes of employers toward hiring military family members. Many employers are understandably resistant to hire and train someone if they believe that person will stay only a short time. Sometimes even the association of that person with the military creates a perception of instability. Often public transportation is needed, particularly for junior enlisted families, because the cost of purchasing, operating, and maintaining a second car outweighs the income they will make.

5. Relocation obviously also has personal and career implications for the spouse. Sometimes spouses will have a feeling of being diminished, as they are unable to influence their own lives; they may lack support systems and connections; and they sometimes become "discouraged workers" because of their inability to find satisfying work, so they end up lowering their career goals. In addition, if they have been working and then have to relocate, the loss of income after the move can be devastating to the family, sometimes losing as much as 10% to 20% of their income in the first year after a move.

One study (Russo et al., 2000) found that when a spouse is employed, the family actually seems to adjust better to relocation.

Human service providers must consider both the burden and the value of spouse employment among those military family members in their client population. Encouraging spouses to develop realistic expectations and to build their own employment-related support network is critical. For many, gaining required basic education and job training will be a necessary first step. (p. 100)

Military spouses are not who they used to be. Wives of service members have a different attitude about their careers and their expectations regarding the role fathers are expected to play in the home, such as sharing the job of raising the kids. Too often the "boot camp methods that wring compliance from soldiers ... alienate wives. Mandating a sense of 'bonding' too often fails [and] efforts to win hearts and minds are transparent—and frequently resented" (Houppert, 2005b, p. xvii). We have to be prepared to work with military spouses from where they are in the world today, not with preconceived ideas of what and who they should be; as stated before, they are straddling the military and civilian worlds with one foot in each sector.

Male Spouses

Civilian male spouses face many of the same "trailing spouse" issues as civilian women married to military personnel. They are a small subgroup in an organization with a strong male tradition, so they often do not benefit from the same support systems as female spouses (Russo et al., 2000). Civilian husbands are significantly different from civilian wives, as they are more likely to have higher educational levels, to have prior military service experience, to be employed full-time or seeking full-time employment, and to be excluded from policy and political discussions of spouse employment issues. "The typical Army husband, with or without kids, is probably the most neglected member of the Army's population" (Sullivan, 2006, p. 52), because most support programs are geared to female spouses.

Family readiness groups are there to provide support but are obviously composed mostly of women, as there are 688,000 active duty spouses, and only 48,000 of those are men. Ninety percent of the male spouses (over 43,000) are either active duty or retired active duty, so only 10%, or 4,800, of male military spouses have no military experience. It is usually difficult for most guys to join these groups where the ratio may be 25 women to 1 man and most of the activities are of little interest to him. Sullivan (2006) also pointed out that because most husbands are working, the female spouses in the groups "don't expect us to need anything" (p. 54). Women also seem to benefit more from emotional support groups, whereas men benefit from knowing what is going to happen, what is needed, and how to competently complete the journey.

Most male spouses are also not comfortable getting too friendly with the female spouses for fear of the appearance of impropriety. Fear of their military wives cheating on them, particularly while deployed, is a major concern, so they definitely do not want to be suspected of acting inappropriately while at home. Gender differences create major roadblocks in connecting and forging friendships because, despite their best efforts, the chasm exists simply because "males are most often supported in different ways than females" (Sullivan, 2006, p. 54). Male spouses may do better with online chat groups, such as Dad Support groups (see http://www.myarmylife2.com). A psychologist interviewed for Sullivan's article stated that male spouses need to be valued for what they can do to reach their goals, they need to feel competent, and they need to receive acknowledgment. One male spouse stated authoritatively, "It's a whole lot easier getting shot at and mortared on a daily basis than to stay at home and worry about her getting shot at and mortared" (Sullivan, 2006, p. 56).

Dual Military Couples

For military families whose children could be orphaned, this new conflict is certainly cause for soul-searching. But it's also a matter of intense interest to the U.S. Armed Services, where dual-military couples and single parents make up a small but rising share of active-duty troops. Between 1990 and 2000, they increased by almost 3 percent to 120,000. (Stern, 2001, p. 4)

The concern arose for the first time during the 1991 Gulf War; although women were then limited to noncombat roles, there were female service members who died piloting transport helicopters, whereas others were killed while sleeping in their barracks when an Iraqi Scud missile hit. Thankfully, no child lost both parents to combat duty during that war. Since the Kosovo air war in 1999, when female pilots flew bombing missions for the first time, the public has grown more accustomed to seeing women in combat.

In writing about the first woman to command a Navy ship while her husband also served in the military, Stern (2001) stated that having orphans is no longer a remote possibility. In addition to the possibility of both parents being killed in war, dual-military couples must cope with many challenges, including being apart for lengthy deployments. The military does have a number of policies and procedures regarding dual military couples.

All parents, whether single or married, must file a Family Care Plan detailing who is to take care of children if parents are deployed. Navy regulations don't allow married couples to serve under the same command, more out of concern that one spouse could end up overseeing the other than for fear of both reaching combat, but neither the Army nor the Air Force have similar rules barring husbands and wives from the same unit. None of the services will deploy a mother of a child younger than 4 months old. "Despite the military's best efforts, it's not easy for children left behind.... These children must adjust simultaneously to new surroundings and their parents' absence" (Stern, 2001, p. 17). Obviously it is much more difficult for those with children to balance work and family.

According to 1998 figures, 22% of military women are married to another service member, whereas only 4% of military men are in a dual military marriage (Russo et al., 2000). A much greater percentage of joint service marriages are within the enlisted ranks. The possibility of retention is usually affected by the perception of each spouse's career intention, as the military more than likely will either retain both or lose both, depending on the effects of policies and programs for either spouse.

A Military OneSource article (*Couples: Balancing Work and Life as a Dual Military Couple,* n.d.) offered suggestions that might be helpful for counselors who work with dual military couples. The article suggested that couples must anticipate the challenges of (a) accepting the certainty of separation; (b) expecting difficult career decisions; (c) acknowledging the likelihood of sacrifices that will be made by their children, extended families, and friends; and (d) understanding the differences in rank, career management fields, and policies and procedures in the different branches of the service.

Some of the coping strategies that might be helpful are also outlined in the article, including (a) focusing on communications; (b) honoring each other's career and personal goals; (c) being prepared to switch roles instead of having rigid expectations about traditional husband and wife duties; (d) taking care of their individual needs through outside activities and support systems instead of assuming all needs can be met by each other; (e) developing career relationships with people who are supportive of their individual goals; (f) taking advantage of professional support services to help manage the challenges; and (g) remembering to recognize and appreciate the benefits of dual-career military life. Some of the actions the article suggested to help dual-career couples be more successful include (a) taking a proactive role in finding joint assignments; (b) seeking agreement on dual-career expectations; (c) meeting all the military requirements for deployment planning; (d) having realistic contingency plans for options for different scenarios; and (e) giving their best to every assignment. It seems clear then that even though dual military couples have specific challenges, they can take active roles in making those challenges work for them.

Kate Blaise (2006) shared many examples of how she and her husband had to sacrifice and accommodate in their marriage as a dual military couple to make it work for them. They signed up for the Married Army Couples program, believing that the Army would make an effort to keep military couples together, which sometimes works. When it works, it means that the Army makes an effort to give them a joint assignment where they would be posted no more than 50 miles apart. Her story of their life as a dual-career couple is full of insights, powerful thoughts, and eventual loss. They were stationed close to each other only when they were both sent to Iraq. When they did finally have time together, she said every conversation degenerated into arguments. The whole idea of a two-career household took on new meaning when she realized that they spent only 2 of their 7 years together actually living under the same roof.

They never imagined, when they fell in love in high school, that they would end up in the military or that world events would send "our fates marching in new and dangerous directions. But we were soldiers, true to our country and true to each other" (Blaise, 2006, p. 103). She said, "Marriage and the military have a lot in common: you have to make compromises and the result is often far from ideal, you are answerable to another person in everything you do and not only does that person play a role in every decision, he sometimes makes the decisions for you" (p. 104). As dual military couples have to do, they had to learn to accept sacrifice and compromise and prioritize what comes first, then second, and then what each had to let go of. It will "challenge you, push you, force you to adjust to unforeseen hardships; if you push back too hard or the wrong time you might jeopardize everything you have worked for" (p. 105), but probably like most military couples, she said, "As important as our marriage was to us both, our jobs had to come first" (p. 105).

Divorce and Remarriage in the Military

A client who was a second wife of a military officer complained to the therapist because she was referred to as "The 31." The first time it happened was in a medical office, and she asked what it meant. The receptionist shared that on the information form, wives were listed under the category 3, the first wife is number 3-0 and the second wife is number 3-1. When divorce happens in the military, the nonmilitary spouse usually takes the kids and goes home, causing considerable difficulty, emotionally, financially, and legally. The issues of custody, visitation, and even the divorce proceedings can all become major problems because of state laws, especially for families who are already stressed.

Although issues around divorce have certainly changed for military families, Armitage wrote in 1984 about a number of concerns that are still relevant, including (a) gaining access to state courts where the divorce and custody are handled is a problem because of residency requirements, jurisdiction problems, and financial constraints; (b) considerations of property settlement, alimony, and child custody are of special significance to military families because most nonmilitary divorcees will not be eligible for benefits when a divorce is final; (c) medical care, exchange (shopping), and commissary (groceries) privileges are immediately cut off, even though the children, if they are still supported by the military spouse, continue to be eligible for privileges no matter with whom they live; (d) the distribution of marital property is determined by the laws of the state in which the action occurs, and there are many variations by state as to the approach to property distribution; (e) the variation in state laws also applies to child custody, original custody disputes, and attempts later to modify arrangements; and (f) the laws of the states granting the original custody decree may conflict with the custody laws of the state in which the noncustodial parent may later attempt to modify the arrangements.

In 1981, the Supreme Court held that state courts could not treat retirement pay as community property because Congress intended military retirement pay to be the personal entitlement of the retiree; however, in 1983 the Uniformed Services Former Spouses Protection Act established as law that retirement pay be treated in accordance with state laws regarding division of property. In most states that act means the spouse must have been married to the service member for at least 10 years to have access to any part of the ultimate retirement benefits.

To understand divorce and remarriage in the military, we should discover just how many families we are actually talking about. Although there is a lot of anecdotal discussion currently about the problems in military families, the recent RAND Corporation (2007) report shows that despite military operations in Afghanistan and Iraq, divorce rates seem to have increased only gradually. The study reports that, after several years of decline, marriage dissolutions among military members began increasing in 2001. The rate in 2005 was the same as it was in 1996. The study also showed that married service members who had been deployed were generally less likely to end their marriages than those not deployed, and longer deployments were associated with greater reductions in risk. At least at the time of the study, researchers noted that perhaps deployments benefit families in some immediate ways, such as providing higher earnings from combat pay and potential for career advancement, along with health care, child care, and housing. However, they noted, "Negative consequences for military couples may emerge later, or families may be experiencing problems that have not been measured; the full impact of these conflicts on military families may not be known for years" (RAND Corporation, 2007, ¶ 9).

Other findings include the fact that women and enlisted are more than twice as likely to end marriages, perhaps because the marriages of female service members benefit significantly less from deployment or the existing programs provide too little support for families of married women. Enlisted service members may be more likely to end marriages than officers, possibly because officers tend to be older and married longer (RAND Corporation, 2007). It is hard for me to believe that there won't be additional long-term consequences of the current military operations and, with the number of service members returning wounded, both physically and mentally, I imagine there will be significant consequences to these military marriages for many years to come.

Remarriage and Stepfamily Data

Although actual current data regarding remarriage and stepfamilies are extremely difficult to obtain, as the questions are simply not asked, a study was done in 2005 that reported the findings of two major surveys of the military family, including a 1999 study of over 30,000 service members and more than 18,000 military spouses, comparing it to a 1992 study that surveyed over 18,000 military members and paired spouses (Adler-Baeder & Pittman, 2005).

The 1999 survey reported that over 86% of male service members were married, whereas just 14% of female service members were married. Of the married service members, 81% were in their first marriage, and 19% were in a remarriage. In terms of rank, 46% of the respondents were enlisted, and 54% were officers. Of those respondents, 52% had residential-only children, and 10% had only nonresidential children. Ten percent were in joint service with their spouses, but for the remarriage couples, the rate of joint service went up to 14%.

Of parents who were in their first marriage, 61% had children in the home, and 7% had nonresidential children. For remarried service members, 58% had children in the home, but 27% had nonresidential children. The study also showed that 49% of single service members in the survey had children: 24% in the home, and 25% nonresidential.

What we can deduce, then, just from these numbers is that there are large numbers of children, spouses, and military members who are struggling as divorced, remarried, or stepfamily members. These conclusions are of value to those studying and working with military families. It is interesting that the remarried and currently divorced members were considerably more likely to be women. Compared to service members in their first marriage, remarried members were slightly overrepresented in the Army and slightly underrepresented in the Air Force. Remarried service members were overrepresented among enlisted pay grades and underrepresented at officer pay grades. Currently divorced members were underrepresented in the Caucasian category but overrepresented in the African American category. The remarried service members were "more likely" to be in joint service, whereas the first-married service members were "somewhat more likely" than remarried members and "much more likely" than currently divorced members to have residential children (Adler-Baeder & Pittman, 2005).

Comparisons to the Civilian Population

Some interesting findings regarding marital trends in the military compared to the general population were also reported. These are also valuable for understanding the relative prevalence of divorce and remarriage in the military. For men in the military, the most significant differences are in the age category of 20- to 24-year-olds, where male service members who have married are double that of the general U.S. population (42% versus 18%). According to the study (Adler-Baeder & Pittman, 2005), married service members proportionally outnumber the general population in all age categories. It follows, then, that the proportions of never-married service members are consistently lower than in the general population. It is notable that 4% of service members between the ages of 20 and 24 years have divorced, and 1.4% have already remarried; this is triple the percentage of divorced and remarried 20- to 24-year-olds in the general U.S. population. The proportions of divorced and remarried male service members in the age category of 25- to 29-year-olds (14% vs. 7% are divorced, and 7.5% vs. 2% are remarried) and in the age category of 30- to 34-year-olds (24% vs. 16% are divorced, and 14% vs. 7% are remarried) are also substantially greater compared to the general U.S. population.

Remarriage Rates for Women in the Military

For women there is a reverse pattern. The number of never-married female service members is proportionally smaller than in the general population in the age category of 20- to 24-year-olds, but the number of never-married female service members is greater than the number in the general U.S. population in all other age categories. The proportion of female service members in the age range of 40- to 49-year-olds who are still in their first marriages is roughly half that of the general population (27% vs. 49%). It is interesting that it was reported that the number of female service members in third marriages is at least double the proportion of women in third marriages in the general population. In addition, the proportion of women in the military who remain divorced or are single is nearly double the number of never-married or divorced women in the general U.S. population (Adler-Baeder & Pittman, 2005).

I have attempted here not to suggest or even guess at the causes of these differences or, by any means, characterize service men and women but rather to report the findings in an attempt to understand this unique population. The results of these studies also cannot tell us if the marriage and divorce rates are the consequence of military life, but I hope they can lead us to a better understanding of the types of issues and concerns military family members experience.

Satisfaction and Retention in Remarried Households

It might seem obvious that families with children reported more problems connected with relocation than did families without children. It even appeared from the review of these studies (Adler-Baeder & Pittman, 2005) that relocation problems may be linked more to the number of individuals in a family unit who must deal with the impact of the move rather than to the marital history of the family members or the parental status. As might be expected, remarried and divorced members who were not parents perceived fewer problems than first-married service members, especially those with children. Also expected, the study showed that residential children in divorced and remarried families increased the difficulties associated with adapting to military life and adapting to relocation issues. Obviously the stress of relocation is a common concern of families with children.

The 1999 study (Adler-Baeder & Pittman, 2005) also attempted to show a relationship between family composition and adaptation to military life. It seems that being in a first marriage versus being in a remarriage made an impact on the satisfaction levels of what they called "personal/family time." When attempting to measure retention intentions, the study found that these intentions were strongest for remarried military members, and their intentions were unaffected by whether they had children present in the home. Within the first-married and divorced subgroups, having children actually significantly strengthened retention intentions. The members most satisfied with military life appear to be those in first marriages with children and in remarriages without children. For remarried parents, in terms of retention intentions and satisfaction with military life, the residential status of children did not seem to matter, but for the currently divorced parent, the residential status of children became significant. Divorced parents with residential children reported the lowest satisfaction with the military and the lowest retention intentions. Divorced parents with nonresidential children reported satisfaction with the military that was about the same as that of remarried parents, and their retention intentions were somewhere in between the high seen for remarried parents and the low seen for divorced parents with residential children.

A possible interpretation made by the authors of the study (Adler-Baeder & Pittman, 2005) was that the experience of divorce might operate like a turning point for military members so that those already more committed to the military self-selected for retention whereas those divorced members who were less committed took the next opportunity to separate from the military. Consistent with the authors' original premise that the combination of remarriage and parenthood is the most stressful, the remarried couples with children who responded to the surveys definitely revealed more stress. Although satisfaction with military life was low for this subgroup of remarried parents with children, it was, interesting enough, not lower than for first-married, child-free members. It is of interest that remarried families with children, although higher in retention intentions, revealed a lower level of satisfaction with military life.

Spouses' attitudes of support for service members' retention were consistently higher for remarried spouses than those in first marriages, and these attitudes were unrelated to the remarried spouse's parental status. Having children, it seems, was associated with significantly more positive views about the service member's retention in the military. Perhaps that indicates a need for the security the military provides for families, regardless of the frequent disruptions. Remarried parents reported significantly more family problems and significantly less satisfaction with military life, whereas first-married spouses, if they were parents, were more satisfied than nonparents. The general conclusion, paradoxically, was that the combination of remarriage with children puts more pressure on families, and although remarried spouses were consistently more supportive of retention than were first-married spouses, they tended to perceive more family problems and felt less satisfaction with military life in general. Given the rates of divorce and remarriage, the concerns, issues, and potential problems faced by military families can be overwhelming.

Challenges for Stepfamilies in the Military

These studies clearly point to a consistent conclusion that the military remarried couple and stepfamily have specific challenges that have important implications for family adaptation and functioning. The military makes substantial demands on its members and, as a consequence, on the families. Not only does the military lifestyle require frequent family relocations but there are also relatively frequent family separations due to duty requirements. Stepfamilies can be expected to encounter more than the typical types of stress as a result of these demands. For children, leaving peers and extended kin for a relocation is one thing, but being separated from a biological parent while also adjusting to a new parent who also may be gone periodically is quite another. Military stepfamilies obviously deserve careful attention.

According to the 1999 study (Adler-Baeder & Pittman, 2005) at least 20% of all service members have experienced divorce, and it is estimated that at least one third of all married personnel are in a remarriage. For such a proportionally young population, these are impressive numbers. Service members marry, divorce, and remarry earlier than the general population, and, as pointed out, the proportions of divorced and remarried service members are greater, particularly among younger age groups and among women service members. Even in the older age category of 40-to 49-year-olds, over half of the women and over one third of the men have divorced. In addition, one third of the women and one quarter of the men in that age category have remarried.

Even though these statistics do not necessarily foretell potential risks, they do clearly indicate that a substantial portion of service members who make the military a career have experienced divorce and remarriage, and for women, it appears to be the majority. Although the nature of the work in the military may result in additional stressors that put couples at risk of divorce, it appears that men in the military who divorce are more likely to remarry than similarly aged men in the United States. It is definitely not clear what factors are related to the high rate of divorce, but one possible reason for the high rate of remarriage is that the support provided for families may actually provide additional incentives for remarriage or may be attractive benefits for potential spouses (Adler-Baeder & Pittman, 2005). Although women in the military experience divorce at greater rates than men, it is interesting that women also are more likely to remain divorced, thereby less likely to remarry. In addition, the number of military women who never marry is more than twice that of women in the general U.S. population.

The same article reported that in the 1999 sample, 42% of military members in a remarriage had children from a previous relationship. This is actually lower than in the general U.S. population, where 65% of remarried individuals have children from a previous relationship. Perhaps this is the result of the earlier marriage and earlier divorce rates of the military. It was also notable that 1 in 12 single service members reported having nonresidential children, whereas 24% of currently divorced members had nonresidential children. Among remarried personnel, 27% reported having nonresidential children.

The remarried military personnel are overrepresented among women, joint service couples, and the enlisted ranks. More of these service members are likely to have children and to have nonresidential children. Because the mean age of remarried personnel is higher than first-married personnel, the increased likelihood of having children is easily understood. Divorce and remarried rates are also higher among lower socioeconomic status individuals, usually in the enlisted ranks. The impact of having nonresidential children while in the military for either single or remarried service members has not been examined, but anecdotally I can attest to a very high level of stress for those families who live overseas and have nonresidential children living back in the States. The sense of helplessness and lack of control of their children's lives and well-being causes considerable anxiety and stress in their lives.

It was found that when spouses of the service members were questioned, those who were remarried and had children reported the most family problems and expressed low satisfaction with military life. Having residential children seemed to increase the problems, particularly those associated with moving. The demanding lifestyle of the military may be especially stressful for children in remarriages, as noted previously, if they have already experienced the considerable change and adjustment demands of the marital transitions of their parents. Interesting enough, as outlined previously, if the presence of children is associated with more commitment to the military, it may be expected that children promote an increased desire for family stability and an increased need for the support services that the military provides. Although the military lifestyle contains elements of unpredictability and change that may negatively influence internal family functioning, it also provides supports that may be attractive to couples with children. Individuals and families who have experienced a period of family disorganization and instability (i.e., divorce and remarriage) may be especially attuned to and appreciative of the resources that the military offers (Adler-Baeder & Pittman, 2005).

The vast majority of stepfamilies today are formed following divorce; children often belong to two households and can benefit from a positive parenting coalition between the biological parents and stepparents. This relatively current study of the marriage, divorce, and remarriage rates of the military demonstrates that a substantial percentage of service members has nonresidential children, but there is no information regarding the impact of a demanding military lifestyle on these binuclear families and coparenting relationships. We can only assume that frequent relocations might result in stressful and expensive relitigation over custody arrangements as noted at the beginning of this section, as some joint custody arrangements impose geographic restrictions on parents.

These geographic restrictions may be in the best interest of the child at the time of the divorce or subsequent renegotiations; however, they are often in conflict with military-mandated duty assignments and often result in a separation of a nonresident parent from his or her children. Even more crucial, in instances of deployment, a stepparent may be left with the often difficult situation of dealing with a former spouse concerning child-rearing issues. Because children usually experience multiple changes after divorce and remarriage, stepchildren may be especially sensitive to other lifestyle changes and stressors associated with military family life. These lifestyle changes due to the military requirements may cause a child to resent the stepparent and further jeopardize already tenuous marital and family relationships. On average, it takes 3 to 5 years (O'Hern-Hall & Williams, 2004) for a new stepparent to transition into a more parentlike role; this transition may be more problematic for the stepparent if the biological parent is the service member and is deployed. If the stepparent is the service member, the disruptions in the family due to trainings and deployment may make the parent–child relationship adjustment even more difficult and lengthy. The children's distress, in this situation, over relocating far from their nonresident parent often also negatively affects stepfamily functioning.

Another consideration, not addressed in the study previously discussed, is the number of families, both first marriages and stepfamilies, that are established through cohabiting relationships. These families are routinely misidentified as single-parent homes. In the general population, about half of first unions begin with cohabitation, and an estimated 75% of stepfamilies begin with cohabitation; conservative estimates are that half of cohabitating couples have children. There has been no attempt in the military to disaggregate this data, so it cannot be said if this figure holds true in the military (Adler-Baeder & Pittman, 2005).

It is because of this data, as well as many years of experience working with stepfamilies in the military, that I chose to include a separate section on understanding stepfamily systems in chapter 6 and a section on working with stepfamilies in chapter 9 of this book. Although the formation of stepfamilies has been increasing since the 1970s, they are still a misunderstood family form in the field of marriage and family counseling. Often counselors believe these families simply should try to act like and look like biological first families; this myth, as well as others, causes undue harm for families in their attempt to become well-functioning second families. The fact that so many military families are remarrying and forming stepfamilies, combined with the normal stress of the military, creates additional concerns and needs for mental health services.

CHAPTER 5

The Children

Unique Challenges

There is a story, even though I do not know that it is factual, that years after Biosphere II was built outside of Tucson, Arizona, the trees inside it started to fall over. It caused a lot of concern for those responsible, because even though they discovered that the roots were only a few inches deep, they could find no sign of disease or mold, or any other reason, for the trees to be so unstable. The scientists finally decided that because there was no wind inside the Biosphere, the roots did not need to grow deep to hold up the trees, as one of the reasons for trees to sink deep roots is to counter the force of the wind. The story may or may not be true, but it makes sense that without a certain amount of stress produced by the wind, the trees could not grow deep roots and therefore stand tall. Perhaps it is true also that without a certain amount of challenge, our children's roots cannot grow deep either. So what are the unique struggles of the military child? Where do they go for help? What it is like to be a nomad, to never have a home? And what are the strengths that result from these challenges?

The National Military Family Association's *Report on the Cycles of Deployment* (Jumper et al., 2006) reported that there are almost 500,000 military children 5 years of age or younger and that more than 600,000 children of service members are school-age. These school-age children primarily attend civilian public schools, and they almost always represent a subculture in these schools in which the staff may not understand the children's life experiences. Although military parents know they must act as their children's advocate, they are often frustrated at the lack of understanding and teacher training to best work with their children. In addition, although much has been done to help military families obtain affordable child care in the military communities, there remains a need for more affordable and available care for younger children and for·children after school. As with all parents, sometimes just a 3- or 4-hour period away from young children can make or break a spouse's week. In addition, Guard and Reserves families report that dealing with their children was one of their greatest challenges, especially during the deployment of the military parent.

There are unique challenges, fears, and strengths of the military child, or the military brat (Wertsch, 1991). First, ask yourself what your first impression is of the term *military brat.* Are you offended by the name? If so, why? When Mary Wertsch (1991) interviewed nearly 100 adults who had grown up as military brats, only 5 objected to the term. Most of those who grew up in the military see it as a term of affection, because it refers to an experience that is too difficult to define but that implies a unique perception of the world. The term *brat* implied to them a world of separateness but a kind of spunkiness that most say are the qualities that got them through the difficult times in their lives.

In the years since I worked in Germany for the Department of Defense, I cannot tell you how many people, when they find out that I worked with military kids, told me they were military brats—and not one was embarrassed or upset at the term. I almost always saw a glimmer in their eyes that signified a recognition that I might understand them just a little because of my experience. In his introduction to the book *Military Brats: Legacies of Childhood Inside the Fortress* (1991), Pat Conroy, the author of *The Great Santini,* wrote, "Military brats of America are an invisible, unorganized tribe, a federation of brothers and sisters bound by common experience, by our uniformed fathers, by the movement of families being rotated through the American mainland and to military posts in foreign lands" (p. xvii).

Nomads

"We think of ourselves as nomads. The term has a nice definitive sound to it, and suggests, somewhat reassuringly, that our experience fits neatly into a known category" (Wertsch, 1991, p. 251). Yet, as she continued to describe the life of military families, she concluded that, of course, they are not really nomads; in fact, there is "no easy label for us" (p. 252). Some of the characteristics, however, of this nomadic lifestyle include the sense of homelessness, not in the traditional sense of sleeping on the streets but of not having a place from which one comes. The questions "Where are you from?" or "Where is home?" are difficult for military dependent kids to answer and are often embarrassing for them, especially when they are attending a civilian school where these questions are the norm. John Bourdette (personal communication, 2007), in telling his story of being a military brat, said that his life was somewhat unique, because he spent his first 6 years on a farm prior to his father's joining the military. Unlike most of his friends growing up, he did have a home, a place where he came from, and he often thought it was sad that his friends did not. Even though these frequently asked questions are always asked with the positive intention of helping new students feel valued or cared for, they are difficult questions, because military brats often have no answer but feel compelled to give one.

I found this to be a particularly troubling issue when seniors in my high school applied for financial aid; the form requires them to identify their home state. In trying to help them identify a home state of their parents, I found they often couldn't give me one. I would ask where their parents pay state taxes, and often the students said they didn't! Military members, in reality, are required to identify their home state in their records, but that may be simply the last state where they lived or the state where the service member's parent resides. For the children, there often is not a home state that has any meaning or emotional tie for them.

Adapting Children

One of the characteristics of military children is their ability to adapt to situations quickly. This adapting child becomes extremely vigilant and very early learns to mimic whatever nuances the new environment provides to fit in quickly. To belong, the adapting child often learns quickly how to find a niche, even if that life skill or personality variable is uncomfortable. The adapting child often lives with a certain level of fear. As these children get older, certainly by middle school, this fear is often right under the surface. It is not just a fear of what might happen to their family or their military parents but a fear of the unknown, of not being accepted, of being behind, of not finding friends, or of not being cool. One of the most common concerns expressed by students when they arrive in a new school is who they will eat lunch with. Another reality for student athletes is that a student could be the star of the basketball team in one school and be sitting on the bench at the next. Houppert (2005b) said as a military brat, she learned to assume and shed identities as circumstances dictated. "The way I saw it, the military family functioned best as a kind of chameleon … [that] straddled two separate worlds. We were both of the military culture and outside it—shifting uneasily in our many different skins" (p. xiv).

While working as a school counselor, I also had the opportunity to coach volleyball for 1 year and tennis for 3 years, so the issue of sports was one I paid close attention to. The Department of Defense Dependents School System in Europe (DoDDS-E) prior to the major drawdown in the early 1990s actually had, I believe, four levels of sports teams in Europe, just like in any state in the United States. When I first went to Germany in 1989, there were approximately 7,000 American teachers in Germany alone. That decreased by more than half after the drawdown and base closings.

The system currently has two sports divisions: the large schools and the small schools. The teams traveled all over Europe playing other schools; it can be compared to a high school state athletic organization, just with larger distances between schools. For example, it was a 12-hour bus trip from Wiesbaden, Germany, to London, England, to play the military dependent schools there. Students who rose to be the stars of athletic teams in Europe began thinking about playing college ball, only to realize at some point that they would not have the opportunities to be seen by scouts or coaches in the States. They didn't go to state tournaments; they didn't go to summer camps. If and when they did return to the States, they were often terribly disheartened, because many realized they were just average when compared to the best in the whole country.

My twin stepdaughters lived with us and attended Heidelberg High School during their freshmen year. They were both athletes, and both were starters as freshmen on their high school soccer and basketball teams. As hopeful college athletes they soon realized, however, that they would need to be in the United States for the remainder of high school, because although they were stars in their overseas schools, they were, in comparison to all college prospects across the country, average to good. They were going to have to be seen by a large variety of colleges to have a chance of playing college ball, which both of them eventually did. Obviously most military dependent athletes do not have the luxury of moving back to the States for the last 3 years of high school just so they have a better chance of being recruited to play college sports.

Another characteristic of adapting children is their relative ease of saying good-bye; they have to learn the skill, and they have to learn it early. By high school they learn how to disengage early, and by the time they actually withdraw from school, their focus is on the future; sometimes it is harder for those left behind. Those of us who worked with these students knew and watched, over and over, how they had learned to stuff their hurt, their loss, and their pain for the good of the families and, just like their parents, for the good of the mission. An adult military brat whom I recently met was planning to make a major career move in her late 40s. For the first time in her life, she was struggling with long-term financial benefits, how this move would affect her eventual retirement, and other issues that she said she never considered in three or four earlier career moves. Most of the adult military brats whom I meet have somewhat of a wanderlust attitude, believing that picking up and moving is a part of life and that life is boring without it.

External Locus of Control

Starting at birth, military dependent children have no control over when and how often change will occur in their lives, but in most cases they learn early how to profit from these changes. I guess the first question that may come to mind is, "Do *any* children really have control over change that occurs in their lives?" And the answer is obviously, "No." The difference here is that for these children, their parents also do not have control over the constant changes, so the subtle message is that all control is external. By the time Isaac, my grandson, had finished first grade, he had already been in three schools. Was that an issue for him? Probably not at that age, but it could have been for a slow learner, an older student, a special needs student, or a student with family problems. The school he attended for most of first grade, although being part of the local public school system, was actually on a military post in the United States, so all the students were military dependents, and the teachers understood their unique needs. Wertsch (1991) discovered that the average number of schools attended by those she interviewed was between 9 and 10 in their 12 to 13 years of school. Although the average military move occurs every 3 years, there are often many who move a great deal more than that, particularly, interesting enough, the higher ranking officers. In both schools where I worked as a counselor in Germany, we had close to one-third student turnover every year in each school; so in a school of 600 students, we lost and gained close to 200 students every year.

Life in the Fortress

As stated in chapter 3, Wertsch's term *Fortress* refers to the physical communities in which military service members live, as well as to the psychological world that is created for the children as they grow up. Although there are certainly other children who share some of the same characteristics as military dependents, this community is unique in its combination of all the characteristics. For example, police officers might have more authoritarian homes and certainly live under the threat of harm. Other families relocate often for job reasons and career moves. Often families with issues such as alcoholism and abuse find themselves moving more often than others. Missionary families may grow up with the sense of mission, and certainly

Department of State and other foreign service workers also grow up with a sense of rootlessness. The uniqueness of military children is that all of these characteristics exist for them throughout their life. The characteristics of secrecy, stoicism, and denial identified by Wertsch (see chapter 3) hold for virtually all military families.

Almost always, like the parent-focused families also discussed in chapter 3, there is a belief that what goes on within the family remains behind closed doors, leading to a sense of isolation and a mentality that is pervasive and sometimes harmful to military children. Most parent-focused military families know that what goes on in the family could have disastrous ramifications to the military parent's career. This isolation often leads to the closing down of the feelings of resentment, hopelessness, grief, and fear that can lead to a denial of self, rage toward self and others, or, more profound, simply giving up. One therapist in Arizona talked about how often the sons in military families that she sees in therapy become alienated from their fathers, often turning to drugs or other acting-out behaviors. Many times the moms are often overwhelmed and may never have bought into or totally understood the culture of the military, so they can subconsciously support the rebellion of the child, eventually sabotaging the family.

Military Brats as Adults

This world of military children leaves military brats with certain legacies (Wertsch, 1991) that may stay with them throughout their lifetime. Often these legacies are seen as either–or dilemmas, leaving them with a need to make absolute decisions rather than to travel the middle road through life. Most adults who grew up as military brats still consider themselves brats and often have difficulty thinking of themselves as civilians, even though they may have never served in the military. John Bourdette (personal communication, 2007) pointed out that, even though it has been four decades since he was a military brat, he can almost always recognize brats within a few minutes of meeting them. "We are the children of warriors. And although it was initially a role not of our choosing, it is a role perpetuated by many of us with pride. … It is an attitude, a way of being" (Wertsch, 1991, p. 350). The following are the four legacies Wertsch found to have lifelong impacts on children of the military.

Time Means Today

In this first legacy that Wertsch (1991) defined as a "distorted relationship to time" (p. 351), today often appears to be all that exists, so that what happens now seems to have no impact on what happens in the future. Time isn't seen as a continuum, but rather something only to be lived in the present. In the civilian world, we begin teaching children fairly early that thinking on a long-term basis is productive and will lead to successful decisions later in life; we tell children that what they do today will lead them to reach their goals sometime in the future. Often, however, military children think in terms of change rather than of time; for instance, "What will happen next?" or "Where will we go next?" Students in middle school and high school often said to me that it didn't matter (but of course it did) how they did academically in this school because the next school would just have different rules, expectations, and requirements. The concepts of permanence and forever don't seem to exist, as the child's experiences relate to either the most recent move or the expectation of the next move (Wertsch, 1991).

It is ironic that military brats also tend to have a very optimistic view of the future, as they continue to believe that the next move, the next location, will be the best. Wertsch (1991) found, in her interviews, that often these military brats had trouble later in life making long-term commitments. They reported making frequent job changes and often getting nervous and bored easily with places and even with people. Adult military brats are often "leaving one foot in the realm of the temporary, and one foot in the realm of potential" (p. 354). The crisis orientation of this warrior society also leads to a sense of dread or expectation of imminent danger, so life should be lived in the present, discounting both the past and the future. John Bourdette shared how the thought process created by the constant moves from childhood seemed to be to live every day as if it were the last and to cram as much into living now as possible.

Taking Charge or Going With the Flow

Often this worldview or lifestyle leads to a sense of external control, as the power always seems to be in the hands of the unknown. The possible lifestyle consequences seemed to be adults who might (a) become very controlling or always know how to cover all bases; (b) buy into the military mentality of needing structure and external control; (c) become the perfectionist, having to get the best grades, be the most popular, and become the head of the corporation; or (d) give in to the sense of powerlessness and simply go along with whatever life presents (Wertsch, 1991). This last group, as high school students, was the group I witnessed in school who would go with the flow, only to often find themselves involved in drugs, alcohol, or gangs, because this brought them into association with others who met their needs for belonging, as well as a sense of being needed by others.

This worldview often also leads to the dilemma of whether to be asser-tive or passive. The highly transient childhood often teaches resiliency, but it may, as noted earlier in the chapter, also teach children how to adapt rather than to assert themselves in new circumstances. This adaptive qual-ity often leaves young people confused about their own values and their own sense of self. They may then find it difficult to stand up for themselves, because they tend to wait for an external authority figure to tell them what to do. Those who move in the direction of taking ultimate control, on the other hand, may not stop with assertiveness but instead perceive that the only way to get ahead, or get their needs met, is to become the aggressor, having to control all situations and even all people in their lives.

Living Within the Structure or Pushing the Limits

Military children often have difficulty reconciling the paradoxical contra-dictions of their life, particularly the need for autonomy versus the need for structure. Despite the strong image of the warrior, military service members, as well as the families, are completely dependent on an external authority telling them what to do. Having lived under the rigid rules of the warrior society, these children often have a powerful need to rebel. Chil-dren of authoritarian families or those who lived within the authoritarian environment of the Fortress seem to have an internalized need to indi-viduate while at the same time internalizing strong controls against indi-viduating (Wertsch, 1991). The need for structure and order is built into the family, the environment, the community, and often the individual.

As mentioned previously, even for those with an urge to rebel, there is an equally strong desire to surrender to structure, order, and discipline. Often service members, many of whom were military brats, comment that when they get out of the military, they are "unimpressed by the civilian work ethic" (Gegax & Thomas, 2005, p. 30) and even "harbor a disturb-ing disdain for the decadent and selfishness of modern American society" (p. 28). In chapter 2, I wrote about why young people join the military; one of the major reasons is often an underlying need for a certain amount of structure in which there is a sense of belonging, security, and safety. Whether it is a psychological need or an environmental need, this sense of structure abounds in military families.

Struggling with these contradictions often has long-term effects, such as pushing the rules to their limits, having problems with authority, and even finding it difficult to function in more stable or established commu-nities after growing up as a nomad. Although the military instills a sense of group identity, it often does not include a sense of community build-ing and belonging that is known in the civilian world. For military brats, "it takes both time and effort to finally appreciate that belonging is not just a matter of passive assignment to a category.... But is a process that is fed continuously, a function of active participation.... Learning this lesson amounts to nothing less than a rebirth into another way of being" (Wertsch, 1991, p. 372).

Idealism

The extreme devotion to the mission and the fact that military parents have given their lives to the mission demand from children self-discipline with an unambiguous drive. Whether the children like it or not, they are part of this mission, and for them to be successful, in school and in life, they have to buy into it. Sometimes this absolutist approach to idealism carries with it a blurring of distinction between important and not-so-important matters. When this absolutist approach is carried into the home, small problems can be magnified into large problems and are sometimes not dealt with in the normal course of teaching appropriate life skills but approached from the standpoint of reflecting one's character (Wertsch, 1991). The end result may be that the child becomes the problem rather than the problem behavior being the problem (see characteristics of parent-focused families in chapter 3).

This sense of idealism also carries with it a loyalty and patriotism unparalleled in the civilian world; although civilians are loyal and patriotic, questions and challenges are expected and respected in a democratic society and condemned and inappropriate within the warrior society. Problems can sometimes also arise because this sense of idealism may incorporate unfortunate myths. Two of these myths are the myth of male superiority (as those predominately in charge are men), which demands a strict adherence to a male conduct code, and the myth that danger and personal sacrifice are the only right ways to live. In other words, having the "right stuff," the characteristics of which tend to be positive for some, might not be appropriate for every child's personality. Often military children believe that if they were to choose a direction for their life that does not include these myths, they would be seen as failures.

Strengths and Their Possible Consequences

The gathering of fighting men should be thanking their children, their fine and resourceful children, who were strangers in every town they entered, thanking them for their extraordinary service to this country, for the sacrifices they made over and over again to the United States of America, to its ideals of freedom, to its preservation, and to its everlasting honor. ... Military brats, my lost tribe, spent their entire youth in service to this country and no one even knew we were there. (Conroy, 1991, p. xxv)

In the introduction to Mary Wertsch's book about military brats, Pat Conroy (1991) questioned who is going to thank these children. This quote is his musing about the answer to that question. Military brats grow up in a world very different from the world in which most civilian kids grow up in the United States, but that experience has given them amazing resiliency and strengths. The following section points out a number of strengths identified by Wertsch (1991) and clearly exhibited by the military dependent students I worked with at the middle school and high school levels.

Taking Responsibility Seriously

Military kids take the notion of duty very seriously. They routinely give their best effort and often do everything in their power to keep their word. A possible downside of this strength is that it may lead to perfectionism or perceived failure later associated with guilt and self-condemnation. These kids will often take on too much and wear themselves out trying to do everything single-handedly, as they have lived a life where they are not allowed to ask for external help and may be responsible for their military parent's downfall.

One of my best tennis players on the varsity squad was also starring in the school drama production, was a straight A student, and was taking two advanced placement classes in her senior year. During one of the trips to and from the tennis practice facility, I noted she was reading Victor Hugo's *Les Misérables*. When I asked if she was reading it for a class, she replied that no, she had read it once in eighth grade but didn't really understand it back then, so she decided she would read it again for pleasure. I have yet to attempt to get through this 800-page masterpiece, yet with everything else on her plate, she was reading *Les Misérables* for pleasure.

Getting Along With Everyone

As we know, military families move a lot, requiring the kids to forge new friendships over and over. They tend to get along well with almost everyone, with perhaps one exception: the more authoritarian personality. They tend to be well suited to careers involving people contact and knowing how to fit in quickly in social situations. A possible downside is that they may wear numerous masks to protect themselves against the loss of friendship or attachments, which they consider inevitable. Many of the adult military brats that Wertsch (1991) interviewed tended to keep relationships shallow and short term, thereby making long-term commitments difficult. One adult military brat who had been divorced six times told me that almost all the adults who had grown up in the military who he knows are in and out of relationships much more easily than nonmilitary adults are.

Being Resilient and Flexible

Many different and sometimes difficult situations arise for military kids that can end up teaching them the kinds of excellent coping skills necessary to deal with almost anything. This resiliency for many leads to healthy and productive lifestyles, in which older teen and adult military brats can make adjustments quickly, can accommodate to difficult situations, and believe they maintain the necessary power to direct their future.

In the process, however, some become ambivalent and lose sight of their personal values, what they really care about, or what they are willing to take a stand for. Among those students who took on this stance, their favorable word was "whatever." When I heard this used over and over, I usually found students who had given up taking control of their life and had already decided they had no power to determine their future. These were, by far, the hardest students to work with.

Being Loyal and Self-Sacrificing

These young people can be extremely loyal to a cause or to friends. Military dependent youth seem to know well the concept of right and wrong; they can be extremely dedicated to matters of principles and will go to extraordinary lengths to defend them. But again there is a downside, as they can also become vulnerable to anyone willing to take them in. The students who arrived in our school with a lot of anger or who had had problems in their previous schools were easily taken in by the druggies or gang members, and this is where their allegiance formed, regardless of the possible harm. They can also be self-righteous to the point where others around them feel guilty or resentful. As adults, they sometimes may even sacrifice their personal happiness, for instance, in a marriage, family, or career, for the sake of making a point or being right (Wertsch, 1991).

Bring on the Challenges

A willingness to take risks is also one of the characteristics of those kids raised in the military, but these kids may not have the cautiousness about them that civilian kids often have. They are generally able to summon up the courage or whatever it takes to leap into a new and challenging situation—they have had to do that, and they can name numerous situations in which they have accomplished something as a result. They have experienced losses so often, they have already learned they can survive and keep going. There is an obvious downside to this strength, as it can become easier to move on to new situations than to put the energy into making the present situation work (Wertsch, 1991). The need for change and excitement becomes a part of their psyche, sometimes leading to an inability to maintain long-term commitments or take unhealthy or dangerous risks with the belief that this, too, shall pass.

Being Productive and Efficient

The young people who early in life internalize this strong sense of discipline can become extremely productive and efficient; they are often amazing in their ability to get things done and to be the best student, the best leader, and the best athlete all at the same time, an example of which I noted earlier. But sometimes this sense of discipline is dependent on an external authority that might eventually trigger the need to rebel. This rebellion may not be tempered with an ability to give up just one thing in their life, but it often becomes rampant and so powerful that everything is discarded.

Living Their Diversity

In having to adapt to so many situations, cultures, ideals, and lifestyles, these young people have learned, very early in life, the inherent value of diversity. They may have lived in different countries, surrounded by different cultures, and have gone to school in some of the most integrated schools available to American kids. They may have had to suffer discrimination and prejudice because they were seen as different, a subculture unacceptable even to others in the United States. John Bourdette spent the first few years in schools in Bermuda, where his father was stationed. Before moving on base, he attended a British school with British kids and the local children. He never saw any signs of being discriminated against in the British school. Only later when his family was stationed at a military base in the United States and he attended a public school did he experience the prejudice of being different from the civilian kids. Military brats learn to value this diversity and to tolerate change and difference, but in doing so they can lose sight of their own values, their own ideals, and their own family culture. Often students would tell me that they knew nothing of their heritage or their family history. Those who stayed connected to their extended families seemed to have a better sense of family values or history.

Taking Care of the World

As might be expected, these military kids can often handle emergencies calmly and competently. Often others around them will turn to them for help. Some almost seem to thrive in crisis situations and may not do the necessary planning to avoid them. One of the adult military brats Wertsch (1991) interviewed made the point that most of what they learned is powerful and useful, but it is a matter of moderating their behavior so that it becomes a part of "a strong healthy life, a life of self-examination and self-awareness" (p. 396).

Major Challenges

Permanent Change of Station

A military spouse told one of the therapists I interviewed that "every house I have lived in I have planted fruit trees to make it feel like it is mine—but soon I have to leave, so I never get to pick the fruit." A planning guide called *Military Families on the Move* (Military Family Research Institute, n.d.), written for kids in the midst of transitions, addresses three issues: Saying Good-bye, What's There?, and How to Move. Written for kids, it starts by stating, "Right now you might feel like your life is out of control. And, in a way, it is—you have no control over the fact that you and your family are moving. However, you can do something about it" (p. 1). The authors made the point that children "just have to accept the fact that even though [they] don't want to move, it is something [they] have to do. But [they] do have some control.… Either look forward to this move or … hate it. Guess which is better?" (p. 1). The guide goes on to give ideas for students leaving school and leaving friends; for instance, a suggestion of bringing a camera and taking pictures of everyone and everything that concludes with, "So, stop worrying and start exploring. You not only have a new installation and town to discover, you might have a whole new country and a whole new continent" (p. 3).

These resources are vital for families and students and can be especially helpful if used with groups of students, either in school or in the community. What is also especially helpful, I believe, is giving permission to kids to have sad or mad moments and explaining that these feelings are a normal part of life and a normal part of any transition. "Everyone has bad days. It's totally normal. Besides classes, tests, homework, sports and clubs, you've got a ton of other things to think about, too. That's a lot to handle; but it's a part of life, right?" (p. 5).

My concern is that these feelings may be taken too lightly, and there are young people who simply do not handle change and transitions easily. Are the feelings recognized and validated, or are they tolerated or dismissed? Are the children just expected to shape up and get with it? Parents, during a transition, have a mountain of concerns to think about and sometimes may not have the patience or time to consider the child who is resistant, has more fears than others, or simply has made attachments that are difficult to break. Fenell and Fenell (2003) outlined a conceptual model of a five-stage transition cycle for families, which includes the following:

1. *Involvement:* The student is currently in an environment, school, or community where he or she belongs and feels connected.
2. *Leaving:* The student begins to disengage from activities, friendships, and responsibilities as soon as the parent receives orders that they will be leaving. This is often a confusing time, as the student has to deal with issues of loss and loyalty.
3. *Transition:* This stage begins after the move has taken place; the chaos is magnified because there are no support systems or friendships to fall back on. The student wants to fit in but often is unclear how, so the feeling of vulnerability is enhanced.
4. *Reentry:* After a time, the student can begin to accept responsibility for developing strategies to reengage with the new school and community, even though there is a lot of ambivalence and mood swings from optimism to discouragement.
5. *Reinvolvement:* The student can once again feel a sense of belonging and will begin to find ways to make sense of the new school while establishing new friendships.

These five stages, along with the Transition Journey outlined in chapter 8, fit nicely together. It is imperative for the school counselor, as well as the teachers, to be actively involved with the student at each stage of this transition. These transitions create a great deal of stress for students academically as well as emotionally, so counselors also need to be aware of the resources available, such as those through the Military Child Education Coalition, which is addressed later in this chapter.

Deployment

Although there is a major section on deployment in chapter 7, I chose to include a section on the effects of deployment on children in this chapter. Rachel Robertson (n.d.), the author of an article titled *Helping Children Handle Deployments* stated,

> Children are especially vulnerable because they often don't know how to handle all the changes and uncertainties. Our kids sometimes seem a bit restless, often moody and occasionally downright unmanageable. It is important to remember that these behaviors are often the way children express negative feelings like fear, worry, anxiety, and loneliness. Children show us how they are feeling by their actions more than their words so we must pay careful attention to body language and behavior. While parents need not allow

inappropriate behavior, simply punishing these behaviors won't stop them and may actually compound them. (¶ 1)

The following suggestions outlined in the article by Robertson (n.d.) are consistent with information from the National Association of School Psychologists (2001) and the American School Counselor Association (Collins, 2005). I believe they can be used by counselors to effectively help parents work with their children during deployment.

1. Maintain consistency and a routine to eliminate the sense of insecurity felt by children because of the uncertainties regarding the deployment. It can be beneficial for them to have a predictable routine and home life.

2. Maintain good communication with honest age-appropriate discussions on a daily basis by answering questions and being willing to listen and express feelings. Sometimes helping parents learn communication skills, such as reflecting, listening, and questioning, can help ease tension and relieve concerns.

3. Pay attention to the needs of the children and continue to have good times together, which can take away some of the pain of the loss of a parent. These times can be difficult for the spouse who stays home, so working with that parent may be a priority. Helping the nonmilitary parent plan special events or even start new hobbies can be valuable to reinforce the message that life goes on even while the military parent is gone. It is easy for the children to feel neglected during deployments, because one parent is gone and the other is more than likely busy and stressed. Both the children and the caretaker parent need many opportunities to feel loved and special during deployment.

4. It is crucial to maintain a healthy lifestyle. It can become easy for the stressed parent to neglect the nutritional foods, the regular exercise, or the required sleep, for both the parent and the children, and fall into unhealthy routines, such as spending too much time in front of the television. It is obviously important for parents to take care of themselves so that they can take better care of their children, which includes getting plenty of exercise, sleep, and healthy food. "Your lives are already in such chaos from all the changes in a deployment; establishing a daily routine to ensure you get the basics can go a long way toward keeping yourself and your kids less stressed" (¶ 14).

5. The parents who are left in charge of the household and the kids should not treat their kids as if they are adults. The children need to be able to remain kids. It is not fair to discuss adult fears in

depth with the children or expect them to take the place of the deployed spouse. It is wise to be careful how much exposure the children have to the news, particularly information about military events. A couple weeks after the events of September 11, 2001, when the whole country was glued to the television, my then-4-year-old grandson saw the American flag while they were driving and said to his Air Force father, "Dad, look there's a flag. That's a really bad thing!" Shocked that his son would see the American flag in a negative way, my son asked, "Why do you think it's bad?" To which his little one replied, very confidently, "Because on TV, whenever you see the flag, people are crying, so it must be bad." It is impossible to know what young children will remember, imagine, or deduce from information and images they see through the media.

6. A need for reassurance is obviously important, as children will so often feel a loss of control and stability. Not only have they experienced a major change in their life but they could do nothing to prevent it from occurring. To build trust, help parents remind the children that both parents will always love them and that together they can survive this deployment.

7. It is essential to help parents create a good behavior plan. Understanding why children misbehave may be all it takes to move from being punitive to being an effective parent. Knowing that it is important to set limits and have consequences is one thing, but understanding the difference between logical consequences and punitive consequence is another. Parents who attend parent education classes, either on base or in the community, can find a source of support and effective parenting tips to help them relieve the concerns about whether they are doing the right thing. A program on filial play that teaches parents how to actively play with their children can make a major difference in the way parents and children interact.

8. Help parents maintain or even increase their physical and emotional expressions of love, including hugs, high fives, and statements such as "I love you," which can go a long way in helping children cope with difficult situations. If these decrease or are abandoned, the message to the children may be that the change and even the loss of the military parent may be the fault of the children.

Developmental Age Differences

Pincus, House, Christenson, and Adler (n.d.) stated that the response of children to extended deployment is very individualized and depends on their developmental age. It is reasonable to assume that a sudden negative change in a child's behavior or mood may be a predictable response to the stress of having a deployed parent. Some of the possible changes outlined by age in their article are listed next, with suggestions for interventions.

Infants (younger than 1 year of age) may refuse to eat and appear listless; they must be held and actively nurtured to thrive. If the primary caregiver becomes significantly depressed, the infant can be at risk for apathy, unwillingness to eat, and eventual weight loss. Early intervention becomes critical to prevent undue harm or neglect. Counselors can assist with teaching and modeling parenting skills and by eliciting family or community support. The primary caregiver may also benefit from individual counseling.

Toddlers (from 1 to 3 years old) may begin to throw temper tantrums or increase the amount of crying for what appears to be no reason; they may appear sad or irritable. They usually take their cue from the primary caregiver. If the nondeploying parent is coping well, they tend to do well. If the primary caregiver is not, toddlers may become sullen or tearful, throw tantrums, or develop sleep disturbance. Toddlers usually respond to increased attention, hugs, and hand-holding. The parent may also benefit from sharing his or her day-to-day experiences with other parents facing similar challenges. It is essential for primary caregivers to balance the demands for caring for children along with their own needs.

Preschoolers (from 3 to 6 years old) may revert to younger behaviors, such as baby talking and thumb sucking, even in areas or skills that they have mastered, such as potty training or sleeping alone. They may also be clingy or irritable, appear depressed or sad, be aggressive, or begin to have somatic complaints as well as fears about the caretaking parent or others leaving. Caregivers will need to reassure them, not just with words and extra attention but also with physical closeness, such as hugging and holding hands. It is also important to avoid changing family routines unless they are extremely emotional and the change is for a short period. Concerns and questions regarding the military parent and the deployment should be brief, matter of fact, and age appropriate but consistent, with no sense that the questions or concerns are unacceptable or a nuisance. This will help to contain the anxiety of children's overactive imagination.

Elementary school age children (from 6 to 12 years old) may whine, complain, become aggressive, or otherwise act out their feelings. They may focus on the military parent who will be missing a key event; for example, "Will Dad be here for my birthday?" Depressive symptoms may appear, including sleep disturbance and a loss of interest in school, eating, or even playing with friends. They will need to have permission to talk about their feelings and will need more physical attention than usual. Expectations regarding school performance may need to be loosened a little but should not be given up. Working with the teachers or the school counselor so the school is aware of the deployment is essential, and keeping routines as close to normal is important, both at home and in school. A therapist in San Diego who works with children talked about the cumulative effect for the kids who were either always preparing for a parent to leave or looking forward to the parent to come home. This seemed particularly difficult for boys between the ages of 10 and 15 whose fathers were deployed, as they were expected to take over as the man of the house. Often this was an assumption made by these boys, not because they were specifically told to by either of their parents but because of their heightened sense of responsibility. Difficulties often result, however, when the dad returns and naturally displaces the son as the head of the house.

Teenagers (from 13 to 18 years old) may be irritable, rebellious, fight or participate in other attention-getting behavior; they can also become parentified to take care of the nondeployed parent. They may show a lack of interest in school, peers, and school activities and are at greater risk for promiscuity and alcohol and drug use. Although they may deny problems and worries, it is extremely important for caregivers to stay engaged, give them permission to express their feelings, even if negative, and be available to talk about their concerns. At first, lowering academic expectations for them may be helpful, if worked out with teachers and the school counselor, but they should be supported to return to their usual school performance as soon as possible. Sports and social activities should be encouraged and maintained to give structure to their lives. Likewise, additional responsibility in the family, appropriate with their emotional maturity, will make them feel important and needed, as long as they do not have to give up their healthy teen activities to solve or rescue the family. It should be noted that, unfortunately, some children might have great difficulty adapting to the stress of a deployed parent. The authors also pointed out that children of deployed parents are also more vulnerable to psychiatric hospitalization, especially in single-parent and blended families (Pincus et al., n.d.).

Living in a Democratic Society

A therapist in Tucson, Arizona, who works primarily with adolescents explained that when families live in such an authoritarian structure as the military, they aren't often faced with major life decisions or choices, such as when to buy a house or whether to relocate to enhance the career of a spouse. At the same time, they have to survive in our mostly democratic American society. This therapist tries, when working with families, to point out to the parents that they might be comfortable living in the authoritarian military structure but that the kids, particularly those who are rebelling, might see the world in a different way. What often happens in many of the families he works with is, if something is not working, for instance, teens not abiding by their curfew, the parents simply tighten up the rules and become more rigid and strict. Parents often use this approach because of their fear of losing control and losing their rightful place as the head of the household.

If the therapist can help parents learn to listen to their kids and be actively interested in what they think, believe, and need, the parents begin to see that they don't have to lose their authority to stay in control. By acknowledging the needs of the children and then investigating alternative solutions, the family can lessen its stress and often its power struggles. Children of the military, whether they live on base or not, live, at least part of their life, in a democratic society; they go to democratic schools, and their parents are serving the mission of defending a democratic nation. It is understandable, then, how those who face strictly authoritarian parenting or home life might be confused and perhaps become rebellious.

McKay and Maybell (2004) wrote about, and teach, what they call the "Democratic Revolution" and its impact on families; they defined the democratic revolution over the past half century or so as the "upheaval in all of our social institutions: government, education, the workplace, race relationships, gender relationships and families" (p. 64). This revolution has taken the traditional roles of domination and submission that previously defined most social institutions and relationships and moved them toward egalitarian democratic relationships. Most people in the United States now operate from an equality identity that includes attitudes of equal values and respect. These societal changes require not only a new attitude toward one's self and others but also a new set of knowledge and skills (McKay & Maybell, 2004).

The military is perhaps the one institution that has not changed to an egalitarian institution: it never will, and it never can. But there have been changes, outlined in chapter 2, since the onset of the all-volunteer military that have moved even the military in a more egalitarian direction to provide the necessary and expected services for the family. Regardless of how the military must and will organize itself and its members, the family still lives in a democratic society and, for the most part, expects to be treated as such. As McKay and Maybell (2004) explained,

> Being in a democratic, equal relationship—adult to adult or child to adult—does not imply that each person is the same. Sameness is not the definition of equality. … Equality refers to respect and dignity to which every family member is entitled. Furthermore, while each person has rights, no one has the right to do whatever she or he wants. There are rules in families and in society. (p. 65)

The U.S. society is in a time of transition, when those who have traditionally been in a superior role may be trying to maintain that position through power and control, and those who have been in an inferior position are attempting to overthrow this oppression. The result is often "tension, conflict, anger, and even violence ... as we move from the old autocratic tradition to a new democratic one" (McKay & Maybell, 2004, p. 65). I believe these are valuable insights into the children of the military, many of whom may view the world outside of the military more appealing and often rebel against the rigid structure they are forced to live within. This theoretical framework can be a useful tool for helping families move from the kind of rigid superior–inferior structure that often is brought from the military structure into the home to a more egalitarian structure that encourages and respects each individual in the family.

Parenting Styles

It can be helpful to work with parents within this framework to understand their parenting styles and perhaps make modifications in their parenting from those styles that are discouraging for their children to those that are empowering and encouraging. McKay and Maybell (2004) described three of the most common parenting styles: the coercive parenting style, the pampering or permissive parenting style, and the respectful leadership style. The first two are often discouraging to the healthy development of children; the third can be a respectful and encouraging style.

Coercive Parenting

The coercive parenting style is often the style used to control children "for their own good" and is often the style of parenting used in parent-focused families. The parents are in control by giving orders, setting rules, making demands, rewarding obedient behavior, and punishing bad deeds. The model is "limits without freedom." These parents usually have the good intentions of wanting to make sure their children avoid the mistakes in life that they perhaps made or they see others making, and they want to teach their children "the right way" before they get hurt. If the children accept a subordinate identity, this style can work, at least for a while, particularly while the children are young. For those kids who want to be acknowledged for who they are and who want, at some point in their life, to be respected as an individual, this style results in conflict and power struggles. "Kids tend to become experts at not doing what their parents want them to do and on doing exactly what their parents don't want" (McKay & Maybell, 2004, p. 71). Often the results of coercive parenting are either kids feel they lose and try to get even, resulting in a constant war of revenge, or kids submit to the coercion and learn to rely only on those in power to make their decisions—sometimes shifting the power to peer groups or negative influences.

Pampering or Permissive Parenting

Parents use the pampering or permissive parenting style to make children comfortable and happy by letting them do whatever they please or by doing everything for them; this style is "freedom without limits." The impact of pampering can easily move children toward seeing themselves as the prince or princess and their parents as their servants. They can develop a "strong sense of ego-esteem with little true self- or people-esteem" (McKay & Maybell, 2004, p. 72). These children tend to be underdeveloped in their social skills and become too dependent on others. Often parents eventually feel they are doing too much, which then leads to conflict and power struggles. Because there are few limits, children begin to believe they can do anything they want, so they develop little internal self-discipline or self-responsibility. Sometimes these first two parenting styles exist in the same family where one parent is the authoritarian (in a military family, usually the military parent) and the other is the permissive parent who tries to make up for the harshness of the authoritarian parent by lessening the rules when the military parent is absent.

Respectful Leadership

The respectful leadership parenting style is the only encouraging style for children; it is the style of "freedom within limits." As leaders of the family, the parents value the child and value themselves; mutual respect is the guiding principle in all areas of parent–child interaction. The parents focus on giving choices instead of giving orders. They have encouraging attitudes, and their goals are to be accepting, to build on strengths, to accentuate the positive, to promote responsibility, and to instill confidence in their children. These kinds of parents, both in the civilian and military worlds, raise respectful, responsible children. Helping parents understand the long-term consequences of their parenting style can be the best lesson they may ever learn. Almost all parents' goals for their children are those listed in this last section, particularly promoting responsibility and confidence, but the difference is the actions they use to achieve those goals. Helping military parents realize that they can reach these goals by changing their parenting style can be extremely valuable.

Development of Problems

In 1984 Rodriguez wrote that in such a rank-privileged and rank-oriented social system as the military, the mix of "caste formation" and egalitarianism might create a difficult dichotomy, particularly for children and adolescents struggling to find their identity. This difficulty is sometimes exacerbated by parents' concerns about the child's misbehavior, which might affect their status in the military, and by parents' communications about whom it would be safe or acceptable to associate with, especially within the rank hierarchy. Particularly in parent-focused families, children are sensitive to this parental anxiety and the anger that follows when they break community rules or military social norms; they generally react to these codes of conduct by either complying with them or angrily defying them.

In some military communities, particularly those that are isolated and where rules are strongly enforced, children have little room to make mistakes or test the limits of authority in a normal manner, without imperiling the family status or the military parent's career. This is particularly true when the parents are involved in a struggle for upward professional or social mobility. Wishes for a better socioeconomic and class status cause such parents to integrate the changing power of income with an altering sense of status, charged with constant stimulus for competition and achievement. Promotion and the failure to be promoted in this milieu become issues for the active duty member and family, for their place in the community, and in the effective functioning of the military unit (Ridenour, 1984). This often leaves the child or adolescent with no choice but to internalize the identity and role conflicts or act them out behaviorally.

This is a common theme in problems brought to child mental health clinics by military families. It is exacerbated by parental and community inability to provide assistance, for a number of reasons. Sometimes the difficulties are not recognized or are minimized, sometimes the parents are not physically present or emotionally available, and sometimes the community support systems are inadequate or unresponsive (Ridenour, 1984). In the 1980s, clinical findings of common behavioral and emotional reactions of military children were generally attributed to military family life, which lead to the designation of a "military family syndrome." These problems were usually found in vulnerable families with a predisposition to develop dysfunctional patterns consisting of continuous separations, transcultural experiences, child abuse and neglect, parental alcoholism, post-traumatic stress disorder of the military parent, poverty, single-parent families, cultural integration problems such as racism, and problems experienced by children of racially or ethnically mixed marriages.

As therapists and other mental health professionals, we know that the family environment affects the development of psychosocial problems (Jeffreys & Leitzel, 2000). A caring relationship and low family stress is associated with resiliency, and if children have an emotionally supportive relationship with their parents, they are more likely to demonstrate high levels of self-esteem and healthy psychological development. They also have the ability to incorporate their parents' attitudes, values, and role expectations into their lives. In the study of military families reported by Jeffreys and Leitzel (2000), when the family climate promotes the participation in family decision making, it is positive for adolescent identity development. Effective communication patterns facilitate family interaction and are associated with social competence. This finding is consistent with the concept of McKay and Maybell's (2004) respectful leadership style of parenting.

Military Youth Satisfaction

It is important to again emphasize that most military families do an extraordinary job in raising their children. And although there are specific circumstances that can cause more difficulties for some children than others, the majority of families and children live exciting, adventurous, and productive lives. In the study discussed earlier (Jeffreys & Leitzel, 2000), the adolescents who were living with one parent and one stepparent had the lowest family satisfaction, followed by those in single-parent families and then two-parent families. The youth satisfaction among branches showed that adolescents who had a parent in the Air Force reported the fewest risk factors and that those with parents in the Navy were most at risk. Those living overseas reportedly were more at risk and reported more moves but felt more safety in their places of residence, but they had greater concerns about moving to installations with more violence and higher crime than those who lived stateside. Those overseas also reported a greater potential for obtaining support because they lived on base. Children of officers seemed to feel less at risk than others.

The preponderance of respondents to this survey reported being "healthy, engaging in weekly exercise, participating in appropriate school and community activities, doing homework and getting good grades in school" (Jeffreys & Leitzel, 2000, p. 234). Furthermore, they recounted being happy with their school, home, and community environment, which led the authors to conclude that in comparisons to civilian adolescents, "military adolescents are doing at least as well as and, in some cases, slightly better than their civilian peers on most of the indicators measured" (Jeffreys & Leitzel, 2000, p. 234).

Tips for the Schools

A result of the global military activities of the past few years is that families "today are experiencing a phenomenon that has not been experienced since the early 1990s" (Collins, 2005, ¶ 1). Professional school counselors are being faced in many civilian and military communities with the challenge of helping families and communities deal with the effects of deployment. The most important role of the professional school counselor is that of an advocate for the child, for the family in distress, and for the staff members who work with these students. For instance, Collins (2005) outlined the following issues to be aware of during deployment, when students often feel that the safety and security of their lives are gone, and then shared a few examples of how school counselors can intervene and provide support for students during deployment.

Some students will struggle with feelings of loss and grief, whereas others seem to have strong coping and resiliency skills, but all must learn to cope and adjust to life without the deployed parent and be ready for the reunion. This time is usually an emotional roller coaster filled with anticipation and anxiety. At the preschool and elementary school levels, schools could create bulletin boards where students bring pictures or write something about their deployed parents, and teachers might be encouraged to incorporate information or activities within their lessons regarding the deployment.

At middle schools and junior high schools, similar kinds of projects can be adapted but geared to the older student. Students at this age could also be encouraged to write poetry or short stories. Counseling groups can be effective for those students whose parents are deployed, as it gives them a safe place to express their emotions without causing undo concern for their at-home parents.

At the high school level, counselors would certainly want to have small group counseling or support sessions with the children of those deployed. They could encourage the teachers to do classroom guidance activities and the staff to be sensitive to the students by monitoring what happens in the classroom, including keeping news reports to a minimum or creating alternative assignments for those students for whom watching the news might do more harm than good.

It is also important to encourage all staff to be careful of voicing their personal opinions about the war or the political situation and to have resources available from the local military installation to help the students and families. Collins (2005) said, "Working with families who are deployed is just like putting together a puzzle; you must help them work at finding the pieces that belong together until the picture is complete.... You don't have to work miracles; you just have to have some puzzle glue handy" (p. 3).

Best Practices

In the April 2007 edition of *The Voice for Military Families,* Patricia M. Barron, deputy director of Government Relations of the National Military Family Association, gave examples of best practices from a number of school districts around the country that have "stepped up to the plate and shown exceptional support and commitment to these families" (p. 1). In Alaska and Virginia, students may be exempt from taking the state exit exam if they have passed another state's exam and if they arrived in the state with only one or two semesters remaining until graduation. Virginia has revised its regulations permitting students to receive credit for what they call "academic accountability" tests taken in other states, which basically grants reciprocity to mobile students who have passed similar content-based tests administered as part of another state's system. In New Mexico, hand-carried paperwork is acceptable for placement until official paperwork arrives, and in Alaska, a physician or clinic listing required immunizations is an acceptable method of verifying the required shots. In Florida, if students transfer from an out-of-state school and do not meet the regular age requirement for kindergarten and first grade, they will be allowed to enroll if they met the age requirement in the state from which they transferred. These and other best practices are ways school districts can make the movement of military families less burdensome.

One of the best resources for school counselors is the work done by the Military Child Education Coalition (MCEC). Since 1999 the coalition has been working directly with school districts, the different branches of the military, professionals, and parents to make the transfer of students from one school district to another a more smooth and hassle-free process (Military Child Education Coalition, 2001). The coalition has been successful in creating a Memorandum of Agreement between school districts and the military that outlines the following goals: (a) to improve the timely transfer of records; (b) to ease the student transition to new schools; (c) to promote practices that foster access to extracurricular programs; (d) to establish procedures to lessen the impact of moves at the end of the junior year through the senior year; (e) to communicate variations in school calendars and schedules; (f) to create and implement professional development systems; (g) to continue strong child-centered partnerships between the installation and supporting schools; (h) to provide information concerning graduation requirements; and (i) to provide specialized services for transitioning students when they are applying to and finding funding for postsecondary study (Military Child Education Coalition, 2001). The MCEC provides regular training for school counselors and has, in addition to numerous other resources, created a checklist for the student transferring schools so parents know what records they need to bring with them from one school to the next.

Special Needs Students

A concern about special needs students was addressed by a number of therapists I spoke with who work specifically with military families who have kids with unique needs. The major concern is that a diagnosis is often delayed, and therefore intervention either has not occurred or did not begin early enough in the child's education. This seems to happen for a multitude of reasons but often relates to either the unavailability of services or the rotation schedule. Families are not getting in to see the right people prior to the next Permanent Change of Station. Families, especially the parents who are having children at a very young age, often don't know what to ask for or know that services are supposed to be available.

As a counselor in Department of Defense schools, at both the middle and high school levels, I frequently had new students entering the school who had never been evaluated for their special needs. Often the reasons were the parents didn't know that there was a problem or that services were available. There are also some parents, as is true in civilian schools, who do not want a diagnosis because of the fear that their child will be labeled, therefore treated differently. There are parents, although relatively few, who are anxious about their child being viewed as different, as it often means to them that their child is weak or reflects poorly on them as parents.

These are difficult situations to deal with, but often by sharing information regarding the long-term benefits of a diagnosis and special needs services can bring the parents around to working collaboratively with the school. Although it is difficult for students who have a history of failure to turn that barrier around, once identified, evaluated, and enrolled in special needs classes regardless of the age or grade, they at least have a chance of success. It is also important, as most school counselors know, that a special needs diagnosis with a transitional Individualized Education Plan (IEP) can go with the child to higher education so that they can immediately qualify for additional services even at the college level.

Department of Defense Schools

It should be noted that those students who spend time in the Department of Defense Education Activity (DoDEA) school system perhaps have the best of both worlds. Fredricka Schouten (2004) wrote that the Department of Defense schools "inspire fierce devotion and with good reason" (p. 7D). Students consistently rank near the top on federal reading, writing, and math tests. Fifty years after the legal end of school segregation, these schools are also models of integration and minority academic achievement. In 2003, Black and Hispanic eighth graders outperformed peers in reading in all 50 states. "The consistency with which this school system delivers high performance and produces outstanding outcomes for these kids and their families is unprecedented" (p. 7D).

In 2004 the Department of Defense school system enrolled about 100,000 children at over 200 schools around the globe, in either the DoDDS-E or DoDDS-P (Department of Defense Dependent Schools–Pacific) system or the 69 Department of Defense Domestic Dependent Elementary and Secondary Schools (DDESS) in the continental United States. There are some obvious advantages for these students; for example, at least one of their parents has a full-time job, and at least one has a high school diploma. Unlike the civilian high school where I also worked as a counselor, there are no homeless kids in military dependent schools.

In addition, unlike civilian schools, the failure of a parent to participate in school activities, for instance, not attending a parent–teacher conference, means the school might call on the commanding officer for help in engaging the parent in school activities. It was not uncommon for me, as a school counselor, if I could not get the parent to come in to discuss a child's problems, that I, or the principal, would contact the commanding officer—and that officer would often accompany the parent to the next school meeting. Where in the public school system would a school have that kind of leverage? Schouten (2004) pointed out that in 2004 nearly 64% of the Department of Defense teachers had master's degrees, compared with 42% of teachers nationwide, with considerably higher pay than most public schools, sometimes as much as $10,000 more annual salary than in a similarly sized civilian school district. The schools also share a common curriculum around the world.

Problems, however, cannot be overlooked. Students move constantly and, interesting enough, are just as likely as students in other public schools to live under the guidelines for poverty. Nearly one in four qualify for subsidized school meals. Obviously the constant worry of many students who fear the loss of a deployed parent halfway around the globe is an additional concern, but the schools become like a family, as everyone understands the difficulty of being in the military.

Schools, whether civilian or Department of Defense, must be interested and involved in the lives of the military dependent kids—not just to offer them the required educational curriculum but to support their emotional, psychological, and social needs. For all students to be successful in schools, the three domains of academic development, career development, and social and emotional development, as outlined by the American School Counselor Association's National Model, must be a part of every school counseling program (American School Counselor Association, 2003).

CHAPTER 6

Other Military Families to Consider

Reserves and Guard Members and Their Families

To most civilians the concept of the Reserves and the National Guard are more than likely interchangeable, so first I want to identify the mission of each and the differences between the two components of the military, both currently referred to as "suddenly military" and "citizen soldiers." Although the National Guard is part of the Reserves forces, it is the oldest component of any uniformed services, tracing its roots back to 1636 with the earliest English colonies in North America (*About the National Guard,* n.d.). The first guard was organized into militias and drew on English military tradition for its formation. These militias protected the citizens from Indian attack and foreign invaders and later helped to win the Revolutionary War. The National Guard made up 40% of the combat divisions in France during World War I, and in World War II the Guard was among the first to deploy overseas and the first to fight in combat. After World War II the aviation units became the Air National Guard. Almost 23,000 Army and Air Guardsmen were called to active duty during the Vietnam War, and over 75,000 were a part of Desert Storm in 1991.

The Guard maintains a unique dual state–federal force rooted in Article One of the U.S. Constitution. Soldiers and airmen in the Guard swear an oath to protect and defend the Constitution not just of the United States but also of the state in which they serve; in peacetime the Guard is commanded by the governors of the state to which they are affiliated. The Guard has the right to help during natural disasters, state emergencies, and civil unrest; this last responsibility is unique to the Guard, as civil laws restrict how federal troops, including Reserves components, can enforce state laws.

In addition to the Army and Air Force Guard components, all four branches of the military—Army, Marine Corps, Navy, and Air Force—have a Reserve component. The Army Reserve component's mission is to provide trained and ready units with combat service support and combat capabilities necessary to support national strategies during peacetime, contingencies, and war (Army Reserve, n.d.). The Air Force Reserve command supports the Air Force mission to "defend the United States through control and exploitation of air and space by supporting Global Engagement" (Air Force Reserve Command, n.d., ¶ 2). All Reserves components provide integral support of the day-to-day operations of all four of the services. There are a number of categories of Reservists, including the Ready Reserve, who may be recalled to active duty to augment active forces in time of war or national emergency; the Standby Reserve, whose civilian jobs are considered key to national defense or who may have a temporary disability or personal hardship and therefore are not called into active duty; and the Retired Reserve, former officers and enlisted personnel who receive pay after retiring from active duty or from the Reserves and are waiting retirement at age 60.

Almost half of all Reserves and Guard members are younger than 30 years old, with 30% between the ages of 31 and 40 and 20% between the ages of 41 and 50. The Reserves and Guard components who are not on active duty traditionally train one weekend per month and one continuous 2-week period annually (Pryce, Ogilvy-Lee, & Pryce, 2000).

Total Force Policy

A policy called the Total Force Policy emerged after the Vietnam War to make sure that the U.S. military would never be used in foreign armed conflict "without the activation of significant numbers of Reserve military forces. The total force policy was to ensure commitment of the American citizenry in support of its military in any extended commitment … as military members would come from both the active and Reserve components" (Pryce et al., 2000, p. 29). This policy went into effect at the inception of the all-volunteer service so that Guard and Reserves units would be eligible to be called up as needed and deployed anywhere in the world and that active duty units would no longer be the first in line to meet mission needs. As has become obvious in the past few years, the combined effect of increased mobilizations and deployments and the unusual number of recent natural disasters have taxed the resources of the Reserve component. Increased and extended absences from home and family, potentially dangerous and tedious duty, and disruption in civilian employment are challenging the total force policy and raising questions that remain unanswered. (Pryce et al., 2000, p. 27)

In addition to the impact on the members of the Guard and Reserves from increasing absences and lengthening deployments, the disruption of civilian employment, and differences in pay between civilian and military jobs are the effects being felt in communities throughout the United States. Some rural areas are being challenged by the loss of police officers, teachers, firefighters, dentists, engineers, lawyers, accountants, medical providers, mental health professionals, and others. These rural areas are also often bearing the prospect of large number of casualties from community-based Reserves units, such as the Scud missile attack in the first Persian Gulf War where one community lost 22 citizen soldiers.

As noted previously, the National Guard answers to two masters (Henderson, 2006). The state governor can call up the Guard units based on the need of the state to respond to emergences such as riots and natural disasters, and the president of the United States can also call on the Guard. At times in our history, the Reservists in the Ready Reserve were on inactive status and virtually never trained, so it was easy for their families to forget they even had a connection to the military. The Reservists in the Selected Reserve, on the other hand, serve about as often as the active National Guard members, who drill one weekend a month and 2 weeks a year. In recent decades both Guard and Reserves members were called up mainly for stateside emergencies, with only a few deployed in the 1990s, mostly in Bosnia, Central America, and South America. The norm has been, for most Reservists and Guard members, that they live and work in the civilian world, but that world has changed.

Since September 11, 2001, 475,000 members of the Reserves components have been mobilized; 79% of those have been Army (Lukach, 2005b). Although the military system was designed primarily for regular active duty forces, many Guard members and Reservists discovered in the past decade that they are being forced to overcome bureaucratic hurdles unique to their status. As one Special Forces soldier wounded in Operation Enduring Freedom (OEF) put it, "Bullets don't discriminate between active duty and Reserve components, and neither should the Army" (¶ 2). Although the current level of lengthy and repeated deployments to overseas assignments obviously has repercussions for all military members and families, the suddenly military are affected differently. The majority of these service members has either left or put their civilian careers on hold, causing tremendous instability in the family and to their finances. If the citizen soldier is also the sole provider or a single parent, the employment concerns are even greater. Also, the families of Reserves and Guard members are not typically part of the military network or social culture, because they live off base or miles from the nearest installation. This leads to further heightened feelings of isolation, as access is difficult to support systems or installation family programs. Families must then face the task of juggling the mission demands while attempting to keep both the home life and the professional life stable. All of these differences require different life management and stress-reducing solutions.

I had an opportunity to spend some time with a member of the U.S. Army Reserve who had been activated from Silver City, New Mexico, to Ft. Sill, Oklahoma, from January 2006 to February 2007. Suzanne Thomas is a physical therapist in private practice in New Mexico, having opened her practice only 2 years prior to her activation. In the 17 years she has been a member of the Army Reserve, she had never received orders for active duty, so this was a new experience for her. Although she is a part of a Reserve Unit out of El Paso, Texas, she was activated as a single soldier going to Ft. Sill to replace an active duty physical therapist who had been deployed to Iraq. This was a concept I had not considered, because we hear so much about the Guard and Reserves members who are being deployed to combat zones, but according to Suzanne the majority of Reservists who are in special fields, such as the medical corps, actually are sent to other installations within the United States to backfill positions being vacated by active duty personnel being deployed to combat regions.

Although Suzanne did not leave children behind, it was necessary to close her physical therapy practice, lay off her four employees, and shut the door to a business that had only shortly before started producing an income. In addition, she had not just the rent and upkeep to maintain on her home but the rent and maintenance on the building she was renting for her physical therapy business. Although her income during her activation easily covered the expenses of her home in Silver City and her day-to-day expenses in Ft. Sill, it did not even come close to covering the expenses of her business. And although she did not have children to consider, her greatest concern was the displacement and stress her leaving meant to her employees and their families.

Clinicians working with Guard and Reserves family members can be invaluable in assisting them in finding solutions to cope with these unique uncertainties, understanding, all the while, that in addition to their unique struggles, these suddenly military who are being deployed into combat zones are equally susceptible to post-traumatic stress disorder (PTSD) and other combat-related mental health issues. Pryce et al. (2000), in reviewing the literature on issues facing Reservists, found in one study that one third of Reservists reported leaving the service because of conflicts with family and the encroachment of service on personal time. Other studies show the factors that contribute to differing levels of commitment to military service include (a) the differential between civilian pay and military pay; (b) the impact of the deployments on employers who have come to expect military absences to be just 2 weeks per year; (c) upward mobility promotions, work opportunities, selected work hours, and impact on vacations; and (d) the fact that military installations are often not found in more rural and smaller communities, so the network of social support is not available (Pryce et al., 2000).

Family Challenges

In remarks made before a House Committee on Government Reform, one injured Reservist who had been activated reported that he was essentially forced to go off active duty orders every 3 months and apply for new orders, contributing to a multitude of problems for him and his family, including no pay, no access to a base, no family medical coverage, and the cancellation of all scheduled medical appointments, which significantly prolonged his treatment and recovery and his return to civilian life (Lukach, 2005b). The *Report on the Cycles of Deployment* (Jumper et al., 2006) stated,

> A predeployment briefing held the same weekend that the service-member deploys is not meeting the need for these families to make transition from weekend warrior to active duty.... Most active duty family members are used to the military lifestyle; the suddenly military families often are not; many are lost in the military bureaucracy because they do not necessarily know how the complex support systems work. (p. 9)

Guard and Reserves spouses report that balancing the spouses' career and family responsibilities were the greatest challenge they faced, along with the service members' employment-related issues, such as the disparity between civilian and military wages. Julie Burger, senior advisor for the Armed Forces Emergency Services and chair of American Red Cross Get to Know Us Committee, said, "The largest portion of troops we serve are the National Guard and Reserves. ... They are the ones that are right now dealing with a lot of difficulty, perhaps more so than active duty military who leave their family on the base with legal counseling, medical care, and other services they have access to right on the base" (Hallman, 2004, ¶ 5). Because of the organizational structure of the Guard and Reserves units, the services and experiences are quite different depending on what state the citizen soldier is deployed from.

> We weren't prepared, and neither was the Guard…. Unlike active duty military, the National Guard had no functional family support system or services in place…. Each week, I heard of a friend's husband or son: wounded, maimed, shot, hit, hurt, burned, amputated, decapitated, detonated, dead. A glossary of pain. I checked icasualties.org all the time, cursing and crying as the numbers rose relentlessly. (Bannerman, 2005, pp. 5–6)

On the other hand, a grandmother in New Mexico has been contacted almost weekly by volunteer members of the Guard unit in the Midwest where her daughter is based, because she is taking care of her two small grandchildren while her daughter is deployed. The unit has also sent a children's video and books for the kids about deployment for the grandmother to use in talking with the children.

Finances

The deployment of part-time soldiers who, in 2005, made up about half of the active duty troops, is taking a financial toll (Bowman, 2005). Forty-one percent of National Guard and Reserves members are losing thousands of dollars through a pay gap between their civilian salary and military pay. "While part-time soldiers assume some risk of being called to active duty when they sign up, today they are serving tours far longer and more frequently than their counterparts in past wars" (¶ 4). Many are serving their second or third rotation. Bowman (2005) stated that the Department of Defense has played down the economic impact to Reservists and Guardsmen, saying most have suffered losses of no more than $3,000 to $4,000, but he believes that, especially for self-employed Reservists, it may be more like $6,500 and up to $25,000 for, as an example, a physician in private practice.

Suzanne Thomas has estimated that she lost close to $100,000 as a result of closing her business, laying off her employees, maintaining the building while she was away, and then having to reopen the business 13 months later. Five months after reopening her practice, she was not even close to the level of clientele she had prior to her activation to active duty. "The war in Iraq and the war on terrorism carry a hidden cost on Reservists and members of the National Guard who have been called to active duty. Besides the emotional burden, the deployments can put unexpected financial hardships on military families" (Decker, 2004, p. 1). A recent survey commissioned by the Pentagon found that 31% of the families of Reservists and National Guard members see a decrease in income when a spouse is called to duty.

The 1994 Uniformed Services Employment and Reemployment Rights Act states that employers cannot terminate employees or hire permanent replacements and that an employer must give the same or a comparable job back to employees once they have returned from a military deployment (Decker, 2004). For large business and governments, that may not be such a burden, but for small companies it is often difficult to enforce. In addition, the Service Members Civil Relief Act precludes creditors from gouging service members and puts a ceiling of 6% on credit card interest. The act also allows service members to break a car lease or rental housing agreement and prevents service members from being evicted from rental property or having an automobile repossessed while on deployment (Decker, 2004).

Mental Health Issues

In addition to the financial issues, mental health experts (National Military Family Association [NMFA], 2006) believe that postdeployment problems may often not surface for several months or years after the service member's return. Members of the NMFA are especially concerned that services will simply not be available to the families of returning Guard and Reserves members, as well as service members who leave the military following the end of their enlistment. There have been reports of Vietnam and even World War II veterans showing up at Veteran Administration facilities in need of counseling after viewing news reports of the war in Iraq. This only serves "to remind all of us that PTSD and other mental health effects of the war can linger for years, thus requiring the availability of care for many years" (p. 11). Often the isolated Guard and Reserves families do not have the benefit of the safety net of services provided by Military Treatment Facilities and installation Family Support Programs.

When the suddenly military look to resources in their communities, they often discover that the local providers may not have an understanding of military life or an appreciation of the service member's choice to serve. When dealing with the consequences of deployment, families want to be confident that the service provider understands and is sympathetic to the issues they face. More education for civilian health care providers, as well as for religious and education professionals, is necessary to broaden the support for military families and improve the quality of the mental health services they receive (NMFA, 2006).

Given the concerns, problems, and issues that the Guard and Reserves members have to face in this current level of activation, one wonders why they remain. Certainly for those who are deployed into combat zones, reasons for separation from their component might be many, but as Suzanne Thomas said, "There are many hidden benefits, including medical care, health insurance and a good retirement plan that we can count on, but more than that, just like everyone else, I signed on the dotted line to do what was right for my country and I am glad I had the opportunity to fulfill my duty."

Stepfamilies and Remarried Couples

As we saw from the information presented in chapter 4, the rate of remarried couples and stepfamilies in the military is significantly larger than in the general U.S. population. Over the past 30 years, I have studied, taught and written about the issues faced by those who go through a divorce and then remarry and the impact these transitions have on families and children. The experience and information gained through those years was invaluable to me as a high school counselor, particularly in the military dependent schools, because so many of the children I worked with were struggling with stepfamily issues while in the midst of living in the military world. Therefore I included a major section in this chapter about the issues faced by stepfamilies and another section in chapter 9 about working with stepfamilies.

Visher and Visher (1996) defended the use of the term *stepfamily* by stating, "None of the attempts to coin euphemistic substitutes for stepfamilies appear to have the advantage of describing a family unit which includes all equally—the remarried parent, the stepparent and all of the children who are simultaneously children of one of the couples and stepchildren of the other, or a child of both" (p. 2). On the other hand, Carter and McGoldrick (1999) used the term *remarried families* because, as they said, it "emphasizes that it is the marital bond that forms the basis for the complex rearrangement of several families in a new constellation" (p. 417). I will use the word *stepfamily* here to mean any family in which there is at least one adult in the role of stepparent, whether the children are living in the same house or not. The stepfamily is not easy to define and is often very confusing to understand—but they are all stepfamilies.

In the military, the actual number of stepfamilies is not kept track of, as questions on surveys are asked regarding the marital status of individuals, but not whether it is a first, second, or subsequent marriage. Questions are also asked if there are children who reside in the home or reside outside the home, but no mention of whether the adults in the home are living together or remarried. So because we know that rates of divorce and remarriage during childbearing years are quite high in the military, we can only assume that a great number of stepfamilies are being created. Certainly in my experience as a school counselor, it seemed that virtually every other student I worked with was, in some fashion, a member of a stepfamily.

Another confusion in stepfamilies centers around what each person in the family should call each other (O'Hern-Hall & Williams, 2004). If being in a stepfamily is perceived as negative, the family may attempt to hide it by forcing children to call the stepparent either mom or dad, often leading to loyalty confusion. However, there are instances, after a death or desertion of a parent, when addressing a stepparent as mom or dad comes naturally and can be not only appropriate but very healing. At first, no one knows what to do about introductions, what to call one another, or even how to talk to one another. One 4-year-old boy, while playing in the yard with his friend close to where his stepfather was working, remarked, "I'm going to see my dad tonight." When the playmate remarked in a surprised voice, "But I thought that was your dad!" pointing to the stepfather, the youngster replied in a rather cool manner, "No, I mean I'm going to see my ex-dad!"

Dynamics of the Stepfamily System

Before addressing some of the common concerns of stepfamilies, I believe it is important to discuss the dynamics of the stepfamily system. There is never one system in any family or group of relationships, but the number of possible relationships and interactions available in a stepfamily is often overwhelming. In a biological family with two children, there are 6 possible interactions or dyads: dad–mom, dad–first child, dad–second child, mom–first child, mom–second child, and child–child. If this family of four divorced and both parents married two new spouses who both had two children, the minimum number of possible interactions or dyads would increase to 25. I won't attempt to list them. As in any system, in a stepfamily there are combinations of subsystems that continue to exist, overlap, and intertwine; the most common of these are as follows:

1. *The divorced spouses' subsystems:* The divorced spouses' subsystems often are held together by a commitment to the children, by years of common history, by common friends, and, hopefully, by genuine concern for each other. These subsystems can, on the other hand, be held together by residual revenge, distrust, and anger. The more years the first marriages were intact, the more difficult it is for people to disengage. If there is ongoing contact, as is usually true when there are children involved, the old patterns often continue. If these established patterns are negative, the stresses and tensions between the ex-spouses (or coparents) are

usually carried into the new marriage. In military families, with members who live a great distance from each other, the distance either can be healthy for the establishment of the new couple and the new family or can create considerable tension because of the difficulty for one or the other parent to be in contact with the children on a regular basis.

2. *The single-parent and child(ren) subsystems:* These subsystems include the two remarried adults and their respective children. These are naturally strong systems, particularly if there have been many years since the end of the previous marriage(s). The stress and anxiety that these single-parent families went through during the divorce and the early stages of being alone often bring parents and children close together based on their mutual interdependency. For military families, this may have been particularly difficult for the military single parent who had custody of the children and was constantly moving and adjusting to new environments. For the spouse of a military service member, the process of divorce and establishment of a single-parent family can be extremely stressful, as they are thrust back into the civilian world, often losing the security of the military community and benefits. For a military family where each newly married spouse has children in the home, a great deal of stress can be created each time a move is anticipated and then carried out.

3. *The children and the out-of-home parental system:* This system includes the other biological parent in a single-parent system or a new stepfamily system. The children may move back and forth, either regularly or occasionally, but almost always with residual tension during the transition time from one household to another. This is obviously a particularly difficult system for the military family where either the service member is frequently moving to a new duty location and leaving his or her children behind or the children are living with the military member and new spouse and have to leave the biological parent behind. Sometimes this means moving across the country or to a different country, not just across town.

4. *The biological sibling subsystems:* The alliances between biological siblings may be particularly strong, as they have come through the crisis of a divorce or death of a parent together. As in the single-parent subsystem, these alliances are often very strong because one parent may be perceived as having abandoned them for another adult. On the other hand, if the children have the common belief that they could break up the new marriage (many times out of the mistaken belief that their mom and dad would then get back

together), they may work together to create extreme tension in the remarriage, even if it is on a subconscious level. Often these sibling subsystems bond closely in a military stepfamily because of the geographic disconnection with the rest of the family and possibly a belief that they are now less important to the in-home parent, who will be in the honeymoon stage of a new marriage. They also soon learn that their life will be dictated by the larger system of the military.

5. *The stepsibling subsystem:* The stepsiblings subsystem, at first, is quite uncomfortable, many times because of what they perceive to be the unreasonable demand placed on them to act like a family. As the two family constellations attempt to integrate into one system, stress and tension often result. If the ages in the group are quite different, the competition may be less. If one group does not live under the same roof, the competition will most likely be strongest when the two subsystems are physically together. If there is a blending of children in the same household close in age, there will usually be rivalry and competition for a particular place of significance, for instance, the oldest child or the youngest child position. If the blending of these stepsibling subsystems in the military happens on a full-time basis, the family and children, over time, can adjust well, as they may experience the new life as an adventure to be faced together. If, however, they come together only on rare occasions, such as during summer visitation or holidays, it often takes a major transition period to adjust each time the whole family is together, causing untold agony for everyone in the system. The newly remarried couple has a lot of work ahead to make these times enjoyable and comfortable.

6. *The new couple subsystem:* The new couple is the most fragile of all! These two people are struggling with their children, the loss of their identity as single persons or single parents, and people who hold prior claims to them (ex-spouses, in-laws), and, at the same time, they are attempting to do something that young adults are supposed to be doing—coupling. The experience of already failing in one marriage makes a remarriage particularly significant, and often the relationship with the ex-spouses can either make or break the new marriage. A significant predictor of intimacy in the remarried couple is the nature of their relationships with their ex-spouses (Carter & McGoldrick, 1999). The process of coupling, with everything that it entails, from romantic dinners to long talks about the future, takes on quite a different flavor when there are a number of children constantly present. It is

hard enough to make the necessary accommodations while overcoming the fears of marrying again, but the additional factor of parenting, and particularly parenting somebody else's children, can be almost overwhelming. The couple often will do anything possible to avoid arguments, at least anything that may be seen as destructive to the couple. Therefore, the couple may find themselves "timidly and anxiously estranged, living through their days with suppressed yearnings and muffled screams, exchanging the contentious and exhausting pressure of their inner lives for an uneasy peace" (Napier, 1978, p. 147). For military stepfamilies, they have to do all that but also add on the stressors of being in the military, including a possible Permanent Change of Station, the new environment, the new job, the new school, and more than likely numerous deployments.

7. *The stepparent and stepchildren subsystems:* Although this subsystem obviously exists in any new stepfamily, it is particularly difficult in a military family, because this family, more than likely, will live some distance from the other biological parent. The newly remarried biological parent, with whom the children may reside, may be gone for long time periods, either for training or for deployment. Although civilian stepchildren and stepparents have to learn to get along with their new stepparent, they often have the biological parent available to help with the normal day-to-day difficulties that arise. In functional stepfamilies, the child-rearing responsibilities need to be worked out so that the bonds to the biological parents are validated (Carter & McGoldrick, 1999). Therefore it is usually advised that the biological parent remains the disciplinarian in new stepfamilies until a relationship is established between the children and the new stepparent. This may not be possible with military families when the biological parent is the one gone for extended periods of time, which increases the tension, distrust, and misunderstandings between the children and the new stepparent. I found these relationships between the stepparent and children particularly difficult for the students when the military biological parent was frequently absent. The stepparent, often with little or no understanding of the military, was required to take over every aspect of parenting, from enrolling the child in school, giving permission for extracurricular activities, and managing the household, sometimes with stepchildren who are angry about being in the family, about being in a foreign country, or about being far away from the other biological parent. This relationship between the children and the stepparent has to

be defined and worked out as their connection evolves (Carter & McGoldrick, 1999) rather than be demanded or expected within a given time frame.

Characteristics of Stepfamilies

Understanding the difficult relationships in stepfamilies is one thing, but understanding how stepfamilies differ from first biological families is also important. John and Emily Visher (1996) defined the structural characteristics of stepfamilies, and this work continues to be the seminal work in the studies and writings about and for stepfamilies. Most current work continues to rely on their work. The Vishers' work, as well as information from O'Hern-Hall and Williams (2004), is expanded upon and offered here in an attempt to assist in the understanding of the turmoil and joys of stepfamily living as it applies to those in the military.

A Family Born of Loss   All members of this system have lost relationships, dreams, expectations, or life goals. Whether through divorce or death, no one in this relationship comes in without some degree of loss. In American society, most young people grow up with a certain set of expectations and beliefs about their adult life. Even after the past three or more decades of a rising divorce rate, our society still holds on to the so-called ideal way to marry and raise a family, and that does not include a second marriage or stepchildren. When one realizes that a decision has been made to divorce, to remarry, or to marry someone with children, those previous beliefs and expectations have been shattered. Sometimes people rush into remarriage because they find it too painful to go through the grieving and loss of the first marriage. Often, however, the negative aspects of the first marriage come back to haunt them in the remarriage, but this time with an additional burden—the fear of failing twice (O'Hern-Hall & Williams, 2004).

The lives of military families are already filled with loss—transitions, moves, new schools, new friends, even a new culture. Entering a stepfamily in the military for children brings the loss of one biological parent, at least geographically, and to some extent at least a partial loss of the in-home biological parent, whose attachments appear to have switched to the new spouse. In addition, the children must enter a world where they don't know the rules or how to play the game. These children have experienced a major loss in their lives, some having adjusted and properly mourned, and some obviously have not. Even for those who have come through the end of a nuclear family, the view of the stepfamily is one of loss, not gain, as the parents may have expected. They may now have to grieve the loss of a special role in the single-parent home, such as the difficult but powerful role of head of household or a special functional or emotional caretaker of the single parent. Children will have to grieve the loss of the parent's time and that certain closeness established during the single-parent journey. When the parent marries into a military family, the children also may have numerous other losses, including the other biological parent, the extended family, and perhaps the friends they have grown up with.

Previous Histories   There are always existing traditions and values that have nothing to do with the newly married couple's relationship and many times get in the way of starting over. Each member brings into this relationship a personal lifestyle. When one member of the newly married couple is in the military, entering this warrior society for the new spouse will be like becoming a member of a new culture. If both spouses come from a military structure, then the adjustment could be easier. Most young singles, coming into first marriages, have not had a sufficient length of time to develop personal traditions and values as an adult and therefore might have difficulties in their first marriages as a result of incomplete separation from their family of origin. Remarried couples, on the other hand, may never have dealt with the separation issues from the family of origin but now may be faced with the incomplete separation from the previous marriage.

As the traditions, values, and lifestyles merge, there will be differences in the rituals around events such as birthdays and holidays but also in the more subtle struggles of everyday life such as role assignments, language, and personal needs. These struggles can be greatly exaggerated when either the new spouse or the new spouse's children become members of a military family but had no background or experience with the military. Although the structure of the military appears to be stable and secure, the new family soon finds there may be fewer choices or lacks the sense of freedom that they may have had in the first family.

Parent–Child Bonds Predate the Couple   The single-parent families have gone through crises together and usually have built strong boundaries against the outside world. To introduce a foreign element, the new stepparent, is much like introducing a foreign element into a physical body—it will be rejected if at all possible. The parent of this previously single-parent family may even participate in this subtle, subconscious rejection of the new spouse, at the same time expressing excitement for the new relationship. If there is tension between the children and the stepparent, the biological parent is torn between the new spouse and the children, often causing marriage problems. Too much togetherness of the parent and child, too much siding for "my children," and too much parenting of the children without involving the new partner will result in the stepparent feeling rejected, isolated, and of little value to the system. A difficulty in military stepfamilies is the resentment by the children if the stepparent is the military member and the perception that it is because of him or her that the family is being forced to move, relocate, and endure other hardships or inconveniences consistent with military life.

A Biological Parent Exists Elsewhere   Even following the death of that parent, the biological parent exists with power and influence. Back in 1979, Furstenberg wrote, "We have no set of beliefs, no language, and no rules for a family form that has more than two parents" (p. 1). Although much has been written about stepfamilies since then, it seems there is still no concrete set of norms or rules that govern how stepfamilies should merge and grow. And although stepfamilies seem to be even more prevalent in the military, particularly for certain age groups, this lack of understanding and guidelines has the potential for creating havoc with military family life. Often stepfamily boundaries are ambiguous and constantly changing. These boundaries do not exist within the confines of a single home but often extend far away from that home; when the two homes are constantly changing and often thousands of miles apart, the children can easily have a sense of being stranded.

The accepted pattern of one person in the role of father and one in the role of mother has to be redefined to understand that some aspects of the father's role may be assumed by the stepfather, whereas some aspects of the role of mother may be assumed by the stepmother. When children are living in the same home as a stepfather, he may assume much of the physical maintenance, although the child may still receive much love and caring from the biological father. There are many combinations of these shared roles, but they must be worked out to everyone's understanding and acceptance. If the out-of-home parent is unwilling to give up any of that role or is unwilling to give permission for the child to care for the new stepparent, the child can be caught in very difficult loyalty conflicts. Whether the children maintain two separate places of residence, only occasionally visiting the out-of-home parent, or have virtually no physical contact, the need for an emotional attachment is still primary. Although the numerous transitions made by the military family are a requirement of their lives, maintaining the attachment with the out-of-home parent, if possible, is essential.

Two Households   If children have contact with both biological parents, they are, at least for periods of time, members of two households. Although ongoing contact with both parents is extremely important, this movement between the two households may, at times, increase the insecurity and instability for children. A deep sense of disloyalty may arise when the child makes statements of preference between households or parents. As children begin to feel comfortable and genuinely cared for by a stepparent, they might have loyalty issues again, as children can feel guilty about the positive feelings they have toward the stepparent. Many times competition between households is rampant as each parent tries to outdo the other as the best parent. Again the children are caught in the middle. These issues often lead to difficult transitions each time the child goes from one home to the other.

When one family is in the military and one is not, children can definitely have culture shock by going from one household to the other, as these homes may be miles apart physically and even further apart in parenting styles and practices. Each parent can do a lot to help children be prepared for moving back and forth and to help them understand the differences in living styles, not that one is better than another but that they are different and each can be valued.

No Legal Relationship   There is no legal relationship between stepparents and stepchildren, and their relationship will most likely end if the marriage ends. Although things have changed dramatically in the past two decades, it is still necessary for there to be some kind of notarized authorization, or permission, granted by the biological parent for the stepparent to sign for medical emergencies, register children for school, or even sign children up for extracurricular activities. These rights between the biological parent and the stepchildren are also much more complicated in military families, as some rights, such as health care, cannot be signed over to the stepparent by the biological parent. Knowing this can make it very easy for the stepparent to take a back seat in the responsibility for the family, but it also makes it easy for the biological parent and children to view the stepparent's lack of initiative as a lack of caring or desire to be a part of the children's lives.

When things are seen as unimportant or temporary, they usually remain that way, and the stepparent may never really integrate into the system. For a military family, if the stepparent is the military member, the children must be included in all paperwork, and the service member must have the legal authority to take full care of the children, if needed. If the stepparent is not the military member, then it becomes even more important for this new stepparent to have legal authority to make crucial decisions in the life of the children while the biological parent is deployed or away from home for extended periods of time.

Stepfamily Potential

In reading and working with the concerns and problems of military step-families, we may think that these families can never be functional and healthy. There are, however, many aspects of the stepfamily experience that are positive. Our emphasis in counseling is to remember the potential and to guide our clients to that positive family experience of feeling encouraged and empowered. Children in military stepfamilies have a wide range of resources from which to draw comfort, support, care, information, and values. With the increase of stepfamilies, the society has again moved toward a form of extended family with the potential for the wider experience offered by the three or four generational extended families of the early 20th century. Children have the potential to gain an added sense of autonomy that may not always be found in isolated biological families. There is movement, ambiguity, and change built into the system that necessitates and invites autonomy, responsible action, and global awareness.

In learning how to move through the necessary changes and adaptation, children and adults have the potential for learning communication, conflict management, decision-making, and negotiation skills. Children have a chance in a remarriage to view adults who are caring, loving, and, hopefully, appropriately sexually active. These demonstrations of affection may be avoided or nonexistent for many children, at least those growing up in unhealthy biological families. The modeling of intimacy can be invaluable later in life. One young man stated, "You learn that adults have their problem, too. It was a hard lesson to learn, because I thought that adults were supposed to know everything … but they are just as ridiculous as kids" (O'Hern-Hall & Williams, 2004, p. 91). The military remarried couple has gone through numerous transitions of loss, fear, and even failure. If they have moved through these transitions and learned from them, they have much to give each other and their children. This new marriage and the children they bring to it can become an exciting, challenging, and dynamic family.

Understanding the characteristics and difficulties of stepfamily living is another multicultural competency that is essential for counselors working with any family, but it is crucial for working with military families, as divorce and remarriage affects so many in the military. These families are typically younger than the average remarried families in the United States and may not have access to the resources they need on or near the military installation where they live. In addition, as they are faced with frequent moves, they may find one counselor who they feel comfortable working with only to pick up and move to another location and have no one who understands their dilemmas. I included in chapter 9 a section on working with stepfamilies that I hope will complement the information shared here about the characteristics of stepfamilies.

Single Service Members and Their Families

My goal in writing about counseling military families was to address the issues of married military personnel and their families until I began to see that we also have to take into consideration the rest of the family. What happens to the parents, siblings, and extended family when a young person enters military service? For example, how are the grandparents who virtually raised their grandson supported when he is sent off to Afghanistan? Who takes care of the psychological needs of the grandparents who are now raising the children of the single Guard or Reserve member who is sent to Iraq? What support is there for the parents of the young man from New Mexico who, while on leave in San Diego, commits suicide? All of these scenarios actually happened.

When family issues are discussed, Rotter and Boveja (1999) said that most articles written are about the service members who are married but tend to forget that almost one half of service members are single. Wounded service members have wounded families, and those families include parents, siblings, and other extended family, as well as spouses and children. The parents' isolation becomes even greater if their son or daughter returns with an injury or illness or is diagnosed with PTSD and the wounded service member is hospitalized somewhere far from where the parents live. The NMFA (2006) maintained that parents of injured or ill service members need to know their child has access to the mental health services they need, even if they are no longer in the service or unable to access a military installation.

Lyons (2007) reported that the families of veterans in treatment for PTSD are concerned because their ability to help is limited, and they often express a great need for supportive and systemic services. The *Report on the Cycles of Deployment* (Jumper et al., 2006) concluded, "Extended family needs services also" (p. 12). Family members seem to know that there should be a group for them but are unsure where to find it. A common question of the respondents to the survey done by NMFA (Jumper et al., 2006) was "Whose responsibility is it to help [the extended family members] connect to the support that is available to them?" (p. 13).

"Throughout our history, there has been one facet of the military family that consistently bears a unique burden in anguishing over the sacrifices made by military members. Parents of military members are, in my opinion, sometimes forgotten when we speak of the military family" (Rogers, 2006, p. 8). The feelings of the father and mother are often ignored, even though parents feel a special pain when their child is away. The author

(Rogers, 2006) explained that his spouse and children reacted like troopers and, even though naturally upset, took his deployment like a military family, but his parents had a much harder time. Rogers wrote that a parent naturally wants to protect the child regardless of age, as it is inherent in parenthood that we want to right the wrongs and feel a unique emptiness when our children are placed in harm's way.

How difficult it is for these parents to imagine their child being sent into harm's way and they no longer can protect them. Suggestions (Rogers, 2006) for these parents are (a) to communicate often with their son or daughter through letters and e-mail; (b) to learn about the chosen branch of service by browsing the branch Web sites to learn the specific history and traditions of that branch; (c) to get the Web addresses of their unit and information about the family center or volunteer network on the base or installation where their child is stationed; (d) to let their child know they want to stay involved; and (e) to get newsletters from their unit or participate in unit-supported activities, if possible. Rotter and Boveja (1999) stated that boyfriends, girlfriends, and fiancées experience the same anxiety and loneliness as their married sisters or brothers, but they have no formal legal status to gain information or seek support. Therefore, depending on which service branch their significant other is in, they may not exist as far as the military is concerned and may not receive support from the family or other programs, usually because of what the military declares as privacy and security reasons.

Kate Blaise (2006) talked about the pride parents feel when they first see their single soldiers at the end of their first military experience in boot camp, usually leaner with their hair shorn in military haircut, but walking with more confidence and with an air of worldly wisdom about them, "almost like a boy who'd survived his ritual rite of passage and returned home a man" (p. 252). During boot camp, one young 18-year-old told his mom that the Air Force issued him a pair of glasses that he called BCG, or birth control glasses, because they were so ugly no girl would ever look at him. How amazing it was for that mom, who had sent off her tall, lanky, long-haired (from his life as a drummer in his alternative rock band) 18-year-old, to watch him at boot camp graduation, standing tall, confident, and worldly—with his BCG glasses on! She says that 15 years later she still gets tears in her eyes every time the image comes to mind.

Additional concerns, of course, exist for those grandparents and guardians who are helping to raise the children of deployed service members. Fleck (2007) said, "Despite the emotional devastation, grandparents and other relatives who are left to raise a loved one's child don't get the financial support from the government that a surviving parent would" (p. 4). The author told of a story of the family who is rearing the grandchild of their fallen son without the $100,000 death gratuity that would have been given to a spouse. Of the 3,131 soldiers killed in Iraq as of February 3, 2007, 143 service members were single parents. Currently Congress is considering legislation that would allow some or all of a service member's death gratuity to go to the children's grandparents or other guardians, who are currently overlooked. These issues are extremely important to know about, and if possible, counselors should work for change in legislation that would give assistance to these grandparents and other guardians.

Retired Veterans

A therapist who works near a major Army installation in Arizona shared with me that in just a couple months prior to my interview, she had seen three World War II veterans. These vets were experiencing PTSD-like symptoms, even though they were currently all in their 80s. The reoccurring symptoms seem to be brought on again by the constant news reports of the current global issues. They reported that experiences like visiting the World War II monument in Washington, D.C., also brought on similar responses. In addition, as they were getting closer to the end of their life, they find themselves reliving many of their life experiences, and those from the war were becoming particularly difficult.

Another therapist was working with a woman in her 80s whose husband was in the service when they were young. This former military spouse, who had lost her husband to suicide decades before, was courageous enough to seek assistance as she found that she, once again, needed to go back and work on the issues that were brought home by her husband early in their marriage and later by his suicide. This same therapist had spent 2 years working in a Veterans Administration hospital with PTSD clients, most from Vietnam and Desert Storm. Most of the survivors she saw were middle aged or older, often disabled, and often unable to hold jobs, and in most cases, they shared that until they came to see her, they had never sought counseling.

Another client told his therapist the story of his father who, as a young soldier in World War II, was stationed in the winter in Germany and had to unexpectedly kill a German soldier, only to realize that the German soldier was younger than himself, no more than 16 years old. Because the soldiers were not getting supplies, the young American took the boots off the soldier he killed, who was small like he was. Those boots saved his feet that winter, but he never got over the guilt he felt about that incident, and he lived with this in silence the rest of his life. The 2007 Ken Burns' documentary about World War II brought the lives and struggles of these retired veterans to life.

Lyons (2007) stated that particular emphasis has been given to veterans who remain mired in the warrior role and who have been diagnosed with PTSD. He reported that one study found that only 30% of couples report relationship distress if the veteran does *not* have PTSD, whereas the reverse is true, with only 30% of couples *not* reporting distress if the veteran has been diagnosed with PTSD. The presence of PTSD is also associated with lower happiness and less life satisfaction and somatic and sleep-related complaints in the veteran's spouse; studies have found children to also be negatively affected by a father's PTSD, although other variables such as family violence or the father's participation in atrocities are sometimes better predictors of problems.

Studies to date have focused almost solely on male veterans and female partners, but as more women are serving in combat zones, future studies can be expected to help elucidate gender-specific effects that PTSD may have on various family relationships (Lyons, 2007). The Veterans Administration has been overwhelmed with veterans of the Vietnam War who were never treated, and many Alcoholics Anonymous groups across the country are made up mostly of veterans from Vietnam.

One of the first prisoners that John Bourdette worked with when a prison counseling program began in Grant County, New Mexico, was a Vietnam veteran in his late 40s. He had been trying to cope with the memories of his tour in Vietnam since he was 18 with the use of alcohol and drugs. He relayed to John that the first week he was in Vietnam he was forced to kill a child; later he was wounded and even a prisoner of war for a time. Upon returning to the civilian world, the image of the child haunted him continually, unless he was drinking. He told Dr. Bourdette that in the 30 years since the incident happened, he had never told anyone; John worked with this veteran for a number of weeks prior to his being released from jail and believed that they had started to make headway on his recovery. The vet almost immediately moved out of state, and Dr. Bourdette heard about a year later that he had indeed killed himself.

Sherman, Zanotti, and Jones (2005) found that the reexperiencing of symptoms from previous combat is becoming commonplace, as the current news brings us almost minute-by-minute information from the conflict in Iraq. In giving us points about working with the veteran, they believe it is essential, if at all possible, to work with the couple or the family. They stated that it is important to assist the veteran who is reexperiencing these symptoms by educating his partner about the meaning of these episodes, by helping him articulate his needs, and by helping them learn to work together when the reactions occur. They suggested that the veteran might need support in knowing how to share the symptoms so his partner can better understand and, we hope, then avoid personalizing the confusing behavior.

Therapists may need to teach the partner about grounding techniques to help orient the veteran to the present and use the opportunity to educate the couple about problem-solving skills. One of the concerns noted was the safety of the veteran and his caregiver upon reexperiencing PTSD. The authors suggested that, through joint ownership and problem solving, the couple, the family, or possibly a caregiver can develop effective strategies to address these safety issues by creating an escape plan and a means of securing assistance.

This short section is included here because of the growing needs of retired veterans who may only now seek services that they never received after their combat experiences. The hard fact is that, as the mental health needs of our current military increase, these veterans may find themselves needing to enlist the services of civilian counselors rather than relying on the services that were previously available through the Veterans Administration.

PART 3

Working with Military Families

CHAPTER 7

Major Challenges of Military Families

Mental Health Status of the Military

The mental health status of our military service members is obviously a key ingredient in understanding and working with military families. It is essential that counselors understand the stressors and conditions that the service members face to most efficiently and effectively work with the families. Marshall (2006) quoted a recent article from the *New England Journal of Medicine* that reports the results of a survey of approximately 1,700 soldiers, showing that up to 17% said they were returning from Iraq suffering from major depression, generalized anxiety, or post-traumatic stress disorder (PTSD). Marshall continued to say that PTSD can happen not just when the service member is attacked but when the service member watches a buddy or a civilian get hurt or even hears constant stories of violent experiences, all of which is compounded by being separated from family and loved ones. In addition, since the start of the current conflict in 2003, 96 service members committed suicide in Iraq and 15 committed suicide in Afghanistan, which has prompted the military to create an automated phone-in assessment program for the purpose of reaching out to service members and their families who might not otherwise seek help. By January 2007, almost 40,000 troops or family members had participated (*Military Creates Mental Health Hotline*, 2007).

Mental Health Advisory Teams III and IV

The results of three important studies are included here; they were completed in the very recent past and they outline what we currently know about the mental health issues faced by both the military service members and military families. The Mental Health Advisory Team III (MHAT-III, 2006) was composed of 12 people, including subject matter experts in psychiatry, research psychology, clinical psychology, psychiatric nursing, occupational therapy, chaplaincy, social work, and enlisted mental health specialties. The team was in Iraq during October and November 2005. This MHAT was the third such advisory team to conduct surveys and focus-group interviews, with almost 1,500 soldiers, 344 behavioral health and health care providers, and 94 unit ministry team members. The key findings of the advisory team (Harben, 2006) were as follows:

1. Soldiers reported more intense and predictable combat experiences than previous studies as a result of the use of improvised explosive devices.
2. The top noncombat stressors were deployment length and family separation.
3. Their units' and personal morale were the same or higher than in previous studies.
4. Fourteen percent indicated they experienced acute stress, and 17% indicated a combination of depression, anxiety, and acute stress. These rates were similar to the 2003 study but higher than in 2004.
5. Soldiers reported higher acute stress if they were serving a repeat deployment.
6. The suicide rate in Iraq and Kuwait during 2005 was 19.9 per 100,000 members, up slightly from the 18.8 rate per 100,000 in 2003 and higher than in 2004, when it was 13 per 100,000 for the Army overall. There were 22 service members in 2005 who committed suicide in Iraq, with a total of 83 suicides in the Army, up from 76 in 2004 and 60 in 2003 (MHAT-III, 2006). The leading suicide risk factors were relationship issues at home and in theatre, followed by legal actions, problems with fellow comrades, and command and duty performance.
7. Even though service members received suicide prevention training both before and during deployments, the number who perceived this as useful in identifying others at risk declined from 60% in 2004 to 55% in 2005.
8. Soldiers reported that access is better to behavioral health care, and more are receiving care; obviously efforts to reduce the stigma attached to seeking behavioral health care has had some effect, because the number of soldiers who reported they avoided seeking care has decreased.

9. Behavioral health providers were confident in their ability to treat combat and operational stress reactions.
10. Soldiers, in general, reported high job satisfaction and good support facilities, even though they were unhappy with the length of their tours and reported more dangerous combat environment than during Operation Iraqi Freedom I in 2003. Those who had been deployed multiple times said they were better prepared for the subsequent deployments but their families were experiencing more stress because of the multiple deployments.

"Everyone who comes back from a combat environment experiences change" (Harben, 2006, ¶ 15), said Colonel Edward Crandell, chief of the Department of Behavioral Health at Ft. Bragg, North Carolina, and leader of MHAT-III, even though the U.S. Army screens those who deploy on at least two different occasions for mental health issues, and soldiers take part in what is referred to as Battlemind Training, designed to inform them about common signs and symptoms of readjustment after a combat deployment. Crandell (Harben, 2006) pointed out, "It is not surprising that Soldiers react emotionally to the prospect of their deaths or causing the death of someone else. What our Soldiers are experiencing are the inherent stressors of combat that we would expect" (¶ 4). Literature and lessons from previous conflicts clearly show that if we don't identify and treat combat and operational stress on the battlefield, "Soldiers are at greater risk for developing serious problems later" (¶ 4).

During 2006 the MHAT-IV conducted a study similar to the MHAT-III study, and in May 2007 it released its findings from these latest investigations. Harben (2007) reported that this series of four yearly surveys "constitute an unprecedented attempt to measure troops' mental health and improve mental-health services during combat operations rather than waiting to evaluate after the war" (¶ 26). The 2006 study included Marines, for the first time, in addition to Army soldiers, and also examined the ethical behavior of U.S. troops. Many of the findings of the 2005 report were similar to the latest 2006 study, including the high degree of stress related to deployment lengths and multiple deployments for the service member and the family, the fact that the level of combat is the main determinant of the service member's mental health status, and the fact that the suicide rate remains much higher in the Iraqi theatre than in the military overall.

Some of the additional findings were that (a) Army morale was lower than that of Marines, and soldiers had higher rates of mental health problems, partially because Marines have shorter deployment lengths; (b) both groups reported dissatisfaction with the rigid enforcement of rules for things such as uniform appearance in the combat environment; (c) only 5%

reported taking in-theatre rest and relaxation; (d) marital concerns were higher than in previous surveys and were usually related to deployment lengths; (e) suicide training is not designed for combat or deployed environments; (f) approximately 10% reported mistreating noncombatants, and those with higher levels of anger who also experienced high levels of combat stress or screened positive for mental health problems were nearly twice as likely to mistreat noncombatants; (g) behavioral health providers asked for additional training before deploying; and (h) there is no standardized reporting system for monitoring mental health status and suicide surveillance of service members in combat or deployed environments. These findings will have a major impact on the service members upon their return to their families. It is hoped that, with some of the recommendations being made by this latest MHAT-IV (Harben, 2007) team, many of the concerns can be addressed while in theatre, or at least have preparations ready to address the concerns of the soldiers and Marines once they return home.

Task Force on Mental Health Care

In addition to the Army MHATs, the Department of Defense (DoD) established a Task Force on Mental Health Care as a subcommittee of the Defense Health Board in early 2006 to investigate the mental health concerns of military service members and their families. The task force included members of the military, federal government, and nonmilitary or federal members; their task was to "gather as much data as possible in order to have a comprehensive picture of the military's mental health system and knowledge of what constitutes psychological help for our soldiers and their families" (DoD Task Force on Mental Health Care, 2007b, p. 6). During the fall and winter of 2006–2007, the task force members visited 38 installations around the world interviewing service members, family members, behavioral health providers, primary care providers, and community mental health providers. Their findings were reported at a task force meeting in April 2007, and the complete report of the findings and recommendations of the task force is now available from the DoD Task Force on Mental Health Care (2007a) in a document titled *An Achievable Vision*.

Although the recommendations are extremely vital to know, what I believe most important for the sake of this book is the current mental health status of the military. Therefore I am including a short summary of the findings of the DoD Task Force, but I am not including the complete list of recommendations that can be found in their final report. The task force hoped to gather information about the areas of access to care, service coordination, stigmas and barriers to care, resources and efficiencies, policies regarding recruitment, retention, training and prevention, and factors increasing stress. The key findings were as follows:

1. Access to care differs depending on the location and the service; a recurring theme was that access for some type of service might be available on one installation and not at another, even though the installations are not geographically far apart. These findings were particularly true overseas.

2. Access to services is often inadequately marketed so that service members and their families do not know what exists, and, even if they know, the service is difficult, time-consuming, and sometimes embarrassing to access.

3. There is no identified leadership structure for behavioral health geographically, and it was not clear who was responsible for the coordination of the delivery of care.

4. Regarding stigma, it was found that some service members want to see only a mental health provider in uniform, as they believe that person will understand them. Ironically, it was also found that service members don't want to see a mental health provider from a different branch of the service. Additional issues related to stigma were concerns around losing one's security clearance, being seen as weak if one seeks care, and seeking care confidentially, not just to the command but to the general community.

5. Medicare reimbursements are higher than TRICARE, so community providers would rather use Medicare. However, the TRICARE list of providers is often inappropriate, and referrals are made to incorrect providers; for instance, children being referred to adult psychiatrists. It was not clear who was monitoring the TRICARE network between the services.

6. A consistent finding was a shortage of child and adolescent psychiatrists and access to care for mental health or behavioral health services for children and youth, as well as the fact that marital and bereavement counseling services are not covered by TRICARE.

7. The adequate and appropriate care for substance abuse is inconsistent at best regarding location and availability of services; for instance, intensive outpatient services, which is often the most efficient and effective treatment, is not allowable under TRICARE.

8. Services may not be available for the Guard and Reserves components who return home and are no longer near installations where services might be provided, particularly with "conditions like PTSD that have a very long tail on them" (p. 28) and whether

there is an organizational structure to support the mental health needs of the citizen soldier.

9. Resources for military service providers have been reduced because of budget cuts and fewer mental health workers in the military; in some cases many mental health professionals are being deployed, leaving the families at home without services. There was concern that just turning "everything into contract or civilianize[ing] it" will not work, because "you have to have a critical mass of those people to sustain a war fight" (p. 72). The reports, however, of those mental health providers who have been imbedded with the troops show that the stigma could be lowered by having the providers accessible; this seems to be having a very worthwhile impact on the troops.

10. There were concerns that service members were not always being evaluated adequately, and there are some who have been administratively separated from the service instead of undergoing assessments for traumatic brain injury or PTSD.

11. A concern was raised about the importance of the primary care physician in the referral process and whether primary care physicians are trained to assess or detect possible mental health concerns, and then, once issues are detected, if there are adequate and simple ways for the physician to support the service member or family member's referral for additional services.

In addition to these concerns and issues, the task force pointed out that there are many creative and progressive examples of care, dedication, and service and that there was an overall belief that, within the military environment, the great possibility exists of providing the kinds of mental and behavioral health services that will enrich the military service members and the lives of their families. These findings can inform us as to many of the concerns that families we see in counseling might be facing, the types of services that may or may not be available to our clients, and, hopefully, the possible changes and improvements that are being considered by the DoD as a result of these studies.

Deployment

Kennedy (2004) wrote, "The idea of leaving their spouse and/or children is what scares them the most" (p. 1), but every branch of the military offers counseling, support, and advice to family members of deployed personnel regarding the stages of deployment and the emotional ramifications of each stage. The author pointed out that military members and their families are a growing population within the counseling field, as civilian counselors are seeing more and more military dependents. For these counselors to be effective, they will also need to be aware of the stages of deployment and the culture that is known as the U.S. Armed Forces. The author of a news story broadcast on CNN (*Welcome Back to the United States,* n.d.) suggested that even before the troops leave home, the military usually advises them and their relatives that family dynamics can, and most likely will, change during deployment. One anecdotal report from a client during counseling was that when he returned from Iraq, about 30 soldiers were in a large room for their debriefing, and the leader asked any to raise their hands if they thought they were suffering from PTSD. Surely this is a rare occurrence, as we can all guess how many raised their hands.

Some of the challenges military families may face before, during, and after deployment are outlined in numerous publications and on many Web sites available to the families. Dr. Matt Friedman (2006) of the Veterans Administration's National Center for PTSD warned families that after returning home, troops should expect to have some behavioral adjustment issues. A survey (Jumper et al., 2006) by the National Military Family Association of over 1,500 respondents from the Army, Navy, Marine Corps, Air Force, Coast Guard, and Public Health Service found that over one half of the respondents were members of families in which a service member was currently deployed. The survey was conducted to determine the needs of families before, during, and after deployment. The answers fell into the general categories of communication, deployment lengths and numbers, training of support personnel and families, and direct support for the families. The respondents believed that communication between the service members, the families, the unit or command, and the family support providers was essential.

Families believe they are being bombarded by press reports about the war, and they need accurate information to counteract the negative press. Families want to know more information about what the service member is experiencing so they will be better prepared for the homecoming. For example, if the family members know that a particular unit had a great deal of difficulty during deployment, then they can be more understanding of the possible heightened anger or other emotions upon service member's returning home. "Families believe that communication during deployment is directly linked to the reunion process, the reintegration of the family, and the mental health needs of all concerned" (Jumper et al., 2006, p. 7).

The respondents of the survey clearly stated that deployment lengths, the frequency of deployment, and the day-to-day operational tempo of service members were taking a toll on their families. For 25% of the respondents, the greatest stress was felt at the beginning of the deployment, whereas 29% felt the greatest stress during the middle of deployment. "The ability to handle the mid-deployment routine seems to be crucial for families' handling of subsequent deployments" (Jumper et al., 2006, p. 7). For those respondents who said subsequent deployments were harder than the first, 37% stated that the middle of the deployment was the most difficult. Most respondents were experiencing family separations of up to 18 months, with several months of training prior to deployment, 12 months deployed, and at least another few weeks of intense commitment following the return home. Almost half cited that the greatest challenges for the families after the service member's return was that the service member might be deployed again, and virtually all respondents shared a need for mandatory leave after deployment "to replenish their spirit" (p. 8).

A need for more and continuous training of the installation support providers and the families was also requested by the respondents of the study (Jumper et al., 2006), and it was noted that this training should extend into the reunion phase of deployment. Fewer than half of the respondents felt that they received "some" level of family support throughout all phases of deployment. They also mentioned that this continuity of information is most critical to those referred to the Guard or Reserve communities. Family members also expressed a concern for the relationships within the family, regarding both children's issues and concern for the couple; a common theme was the need for marriage counseling and couples' retreats. Family members expected that a certain level of support by the military would be available, regardless of the branch of the service or where the family lives.

Many respondents voiced a concern that the assumption by the military that families already know about the family support resources and how to access them was clearly not the case. Other concerns were raised by the almost 50% of military spouses who are employed outside the home regarding employment problems they had encountered, and many raised the issue of families who need financial counseling.

Stages of Deployment

A number of authors and researchers have outlined specific stages or phases that families go through during the course of the deployment. Kristin Henderson (2006) summarized in her book *While They're at War* the two emotional phases outlined by Kathleen Logan, a marriage and family therapist and former naval officer, that spouses typically go through while anticipating a deployment. These are the anticipation of loss phase and the detachment and withdrawal phase. Rotter and Boveja (1999) outlined the three phases of deployment in a table adapted from the U.S. Navy. These stages are anticipation, separation, and reunion. Pincus, House, Christenson, and Adler (n.d.) outlined perhaps the most comprehensive stages of deployment when studying the impact of extended deployment on military families after 5 years of the peace enforcement missions to Bosnia. I attempted to present here a modified version of the stages outlined by Pincus et al. (n.d.) while incorporating aspects of the work done by Logan (Henderson, 2006) and those presented by Rotter and Boveja (1999) for counselors to best assist families as they go through these difficult periods of the military family life cycle.

Pincus et al. (n.d.) divided the cycle of an extended deployment into five distinct stages: predeployment, deployment, sustainment, redeployment, and postdeployment. Each stage is characterized in terms of time and emotional challenges that, if mastered by each of the family members, will assist them in making the deployment of a military spouse or parent far less stressful. Providing information early, especially for families who have not previously endured a lengthy separation, can help normalize the experience. In addition, helping families understand "the stages of deployment helps to avert crises, minimize the need for command intervention or mental health counseling, and can even reduce suicidal threats" (p. 2). Combining our understanding of these five stages of deployment with the Transition Journey outlined in chapter 8, can be valuable learning for the families as they move through each transition or change in their life and, hopefully, learn from each how better to adjust to the next.

Predeployment The first stage begins when the deployment order arrives and ends when the service member actually departs from the home station. The time frame of this stage can range from several weeks to more than a year. The predeployment stage is characterized by both denial and anticipation of loss, sometimes at the same time, with the spouse sometimes thinking that this surely isn't going to happen. With the increased field training and long hours of preparation away from home, the inevitable becomes obvious. The military spouse or parent who is about to be deployed often begins to more energetically talk about the upcoming mission and the unit that is deploying. Although uncomfortable for the family, particularly the spouse, this bonding is essential for the unit cohesion and will ultimately be necessary for a safe and successful deployment. This spousal discomfort often creates an increasing sense of emotional and physical distance for the couple, with the one staying home often wishing the military spouse was already gone. "It is as if their loved ones are already 'psychologically deployed'" (Pincus et al., n.d., p. 2).

Rotter and Boveja (1999) shared that the most common feelings during what they called the anticipation phase are denial, fear, anger, resentment, and hurt and that the emotional withdrawal that often occurs during the last week before deployment includes feelings of confusion, ambivalence and anger and a sense of pulling away from each other. A common characteristic of the predeployment stage is the need for the family to get its affairs in order. There seems to be a rush to deal with issues such as home repairs, security systems, car maintenance, finances, tax preparation, child care plans, insurance, and wills. In the midst of all the planning and frenetic activity, couples will also strive for increased intimacy, more because they feel they are supposed to than because they truly feel a need to. Plans are made for the best Christmas, the perfect vacation, or the most romantic anniversary—often with such high expectations that any mishap is seen as a catastrophe.

In explaining Kathleen Logan's anticipation phase, Henderson (2006) shared an example of a family who, in attempting to accept the reality of the upcoming separation, decides that the garage reorganization project, begun 2 years previously, absolutely must be finished prior to the departure date. Another spouse found herself bursting into tears at inappropriate times, and a third spouse reported simply being "pissed off" at the military. This kind of increased tension often leads to increased arguing between the spouses. "For couples with a long history, this argument is readily attributed to the ebb-and-flow of marital life and therefore not taken too seriously. For younger couples, especially those experiencing an extended separation for the first time, such an argument can take on 'catastrophic' proportions" (Pincus et al., n.d., p. 3).

It can be therapeutic to help couples and families understand that this anger is often used as a mask instead of having to confront the pain and loss of saying good-bye. As the deployment date looms, the detachment and withdrawal phase begins, often with the spouse feeling like the marriage is out of control (Henderson, 2006), but the spouse's desperation and emotional withdrawal makes it easier to eventually say good-bye. "This is usually not funny until you look back on it. Then you either laugh or cry, and laughing is a lot more bearable" (Henderson, 2006, p. 43).

Fears about fidelity or marital integrity are sometimes raised but more than likely go unspoken (Pincus et al., n.d.). Although couples experiencing long separations may raise this issue, it is an issue brought up by every counselor I interviewed for this book. The situation of being apart for long periods of time in situations of such extreme stress on both members of the couple makes the situation ripe for infidelity. In addition, the small-town atmosphere of many military installations means that rumors can be rampant. The impact of unresolved family concerns can have potentially devastating consequences, including the possibility of a serious accident or the development of a stress casualty for the deployed service member;

spousal distress that interferes with completing basic routines, concentrating at work, or attending to the needs of children; and adverse reactions by the children that might include crying, apathy, tantrums, and other regressive behaviors (Pincus et al., n.d.).

It is often helpful for military couples in this stage to discuss in detail their expectations of each other during the deployment, but if this is not a normal part of their relationship, they may require the intervention of a counselor to facilitate the process. Failure to accurately communicate expectations is frequently a source of misperception, distortion, and hurt after deployment when it would be virtually impossible to resolve.

Deployment   This second stage occurs from the time of the service member's departure from home through the first month of separation. Mixed emotions are common, with spouses reporting feelings of being disoriented and overwhelmed; some may feel relieved that they no longer have to appear brave and strong, whereas others carry residual anger at all the tasks left undone. The military spouse's departure creates an emptiness, leading to feelings of numbness, sadness, loneliness, or abandonment (see the experience of the endings during the Transition Journey in chapter 8). Spouses often have difficulty sleeping and have a sense of anxiety about coping with things such as pay problems, safety issues, child care concerns, or other everyday issues. This is the time that Rotter and Boveja (1999) called the separation phase, during which there is often a lot of emotional confusion, accompanied by feelings of loss and emptiness and a sense of disorganization.

The nonmilitary spouse, usually a woman, spends a lot of time crying and keeping busy but also often experiences changes in sleeping and eating patterns. On the positive side, communication between the service member and the family has greatly improved in the past two decades as a result of the Internet and e-mail, and this has proved to be a great morale boost for families. It is unfortunate that it is common for phone and Internet provider bills to mount, which can further add to financial stress. Another source of anxiety for families is that sometimes several weeks pass before they hear from their military spouse. A grandmother who is caring for her daughter's two small children in New Mexico while her daughter serves in Iraq shared that she begins to get uptight if she does not receive an e-mail on a daily basis. Although she understands that her daughter might not have daily access to a computer, she starts worrying if the e-mail does not arrive. For most military spouses, connecting with their loved ones is a stabilizing experience. For those, however, whose phone calls or e-mail messages end with hurt feelings, the stress of deployment is only exacerbated. It is usually difficult to disguise negative feelings of hurt, anger, frustration, and loss on the phone; a disadvantage of easy access is the immediacy and proximity to unsettling events. Sometimes both members of the couple feel helpless and unable to support each other, at the same time feeling jealousy toward those whom the partner does rely on during the deployment. Even with these possible negatives, most report that the ability to stay in touch greatly helps them cope with the separation (Pincus et al., n.d.).

Sustainment   The sustainment stage (Pincus et al., n.d.) usually begins about 1 month into the deployment, when life begins to settle down, until about a month before the service member is expected to return. This is a time for families to establish new sources of support or reconnect with old ones and begin to establish new routines. The family readiness group, usually available on any installation, can be a way of networking with others; these groups usually meet on a regular basis to handle problems and disseminate information. If the family has friends, family, or other means of support, such as a church or religious institution, it should be encouraged to maintain these contacts.

By the end of the sustainment stage, military spouses usually have a sense of being in control, are more confident, and believe they can handle the challenges the deployment has created. A young 14-year-old who was interviewed for a story in a recent *Military Spouse* magazine (Alpeter, 2007) stated that it was hard when his dad first deployed, but "you have to step up and take more responsibility. Deployment gets easier in that eventually you get used to it" (p. 30). Rotter and Boveja (1999) said this is a period of hope, confidence, calmness, less anger, and less loneliness.

A challenge that often comes up during this time frame is the volume and speed of information provided by phone and e-mail access. Over long distances and without face-to-face contact, communications can be vulnerable to distortion or misperception. Given this limitation, discussing hot topics can be problematic and are usually best kept until after the deployment. Exceptions to this rule obviously include family emergencies, critical illness, or joyful events, such as the birth of a child. In these situations, the best way to communicate is through the Red Cross so that the service member's command can coordinate emergency leave if required (Pincus et al., n.d.).

A spouse shared in a *Military Spouse* article (Pavlicin, 2007) that she discovered that her husband did not need to know every detail of the family's life. After venting to him about things like the washing machine overflowing or the overwhelming things that were happening in her life, she realized that he got off the phone feeling stressed and deflated because he couldn't help with all the reported problems. Pavlicin (2007), one of the most frequent writers about the issues of deployment, also suggested that if spouses have problems that need to be solved quickly, they ought to talk to a friend or neighbor rather than venting in an e-mail; there needs to be some time in each phone call or e-mail to express positive feelings for each other and talk about something other than just problems. Because e-mail is now so widely available, it is often a better means of communication than telephoning, as service members and spouses can be more thoughtful about what is said and can filter out intense emotions that may be unnecessarily disturbing, as long as each takes the time to think through the message and make sure there aren't hidden messages being communicated (Pincus et al., n.d.).

Sometimes this ability for rapid communication can also lead to unanticipated rumors, which have been known to circulate unchecked. Of course, the most damaging rumor would involve an allegation of infidelity, usually very difficult to validate. Other troubling rumors may be about who is handling the deployment poorly, someone having an accident or injuries, changes in the date of return, disciplinary actions, or who calls home the most. These kinds of rumors can be very hurtful, and at their worst, unit cohesion and even the mission success can suffer.

In other situations (Whealin & Pivar, n.d.), communications during deployment may be minimal, so families try to obtain information from the media. Sometimes this will include frightening commentary and images rather than factual information, so families need to be encouraged to gather the information from trustworthy resources.

Despite the obstacles, the vast majority of spouses and family members successfully negotiate the sustainment stage, as they develop a belief that they are capable of making the necessary decisions, feel successful, and begin to look forward to their loved ones coming home. A mom (Pavlicin, 2007) even reported that her family grew in ways she never expected as she watched her teens becoming more confident, responsible, and independent. She also expressed how appreciative she was for the newfound friendships that developed, because they had the time to really get to know each other. She added, "For all the challenges, there have definitely been blessings from this experience" (p. 28).

Redeployment   The redeployment stage is essentially defined as the month before the service member is scheduled to return home (Pincus et al., n.d.). In most writing, this specific time frame is included in the deployment or sustainment stages, but, even though I might have chosen a different name, I find it helpful to separate it, as it brings specific challenges to the family. This time frame includes the last part of the separation stage discussed by Rotter and Boveja (1999), who stated that during the last 6 to 8 weeks prior to homecoming, the expectation of the reunion brings feelings of apprehension, excitement, and high expectations, along with added worries and fear. This stage is generally one of intense anticipation and may include a surge of conflicting emotions, from the excitement that the service member will be coming home to a sense of apprehension. Questions arise such as "Will he [she] agree with the changes that I have made?" Will I have to give up my independence?" and "Will we get along?" (Pincus et al., n.d., p. 7).

Paradoxically, with the separation coming to an end, there may be renewed difficulty in making decisions, often because of increased attention to choices that the returning service member might make. Some spouses experience a burst of energy in an attempt to complete all the "to-do" lists around the home. It is almost inevitable that expectations will be high, often to be left with some disappointment when the parent or spouse returns. The family and spouse must remember at this point that they have established new routines that worked without the military member present, and when he or she returns, there will be yet another transition to make.

Of course we have to be cognizant of the fact that many spouses and families, because of the current conflicts, are being told that they have lost their loved ones and the cycle of deployment ends. Regardless of the stoicism of the military and the preparations for disaster, it is more than life changing when the notice comes that the loved one will not be returning. Kate Blaise's (2006) story of her husband's helicopter being shot down the day before he was to leave Iraq makes us all wonder how these families actually endure.

Postdeployment   The postdeployment stage begins when the service member arrives at the home station, even though the time frame is variable depending on the particular family. Blaise (2006) wrote that Hollywood has an irritating habit of elevating every emotion to a grand passion, with all homecomings showing couples falling into each others arms, kissing passionately, and then magically continuing on with their lives. She wrote that this homecoming is always an adjustment; there is family to catch up with, a new home to establish, and new jobs to get used to. She, as the service member, had grown accustomed to the total freedom that comes with living alone, and that selfishness was hard to break. Even though the shared values and reasons they had fallen in love remained intact, there were changes they needed to work on. When a couple works as a team, they have to learn to bend, and Blaise said she eventually figured out that she had to take "off my superwoman cape and stop trying to do everything all the time" (p. 141).

Typically this stage lasts from 3 to 6 months, starting with the home-coming of the deployed service member. This can be both a wonderfully joyous occasion and an extremely frustrating and upsetting experience. As noted previously, the image of children rushing to the returning parent and a warm embrace of the reunited couple followed by the unit coming to attention for one last time and words of praise from the senior com-mander present is one we have seen over and over in the media. However, sometimes the date of return gets changed repeatedly or members of the units travel home piecemeal over several days. Despite their obvious best intentions, spouses may not be able to meet the returning military mem-bers because of the short notice, the children are sick, they cannot find child care, or they cannot get off work. The returning service members may expect to be received as heroes, only to find that they have to make their own way home.

Rotter and Boveja (1999) wrote that the reunion stage, which includes the honeymoon period, occurs from the first day home until the first argu-ment. There are feelings of euphoria, a blur of excitement, a lot of talk-ing, and reestablishing intimacy. This phase is followed by the next 6 to 8 weeks, which they referred to as the readjustment period, where the couple and the family must begin to start settling in by renegotiating the relation-ship and redefining their roles. Typically, the honeymoon period is a time for couples to reunite physically and emotionally, but the emotional part can sometimes be missing, often from a sense of awkwardness combined with excitement (Pincus et al., n.d.). For some, the desire for sexual inti-macy may require time so the couple can reconnect.

Eventually, service members want to return to their predeployment role as a member of the family, which may require considerable patience to accomplish successfully. They may feel pressure to make up for lost time and want to take back their old responsibilities without realizing that things have changed in their absence. Their spouses have become more autono-mous, the children have grown, and personal priorities may be different. During the deployment, spouses often feel a lost sense of independence, possible resentment at having been abandoned, and may even consider themselves to be the true heroes (watching the house, children, paying bills, etc.) while their military spouses cared only for themselves. The spouses also report that they are more irritable with their mates underfoot, and many express a desire to maintain their own space even while rene-gotiating basic household chores and routines. Pincus et al. (n.d.) reported that one study even suggested that the stay-at-home parent is more likely to report distress than the returning service member.

One of the therapists I interviewed reported that many spouses are angered by the fact that the returning military members want to socialize with the returning troops rather than spend their free time at home. One client shared that at family gatherings, videos were sometimes shown of the deployed service members in bars with women on their laps, and the military members had no idea that these were hurtful to their spouses. For the nondeployed partner who has been in charge of everything and wants the reconnection to be perfect, the need for the military members to maintain a high level of connection to their comrades often feels like another abandonment. Spouses need help understanding that these service members had been through difficult and sometimes terrifying experiences and that their connection with each other can perhaps help them heal far faster than if they tried to put those thoughts and images aside to reconnect with the family. This disparity in perception is an important issue for therapists to be aware of as they work with military couples.

As the fact sheet called *Coming Home* from the American Academy of Child and Adolescent Psychiatry (2005) pointed out, military deployments can significantly change one's life, especially in a combat zone. Deployment almost always involves the loss of comforts that those back home take for granted; it involves hard work and enormous responsibility, and in a war zone there is the constant threat of the loss of life or injury. In addition, the returning service member may have witnessed injuries, deaths, and incredible destruction. What will sustain these service members is their devotion to duty, their connection with fellow service members, and the overarching desire to return to the comforts of their family. Upon returning, these service members may seem preoccupied with their experiences and may either be unable to talk about it or excessively talk about it. They may have suffered physical or emotional injury or disability and may expect and require extra attention and support. Helping the spouse and family members, if age appropriate, understand these issues will go a long way in making the postdeployment period more successful. Jonathan Shay (2007), in the foreword for one of the most recent books written on combat stress, pointed out,

> Valid survival skills and adaptations in the war zone can persist into life after war and put family, neighbors, employers in a quandary. If everyone, including the returning service member himself or herself, has this knowledge and understanding of where these patterns of thought, feeling and action came from and what they were once good for, many destructive misunderstandings and mis-attributions will be avoided all around.... Providing usable education is always the first and most important task of those aiming to protect service members and their families and to prevent the life-blighting

complications of out-of-place adaptations to combat which have persisted into life in garrison or civilian life. (p. xix)

Reunion With Children

The reunion with the children is often also a challenge (Pincus et al., n.d.), depending on their age and understanding of why the military parent was gone. Detailed information is included in chapter 5 regarding typical reactions of children to the deployment of a parent, but the following is a summary of how children, depending on age, may react when the military parent returns. Babies younger than a year old may not know the soldier, be frightened, and cry when held, whereas toddlers (1 to 3 years of age) may be slow to warm up. Preschoolers (3 to 6 years of age), who may have felt guilty and scared by the separation, may have difficulty trusting; school-age children (6 to 12 years of age) may want a lot of attention; and teenagers (13 to 18 years of age) may be moody and appear to not care.

Children are often loyal to the parent who remains behind and do not respond well to discipline from the returning service member. Some children may display significant anxiety up to a year later, triggered by the possibility of another separation. Certainly as we see more and more service members being deployed a second and sometimes third time, these anxieties will, more than likely, increase. In addition, the returning military parent may not approve of some of the new rules, routines, or privileges granted to children by the nondeployed parent.

Robertson (n.d.) recommended that counselors help the returning parent go slowly, talk softly and often with an infant until the child gets used to this new voice, and get down at the level of toddlers to talk to them. She recommended that parents make time to play with their children on their level, because if a parent can get children to laugh, they will make friends sooner. The returning military parent will want to stay nearby while the spouse feeds, dresses, or plays with the small children or infants until the children become comfortable with the parent whom they may perceive as an intruder.

The couple will need to spend quality time alone, as children of any age are more comfortable when they know their parents' relationship is strong. Helping families realize (a) that both the roles and the people will change (b) that everyone in the household will be tired from the added responsibilities as well as the heightened emotions of the deployment; (c) that parenting and decision making will be strained; (d) that there will be a need for private time for the couple to reestablish intimacy; and (e) that it may take weeks to adjust after each and every deployment are key ways in which a therapist can assist the family (Robertson, n.d.). Postdeployment is obviously the most important stage for both the returning military member and the spouse. Communicating, lowering expectations, and taking time to get to know each other again are critical to the task of successful reintegration into the family.

In the event that the service member is injured or returns as a stress casualty, counseling may be essential. On the other hand, the separation of deployment provides the couple with a chance to evaluate changes within themselves and what direction they want their marriage to take, and even though it is a difficult as well as a joyful stage, many military couples report that their relationship is much stronger as a result.

Reflections on Deployment

Pincus et al. (n.d.) shared that if families remember a few key points, they will be able to master the many challenges during the five stages of deployment. These points include (a) anticipating the challenges caused by extended deployment; (b) avoiding the overinterpretation of arguments caused by the pain and loss of separation; (c) avoiding any attempt during deployment to resolve marital issues that preceded the deployment; (d) understanding that the dates of departure and return often slip forward and backward; (e) understanding that establishing or maintaining a support network is essential; (f) remembering that rumors are hurtful and are best not repeated; (g) knowing that breaking up the time is a useful technique to prevent being overwhelmed, including arranging possible regular get-togethers with other families, outings for the children, or visits to or from parents and in-laws; (h) understanding that finding time for at-home parents to spend alone, without the children, will help to maintain their sanity; and (i) understanding that they should avoid unhealthy or nonproductive habits, such as overspending, increasing alcohol use, or giving up healthy habits and routines such as eating properly or exercising regularly.

Pavlicin (2007) added a few more points for the nonmilitary parent and spouse. She suggested that it is important for spouses to keep their life in balance, to find a creative outlet, to nurture their spiritual side, to surround themselves with supportive and positive people, to keep their expectations and consequences high for their children but not be too disappointed if the children do not meet those expectations, to have a sense of humor, and to look for positive blessings.

Deployment extensions add additional stress, and because they are becoming increasingly more common, they "can feel very different from regular deployment situations" (Pavlicin, n.d., ¶ 3). There is usually a host of fresh emotions, including disappointment, anger, frustration, guilt, sadness, physical exhaustion, quickness to tears, and increased fears and worry. Although these are normal, they can also quickly turn to depression, apathy, reduced communication, unhealthy anger, resentment, negativity, and increased physical stress, sickness, or injury. Pavlicin outlined a number of creative tools for what she called the "deployment extension kit" to help spouses get through these extensions, or redeployments, from putting on good dance music, watching a funny movie, surrounding oneself with positive people, creating a worry notebook, scheduling time for oneself, asking a friend to help with difficult situations, expressing their love to those around them, and planning at least one fun activity to do for oneself or with the family during the extension. This might, however, be a time when spouses come in for counseling, as it may be simply more than they can bear, so these suggestions and ideas are offered here to assist therapists who may work with military families prior to deployment, during and after deployment and, in some cases, during those deployment extensions that families find so fraught with difficulties.

PTSD

I did not attempt in this chapter or in this book to write an authoritative or comprehensive review of Post-Traumatic Stress Disorder (PTSD). My goal is to give enough information for the civilian counselor to begin understanding and working with any military family, not just those with major illness or injury, including stress injuries. In fact, my original goal was to focus strictly on the typical issues faced by the military families, most of which are developmental or transitional in nature. However, it has become apparent that it would leave a major subject untouched to not at least address PTSD, even though what is offered here is by no means comprehensive enough for counselors to thoroughly understand or work with service members or their families who are diagnosed with PTSD. I hope this will be enough for civilian counselors unfamiliar with PTSD to recognize certain symptoms and determine if further evaluation and more intensive treatment is necessary.

A Historical Perspective

In the introduction to their new book *Combat Stress Injury: Theory, Research and Management,* Figley and Nash (2007) wrote that the word *friction* was used by a Prussian general and war theorist from the 19th century to describe the physical, mental, and emotional stressors of combat. This Prussian general believed that "no amount of training or preparation prepares combatants for the friction or the unexpected and distressing experiences of combat—not even those veterans of other battles. The friction of war occupies the mind and distracts the war fighter from the true mission" (p. xv). Combat friction, or combat stress, can easily lead to stress injuries unless the combat leaders are fully aware that these are the consequences of war, having little to do with courage, fear, allegiance to duty, or competence. It is important to understand that "attending to the stress injury does not imply a lack of courage, weakness, or competence, and furthermore such attention will decrease the likelihood that the injury will become a stress disorder during and following military service" (Figley & Nash, 2007, p. xv). Combat stress is like no other.

> Everyone in combat experiences combat stress and a large and unknown portion experience combat injuries. As with a physical injury, stress injuries deserve little condemnation ... and sufficient attention in order to avoid stress disorders during and following combat services. (Figley & Nash, 2007, p. xv)

In the foreword to Figley and Nash's book, Jonathan Shay (2007) wrote that understanding stress disorders by military officers is a matter of readiness, and he pointed out that a major problem with the diagnosis of PTSD is the practice of calling it a "disorder" instead of an "injury," which he believes perpetuates the stigma against seeking help. He asked, "When a military service member's arm is shot off, do we say he or she suffers from Missing Arm Disorder? That would be ludicrous, and we do not.... The diagnostic entity we now call Posttraumatic Stress Disorder is an injury, not a malady, disease, sickness, illness, or disorder" (p. xvii).

Friedman (2006) pointed out that those who are most symptomatic actually seem to be the most sensitive to the stigma and, therefore, are less likely to seek treatment. As counselors work with returning military service members and their families, we would be wise to understand that "few realms of human practice show as vividly as military functioning does, that we are just one creature—body, mind, society, culture—at every moment. ... The unity of body, mind, and spirit is nowhere more vivid, nor more painful" (Shay, 2007, p. xviii).

Combat Stress, a Given in War

Nash (2007) explained that combat stress, in and of itself, is a given in combat and that, in reality, one of the major goals of war is to use combat stress as a weapon. He said, "It is seldom the physical destruction of people or equipment that brings victory, but the destruction of the adversaries' will to go on fighting" (p. 13). Stress-inducing factors such as chaos, uncertainty, surprise, hopelessness, physical hardship, isolation, and sleep deprivation are what the military call psychological operations (PSYOPS). "Combat stress is not a by-product or side effect of war that can be sanitized away; war is stress and the greater the tempo of operations and intensity of combat, the greater must be the stress" (p. 13). The information written by Nash, perhaps more than any other, helped me understand that combat stress is a given and something everyone in combat must deal with rather than the consequences or outcome of combat for only some warriors. Because stress in war is a weapon, it may discourage sympathy for those affected by combat stress, because to "inflict suffering on an adversary, the warrior must avoid identifying with that adversary or feeling remorse or sympathy" (p. 14).

At the same time, we know that the consequences, the aftermath of this combat stress, does create havoc in a good percentage of service members' lives. Figley and Nash (2007) believe that the attitudes of the military personnel toward the concept of combat stress forms "an important cultural context in which they experience these stressors" and that adaptations to stress include "the spectrum of so-called normal and reversible reactions to the abnormal challenges of combat and military operations while stress injuries and illnesses are a group of very specific syndromes with highly predictable symptoms and courses over time" (p. 3). Given the fact that combat stress is at the core of war and combat efforts, "it is hard for warriors to not perceive stress symptoms of any kind as evidence of personal weakness and failure" (Nash, 2007, p. 17), as this is the very heart of who they are and what they have been called on to do. To the extent that the stressors of war are absolutely essential, then the greater the ability to master the stressor, the greater the warrior's self-concept.

> To the extent participation in war is perceived by warriors as a test of their personal strength, courage, and competence, admitting to combat stress symptoms may be tantamount to admitting failure ... developing stress symptoms can bring with it considerable shame.... The fact that stress injuries are invisible makes it even more difficult for warriors to forgive themselves for developing symptoms of stress injuries ... [and] accept in themselves evidence of being damaged by combat and operational stress without feeling like they have failed the test of war. (Nash, 2007, pp. 17–18)

The Numbers

Joyce Brothers (2006) reported that a study published in 2004 from the Walter Reed Army Institute of Research found that 15% of Marines and 17% of soldiers (Army) surveyed after they returned from Iraq suffered major depression, generalized anxiety, or PTSD. One of the difficulties in Iraq is that there is no "front" and therefore no safe place to retreat to for mental and emotional respite. Those who have been the closest to combat or have been injured are most vulnerable to PTSD. According to this study, 86% of service members reported knowing someone who was seriously injured or killed, and half said they had either handled or uncovered human remains. More than half said they had killed an enemy combatant, and 10% said they had been responsible for the death of a noncombatant. These are staggering numbers.

Blaise (2006) pointed out the difference in the military since Korea when the "enemy wasn't hard to find; he was sitting a few miles over the border knowing we were sitting on the other side. [In Iraq] we didn't feel trained to hunt out and kill an enemy that excelled at staying out of sight" (p. 138). A study (Lowe, 2007) titled "Bringing the War Back Home" led by Dr. Karen H. Seal from the University of California found more than 31,000 veterans returning from Operation Iraqi Freedom and Operation Enduring Freedom have been diagnosed with PTSD. Those afflicted with mental or psychosocial disorders tend to be the younger troops, with those between the ages of 18 and 24 at the greatest risk. About 13% of those diagnosed are women. More than 30% are minorities, and about 50% are members of the Guard and Reserves.

Criteria for Diagnosis

Matthew Friedman (n.d.) offered a short overview of the history and criteria that is meant to be, by no means, an exhaustive review of findings, research, or treatment but an attempt to introduce the reader to the magnitude of PTSD and to encourage readers to do additional research into the dynamics and far-reaching consequences of PTSD for both the survivor and the family. In 1980 when the American Psychiatric Association added PTSD to the third edition of the *Diagnostic and Statistical Manual of Mental Disorders* (*DSM-III*), the diagnosis was initially controversial, but it attempted to fill in the gap between psychiatric theory and practice. The significant change that occurred in the criteria for diagnosis of PTSD was the stipulation that the agent, or cause, was outside the individual, as in a traumatic event, rather than an inherent weakness in the individual. The key to understanding the scientific basis and the clinical expression is the concept of "trauma." This traumatic event was first defined as a catastrophic stressor outside the range of usual human experience, such as war, torture, rape, the Holocaust, natural disasters such as earthquakes, and human-made disasters such as airplane crashes. These were seen as different from painful stressors that happen in normal life, such as divorce, rejection, or serious illnesses. This differentiation was based on the assumption that individuals have the ability to cope with ordinary or normal stress but "their adaptive capacity is likely to be overwhelmed when confronted by a traumatic stressor" (Friedman, n.d., ¶ 3).

In the field of trauma studies, it is also important to understand the concept of intergenerational or multigenerational trauma (Dass-Brailsford, 2007), which is defined as "the cumulative emotional and psychological wounding that is transmitted from one generation to the next" (p. 5). Dr. Bourdette (personal communication, 2007) pointed out that many of the current service members serving in combat zones are children of Vietnam veterans who, more often than not, did not receive services or heal from their trauma, making it possible that many of the current PTSD survivors are also dealing with residual trauma from an earlier generation. PTSD is unique because of the importance placed on the external agent, or stressor.

Clinical experience since 1980 has shown that individual differences regarding the capacity to cope with catastrophic stress depends on how that experience is filtered through the cognitive and emotional processes before it can be appraised as an extreme threat. The *DSM* diagnostic criteria was revised in 1987, 1994, and again in 2000 (American Psychiatric Association, 2000). The current diagnostic criteria includes the history of the exposure to the external traumatic event, symptoms from each of the three clusters of intrusive recollections, avoidant or numbing symptoms, and hyperarousal symptoms, along with the criteria regarding the duration of the symptoms and the impact on the survivor's ability to function. The criteria (Friedman, 2006, n.d.) for a PTSD diagnosis are as follows:

1. The stressor must be a catastrophic event involving actual or threatened death or injury or threat to physical integrity of self; the survivor's subjective response is marked by intense fear, helplessness, or horror.
2. Intrusive recollection of the event occurs in which memories of the traumatic event remain, sometimes for decades or a lifetime; this is a dominating experience that retains its power to evoke panic, terror, dread, grief, or despair.
3. Avoidance of stimuli and the numbing of responsiveness that consist of behavioral, cognitive, or emotional strategies that survivors use as an attempt to reduce the likelihood of exposing themselves to trauma-related stimuli; these strategies are used to minimize the intensity of the response and may superficially resemble agoraphobia, because the individual is afraid to leave home for fear of confronting these reminders. Because survivors cannot tolerate strong emotions, they separate cognitive from emotional aspects of the psychological experience and perceive only the cognitive. This "psychic numbing" is an emotional anesthesia that makes it difficult to participate in meaningful interpersonal relationships.
4. Hyperarousal symptoms resemble those in panic attacks and generalized anxiety disorders, usually including hypervigilance and

startle reactions, which may become so intense that the survivor appears paranoid.

5. The duration has been shortened from 6 months to 1 month to qualify for the chronic or delayed PTSD diagnosis.

6. The functional significance specifies that survivors must experience a significant social, occupational, or other impact or distress in their ongoing ability to function as a result of these symptoms.

The diagnosis also specifies either acute, if the duration of symptoms is shorter than 3 months, or chronic, if the duration of symptoms is longer than 3 months and if the onset of symptoms is at least 6 months after the stressor (Friedman, 2006).

Assessment

The National Center for PTSD has developed a screening instrument (Friedman, 2006) designed for use by primary care practitioners that would be useful for any counselor to have on hand. The result is found to be positive if there is a "yes" answer to any three of the four questions. The client is asked, "In your life, have you ever had any experience that was so frightening, horrible, or upsetting that, *in the past month*, you …

1. Have had nightmares about it or thought about it when you did not want to?

2. Tried hard not to think about it or went out of your way to avoid situations that reminded you of it?

3. Were constantly on guard, watchful, or easily startled?

4. Felt numb or detached from others, activities, or your surroundings?" (Friedman, 2006, p. 589)

Although the experiences listed in this assessment instrument are the typical reactions to trauma, Foa, Davidson, Frances, and Ross (1999) pointed out that often there are other problems common to those with the diagnosis of PTSD. These include panic attacks, severe avoidant behavior, depression, suicidal thoughts and feelings, substance abuse, feelings of alienation and isolation, feelings of mistrust and betrayal, anger and irritability, severe impairment in daily functioning, and strange beliefs and perceptions. Friedman (2006) reported that the likelihood that a person with a PTSD diagnosis will meet the criteria for at least one other disorder is 80% and that they are also at higher risk for medical illnesses. Some of the typical comorbid diagnoses include major affective disorders, dysthymia, alcohol or substance abuse disorders, anxiety disorders, and personality disorders. The comorbidity diagnosis obviously complicates the treatment decision of whether the comorbid disorders are treated concurrently or sequentially with the PTSD (Friedman, n.d.).

Factors that appear to make it more likely for persons to develop PTSD include the severity of the trauma, the length of the trauma, the relative proximity to the trauma, the amount of danger perceived, the number of times one is traumatized, if trauma is inflicted by others, and if the person gets negative reactions from friends and relatives (Foa et al., 1999). As noted earlier, we might also want to consider the possibility of intergenerational trauma. It is also important to understand that people exposed to traumatic events exhibit a "wide spectrum of posttraumatic reactions, from extreme vulnerability to strong resilience" (Friedman, 2006, p. 589) and that most do *not* develop PTSD. Characteristics such as coping skills, interpersonal relatedness, attachment, shame, stigma sensitivity, past trauma history, and motivation for treatment appear to be relevant for the development of PTSD (Friedman, 2006).

A therapist in Tucson, Arizona, who has worked with a large number of veterans with PTSD found that if her clients have troubled backgrounds, they seem to be more predisposed to difficulty dealing with violence in the military. Another psychologist found just the opposite, where the clients who had not been associated with violence in their youth seemed to have more trouble dealing with the violence they experienced in the military.

In attempting to assess PTSD, longitudinal research (Friedman, n.d.) has shown it can become a chronic disorder and persist for decades and sometimes for a lifetime, as noted in a previous chapter by an 80-year-old client who had come to counseling because of recurring PTSD symptoms. Chronic survivors exhibit a longitudinal course marked by remissions and relapses. It has also been documented that there is a delayed variant in which an individual exposed may not exhibit symptoms until months or years later, with the usual immediate precipitant being a situation that resembles the original trauma. Although Freedman also cautions us that there are problems with the diagnosis of this disorder when considering non-Western European regions and cultures, the information is included here because of its prevalence in military families.

Family Violence

I will attempt here to address only issues related to family violence, not the much larger concerns and statistics regarding violence and sexual assault outside the family by members of the Armed Forces or when service members are the victims. A newspaper article (Alaimo, 2006b) reported that southern Arizona's largest Army installation was experiencing a surge in domestic violence cases, with reports of child and spousal abuse up 42%

from the previous year. Those numbers increased from 80 cases in 2004 to 114 complaints in 2005. The number does not include incidents involving single soldiers, because the military recognizes abuse only among married troops. However, officials said, "The increase is due to heightened awareness of Army aid programs for soldiers and their spouses" (p. B2). That explanation seemed plausible to some victim advocates, but not to others. The article quoted an official from the Connecticut-based Miles Foundation, a national advocacy group for victims of violence in the military, who stated that the mounting stress on military families during wartime may account for the increases being seen.

The Miles Foundation normally receives about 50 reports of domestic violence in any given month, but that has increased to up to 600 monthly reports, with the level of violence escalating (Alaimo, 2006b). The same article reported that a major Air Force base in Arizona also showed a spike in domestic violence in 2005 from 35 incidents in 2004 to 66 in 2005, an increase of 83%. According to DoD 2006 figures, "there were 16,500 cases of domestic violence reported, with 9,450 of them substantiated. That's still a rate of 14 cases of every 1,000 couples, compared with 3 per 1,000 among civilians" (Houppert, 2005a, p. 1).

One study from 2000 reported by Marshall (2006), found that long deployments raise the likelihood of severe aggression against spouses, citing the example in 2002 when four soldiers allegedly killed their wives on a U.S. Army base. Rentz et al. (2006), however, in a review of the literature, found few studies that examined family violence in the military and even fewer that compared violence in the military and civilian populations. The main sources for the national statistics on violence are population-based surveys, such as the 1998 National Violence Against Women Survey and the National Family Violence Surveys from 1988.

The DoD has taken a clear stance against family violence and in 1981 required each branch to establish both a Family Advocacy Program (FAP) to prevent and treat child maltreatment and spouse abuse and a confidential central registry to collect and analyze FAP data (Rentz et al., 2006). All substantiated and unsubstantiated cases are now entered into a confidential central registry in accordance with that directive. Until recently (Ceridian Corporation, 2005), a conviction involving domestic violence was considered a misdemeanor that prevented abusers from ever being held responsible for their actions, but "a major paradigm shift is occurring … [in which the DoD] is changing the military system to hold abusers fully accountable, and punish criminal behavior" (p. 2). Schwabe and Kaslow stated in 1984,

For years a conspiracy of silence by family members, health professionals, and the military allowed cases to go unreported, undetected and/or unresolved by tacitly supporting the victim's reluctance to reveal the source of injuries because they were trained not to make waves and protect the patients' confidentiality. (p. 138)

However, current studies (Ceridian Corporation, 2005; Kozaryn, 2000) find that service members who are reported for abuse are 23% more likely to be separated from the service, and those who remain in the military are less likely to be promoted as fast as nonabusers. DoD officials said that because most spouse abuse is reported early, the chances of successful treatment is good, and, as a result, the careers of the abusers are not impaired (Kozaryn, 2000). The 2003 final report from the Defense Task Force on Domestic Violence recommended that to better address domestic violence in the military, the DoD "must establish a military culture that does not tolerate domestic violence, holds batterers accountable for their actions, and provides victims of abuse with the services they need" (p. 1).

Part of the concern listed in the 2003 report from the Defense Task Force on Domestic Violence (RAND Corporation, 2003) is that the definition of domestic violence by the DoD recognizes only military members and current spouses, whereas ex-spouses and unmarried cohabiting and dating partners do not quality for services through the FAP where the victim usually goes first to report the abuse. Even if family members go to FAP services, the counseling and other assistance is not confidential, so many choose to go to civilian counselors. The National Coalition Against Domestic Violence (n.d.) explained that the only military personnel granted confidentiality are chaplains and that the person who is notified first of domestic violence allegations is the perpetrator's boss.

Another problem the coalition pointed out is that the DoD severity definitions are inconsistent with commonly held characterizations of domestic violence. The DoD prerequisite to be categorized as "severe physical abuse" is "major physical injury requiring inpatient medical treatment or causing temporary or permanent disability or disfigurement" (¶ 12). Obviously this requirement eliminated many, if not most, cases of domestic violence. The National Coalition Against Domestic Violence recommended that the military instillations need to start forming partnerships with local victim advocacy agencies. This process was started in 2003 when the DoD began to develop memorandums of understanding with local communities on how they could work together to stem the problem of domestic violence in military communities (RAND Corporation, 2003).

One of the main reasons that "family violence *may be* more common in the military population compared to the civilian population [is] because of higher overall stress levels associated with the military lifestyle" (Rentz et al., 2006, p. 94), especially with ongoing relocations and deployments that lead to separation from peers and community. These frequent and extensive separations may have a profound impact on marriages, particularly those of short duration, as they present a window of opportunity for the spouse left behind to explore independence and develop other relationships and for those relocated to installations located outside the continental United States where social and cultural isolation is fairly common.

On the other hand, Rentz et al. (2006) pointed out that the military lifestyle also creates a number of protective factors that could reduce the amount of family violence, including the fact that the discovery of severe problems, including criminal conduct, mental health problems, and drug and alcohol abuse, are cause for punishment or discharge from the military. The military also has family health care, housing, and many family support programs that could mediate against many variables associated with poverty and drug abuse that leads to violence in the civilian population. For families with children, having at least one employed parent who is able to function effectively in a structured environment and is required to pass literacy and aptitude tests may also be viewed as a protective factor for child maltreatment.

Related Studies

Rentz et al. (2006) found a total of 103 studies concerning maltreatment and 21 studies concerning spousal abuse. Of these, only 11 studies of child maltreatment and 3 studies of spousal abuse in the military, as well as 6 child maltreatment civilian studies and 3 civilian spousal abuse studies, met the researchers' criteria. In reviewing the studies of child maltreatment in the military, the most common type of abuse was physical abuse, accounting for 33% to 70% of all reported child maltreatment cases. Child neglect cases accounted for 18% and 50% of the child maltreatment cases. The low prevalence of neglect is likely the result of the lack of both the visibility of neglect and a clear definition of neglect, particularly in an environment as mentioned earlier where at least one parent is employed and all have housing. It was noted that child sexual abuse in the military accounted for 6% to 18% of all child maltreatment reports. The percentage of emotional abuse among child maltreatment cases ranged from 0.7% to just over 15%, being the least common form of abuse or neglect reported in military families.

In an attempt to make a comparison between military and civilian populations, six studies by Rentz et al. (2006) were found that showed mixed results when comparing child maltreatment. Two studies suggested that child abuse and neglect were more common in military communities, and one study, over the 15-year period between 1985 and 2000 in a hospital near one of the largest military installations in the United States, showed high child abuse and homicide rates for children of military families younger than the age of 10, with 5 cases per 100,000, compared to an overall rate among civilians in that state of 2.2 for 100,000. On the other hand, two studies found a lower rate of child maltreatment in the military, with 7.4 per 100,000 in the military versus 14 cases in the civilian population. One study reported that the rate of neglect was less than half of that found in the general population.

Other studies confirmed that, when comparing the Army Central Registry and the National Child Abuse and Neglect Data System with the rates of child maltreatment in the U.S. civilian population, the rates in the civilian populations are about double the rates of substantiated maltreatment seen in Army families. The civilian population also had slightly higher rates than did the Army in physical abuse, sexual abuse, and emotional abuse. Two other studies showed that "military families in the study experienced significantly less psychological abuse, threat of abuse, educational neglect, psychological neglect and abandonment" (Rentz et al., 2006, p. 103).

In reviewing the studies of military spousal abuse, Rentz et al. (2006) found that physical violence was the most frequent form of substantiated spouse abuse, with 89% to 92% of all spouse abuse cases associated with physical violence. Substantiated emotional abuse was found to be less common, from 6.7% in the Air Force to as high as 10.6% in the Army. Very little spousal sexual abuse and neglect was found. The researchers examined 6 years of data from the U.S. Army Medical Command Central Registry and found that physical child abuse was twice as common when spouse abuse was present in the family and that child sexual abuse was also more likely among families with spousal abuse. However, no significant differences were found of child neglect in families with and without identified spouse abuse.

All studies reviewed showed that spousal abuse is more prevalent and more severe in military families than in civilian families. It was also found that military wives also were at greater risk for certain marital problems, including husbands who drank and worked late and did not express emotions at a healthy level. The standardized rates of moderate and severe husband-to-wife violence were significantly higher in the Army for men's reports of severe aggression and women's reports of experiencing moderate and severe violence. In one study, questionnaires that were completed by the dependents of civilian and military families pointed to a significantly higher percentage of school-age children from military families reporting parental spousal violence, including slapping, pulling hair, and throwing things at or toward the other parent. This was similar to a study reported in the May 2005 issue of a newsletter from Military OneSource that stated, "Studies have placed the incidence of domestic violence within the military anywhere from two to five times higher than in civilian life" (Ceridian Corporation, 2005, p. 2).

The Military OneSource article suggested that the high rates may be due to the fact that (a) the military population is made up of more 18- to 25-year-old men than the general population; (b) families are geographically separated from their extended families, and they, particularly young spouses, feel the isolation; (c) the fear of confidentiality being breached prevents both victims and abusers from getting help; (d) women often become highly financially dependent on their spouses for income and benefits; and (e) military couples are often married when they are very young, which may instill more emotional dependence. Mercier and Mercier (2000) pointed out that because one third of the military is in the lowest pay grade and younger than 30 years old, those of this age and economic status are at the highest risk for domestic violence.

Additional Variables

Gilligan (1996) wrote that the only two variables that "appear to be among the determinants of violent behavior in general are youth and maleness [and] that these patterns are universal across cultures, historical epochs and social circumstances" (p. 221). In addition, multiple other variables and family stressors exist, such as dissatisfaction with employment, responsibility for a family, deployment, and family separations. It is likely that "no one single factor causes domestic violence, but multiple risk factors may increase the risk of abuse in the military family" (Mercier & Mercier, 2000, p. 5). "We can only understand male violence if we understand the sex roles, or gender roles, into which males are socialized by the gender codes of their particular cultures" (Gilligan, 1996, p. 229). So we have to consider the additional factor of male psychology, which we addressed in chapter 3. There may be more men in the military with the "give 'em hell" (Mahalik, Good, & Englar-Carlson, 2003) script in which part of their socialization results in "violence and aggression [becoming] avenues through which some boys and men compensate for uncomfortable feelings such as shame and hurt.... Therefore, instead of recognizing, understanding, and coping with their hurt or scared feelings, males may externalize their distress by 'taking it out on others' " (p. 125) because "violent behavior can be the most powerful disguise for shame-provoking truth" (Gilligan, 1996, p. 118). Sam Keen (1983) wrote that the "more the identity of the male is rooted in the warrior ideal, the more a society will degrade women and cast the relationship between the sexes as a form of warfare. ... That warfare ... will see the woman as an inferior to be conquered, raped, and dominated" (p. 125). Although certainly the majority of male service members do not fall into this category, our awareness of this can perhaps help us understand one of the risk factors involved in working with family violence in the military.

Rentz et al. (2006) urged caution in interpreting the estimates found in the studies they reviewed in light of the methodological limitation of many of the studies. In addition, the criteria for substantiating child maltreatment and spouse abuse can be somewhat suspect, because the reporting system and the source of referrals may differ somewhat in each branch of the military and certainly differ when comparing the military reporting system and the civilian reporting system. The amount of family violence information published in peer-reviewed journals varies, with no data reflecting an overall higher rate of family violence in the military. Also, statistics presented focus on substantiated cases that are entered into central registries and do not include cases that are never reported to the authorities and those that are unsubstantiated. Given those facts, the estimates will more than likely be an underestimate of what is actually occurring in military communities.

Certainly the characteristics of the Fortress discussed in chapter 3 of secrecy, stoicism, and denial also contribute not only to the violence but also to the hesitancy to report or disclose the abuse. "Understanding family violence in the military is an important concern because of the unique stresses faced by military families on a daily basis that could place them at greater risk for family dysfunction" (Rentz et al., 2006, p. 106). A chapter in a major work on military families written in 1984 (Schwabe & Kaslow) stated that no statistics were found that compared the incidence of military family violence to civilian family violence, with the contention that the concept of the military as a "school for violence" is unsubstantiated. The authors back then wrote that most military service men were technicians and bureaucrats and that although there are those "small organized fighting forces specializing in intense physical combat, the men in these units are highly disciplined and professional and there is no evidence to support the assumption that they are at a greater risk for family violence than anyone" (Schwabe & Kaslow, 1984, p. 129).

The world has changed greatly since 1984, and more and more of our military service members are being faced with the uncertainty and trauma of combat, so although I believe that the recent increases in domestic violence are absolutely significant and cannot be ignored, these statistics also cannot be used to condemn or define all military service members. The current increased stress of the long and multiple deployments, as well as the catastrophic situations service members are finding when they are deployed, must be taken into consideration. It is also important for mental health professionals working with the military to know that there are a number of resources for victims of violence, including each installation's FAP. Another organization called STAMP, which stands for Survivors Take Action Against Abuse by Military Personnel, has been organized to provide support to and struggle for justice for anyone experiencing abuse or mistreatment by military personnel.

Alcohol in the Military

One weekend afternoon my husband and I traveled to a town near our home in Germany and, while there, went on the military base to fill up with gas. While on base we discovered there was a fall festival going on over the weekend, so we decided to take part in the celebration, something pretty common in Germany. In walking through the food tents, we noticed that beer was being served indiscriminately to anyone who asked. Well, it was Germany; beer is always available! As we watched, however, we realized that those working behind the beer table were quite openly giving free beer to kids as young as 12 or 13, without ever asking where their parents were or how old they were. We informed the military police who were on duty, and they said they "would take care of it." Did they? There is no way to know, but what we realized was that even 15 years ago, at least in Germany, alcohol was so common on military installations that these kinds of actions were not considered inappropriate.

Dr. Butler, a therapist in San Diego, shared that one of his clients was a chief petty officer whose job was to deal directly with alcohol-related incidences; this client shared that the military now has a zero-tolerance policy regarding any kind of substance abuse or overuse. The military has come a long way in recognizing the difficulties that alcohol, as well as drug use, has created for service members and has attempted to promote the acceptability of seeking treatment. Despite this, depending on the location and the availability of both drugs and alcohol, addiction issues are also major problems with teenagers in military families. The DoD made a major step in combating this issue early in the 1990s, when it hired substance abuse counselors to work in each school in Europe. These counselors were not school counselors and were not a part of the DoD school system, but they were in the schools to work with the school counselors specifically regarding addiction issues.

In the book *The Viking* (Baker, 2004), the author reported that as far back as the Viking days, an elite group of fighters were known as the *berserkergang,* which basically means "mental state." These fighters believed in their invulnerability and went into battle in a frenzied state, appearing to be able to ignore any and all pain. Their painted faces and appearance of being part creature and part man, according to the author, may have contributed to the legend of the werewolf in Europe and were meant to inspire terror. It was believed that for these fighters to get to that frenzied mental state, they had to ingest a large quantity of alcohol, as well as perhaps even hallucinogenic mushrooms. Throughout military history, at least in Western European traditions, the use of alcohol was not just prevalent but used either to produce the kind of invulnerability necessary to go into battle or to mask the horror that those in combat witnessed.

A retired military psychiatrist shared that alcohol use in the U.S. military goes back to the Civil War, when it was recommended that soldiers be intoxicated to stand in line and fire their weapons. He said that it has been so ingrained in the military culture that there has been a stigma against breaking it. It has traditionally been one method of building unit cohesion, creating the kind of comrades that can be trusted to watch each other's back; it has been an essential, however destructive, component of the military. John Bourdette related the story of his father who was career military but a nondrinker in the 1950s; in one of his performance reviews he was given a negative rating because he was not willing to drink with his commanding officer. That rating almost ended his military career. Although the issue of alcohol is no longer so overt, drinking and even the use of drugs have gone underground and are becoming covert. A 2007 news release reported that service members in Iraq are requesting, in an attempt to get around the rules, that their spouses buy bottles of mouthwash, pour out the mouthwash, fill the bottles with alcohol, and send them to them (Bourdette, personal communications, 2007). Ames and Cunradi (n.d.) reported,

> Heavy alcohol use is a significant problem in the military. Personnel often use alcohol in an attempt to cope with stress, boredom, loneliness, and the lack of other recreational activities. The easy availability of alcohol, ritualized drinking opportunities, and inconsistent policies contribute to a work culture that facilitates heavy and binge drinking in this population. (p. 1)

Rate of Alcohol Use

Illicit drug use and cigarette smoking decreased in the military from 1980 to 2002, but heavy alcohol use actually increased significantly from 1998 to 2002, the first increase since 1988 (Ames & Cunradi, n.d.). In 2002 more than a quarter of adults in the military from the ages of 18 to 25 reported heavy drinking, compared to a little less than 9% of those between the ages of 26 and 55. What is interesting is that young people who entered the military were more likely to be heavy drinkers in high school compared to those who did not enter the military. "Those especially likely to report heavy drinking are young non-Hispanic white men, with a high school education or less, who are either single or married but living away from their spouse" (p. 7).

The rate of heavy drinking also differs by service branch, with the Marine Corps having the highest rate of heavy alcohol use at just over 38% and the Air Force having the lowest rate of slightly over 24%. The Army and Navy fall between the two. The largest negative effects of alcohol use, such as missing work or being arrested while impaired, occur in the lowest pay grades, who, naturally, are the youngest enlisted service members, typically without a college education (Ames & Cunradi, n.d.).

This prevalence of heavy alcohol use also differs markedly from civilians in the same age groups. Of the young men in all branches of the military, over 32% engaged in heavy drinking compared to a little under 18% of civilian men; women serving in the Navy and Marine Corps had significantly higher rates (11.5% and 12.9%, respectively) than civilian women (5.5%). Women in the Army and Air Force did not differ that significantly from their civilian counterparts (6.3% compared to 5.5% of civilian women) (Ames & Cunradi, n.d.).

The Center for Substance Abuse Research (2007) reported that the percentage of military personnel between the ages of 18 and 25 who report using illicit drugs was less than one half of that of civilians (6.8% vs. 18.8%) suggesting that the policies and the enforcement of the policies in the military have been successful in discouraging illicit drug use.

Risk Factors

The risk factors for heavy drinking outlined by the Ames and Cunradi (n.d.) study are as follows: (a) a workplace culture that influences beliefs about acceptable drinking contexts, acceptable drinking behavior, and expectations about the consequences of drinking; and (b) alcohol availability, particularly the availability of alcohol in foreign ports and on U.S. bases where even underage recruits have easy access to alcohol in bars, in the barracks, or in hotel rooms near the base. In foreign ports, alcohol is relatively inexpensive, and bars are often located near the base, and few ports have underage drinking laws. These types of bars have little legal, moral, or ethical standards with regard to the use of alcohol. The kids from the housing areas on base in Germany could walk out the gates, down the street, and buy beer at the gas station from vending machines!

Bray, Bae, Federman, and Wheeless (2005) did a major study of the differences in alcohol use by the military in different parts of the world, pointing out that those in Asian countries have higher heavy drinking patterns than those in other countries. They also pointed out that there are probably many other reasons for differences in patterns of drinking, including "length of military tour, relative isolation of assignments, stresses associated with moves to unfamiliar countries, lack of family support for unaccompanied duty tours, command emphasis on responsible alcohol use, and reasons affecting selection for assignments" (p. 230). I would guess that a combination of these contributes to the increase in alcohol use over the past few years, especially for those who are deployed, away from their families, and serving in very stressful combat areas. As Figley and Nash (2007) stated in their introduction about combat stress and the consequences of the sleep-deprived brain, "Once psychologically injured, sleep loss perpetuates the injury and blocks spontaneous healing, while fatally greasing the slide into alcohol and drug abuse—which often begin as desperate efforts at sleep" (p. xx).

As the retired psychiatrist informed me, there have been major policy changes in the military in the past two to three decades, particularly after the devastating consequences of the use of alcohol and drugs in the military during Vietnam. Thousands of dollars have been spent to counter both the actual drinking problem and the belief about alcohol. Dr. Bourdette, who has been working with addiction issues most of his adult life, urges all counselors working with the military to have some substance abuse training. Just asking service members or families if there is a problem is not good enough. Military members know that from a command level, the use and abuse of alcohol are unacceptable, but as the statistics point out, they are still major issues. All counselors must have training in the identification, assessment, and treatment of addictions to work effectively with military families.

Finances

Financial problems are of major concern in the military, particularly for the young service members. Henderson (2006) wrote, "Young soldiers can always find plenty of businesses happy to take their money, and when that runs out, just as happy to extend credit, lots of credit, at fat interest rates. Dozens of payday lenders near the post supply one and two week loans to soldiers living paycheck to paycheck" (p. 30). She explained that a typical $30 fee for a short-term $200 loan doesn't sound so bad until the annual percentage rate is calculated, sometimes at as much as a staggering 400%.

Businesses regularly extend credit to service members because they know if they try to default, military regulations will let the business garnish the service member's wages. Henderson quoted the deputy director of Army Emergency Relief, who said that the biggest cause of trouble for service members is how they handle their money. Even though they don't make a lot of money, if they manage it well, they can get by, but

> when the transmission falls out of the car, or there's a death or serious illness in the family and they need to buy plane tickets home, or when they get to a new duty station and there are no quarters available so they have to live off post and that means two months' rent in advance and a security deposit … they don't have that kind of cash. (Henderson, 2006, p. 30)

A concern for many in the military, particularly those at the lower enlisted ranks, is that they have bought the stereotype that the military will take care of them. Housing is provided, meals are "free" because they eat in the mess hall, medical care is free, and uniforms limit the expense of clothing, so they tend to regard their actual paycheck as play money or allowance. There is little incentive to save money, leading to the proverbial "paycheck to paycheck" consumer mentality and lifestyle. When life happens, however, they have little to fall back on. According to a recent article ("Due to Debt," 2006), some soldiers are not being sent overseas because they are so deep in debt that they are considered security risks. The Pentagon contends that financial problems distract personnel and can make them vulnerable to bribery and treason, and even suicide.

The problem is attributed to "a lack of financial smarts among recruits [and] reckless spending among those exhilarated to make it home alive from a tour of duty," because when they go to war, they get combat pay, and none of their income is taxed. Added to this is "the profusion of … businesses that allow military personnel to borrow against their next paycheck at extremely high interest rates" ("Due to Debt," 2006, p. 2). The news article reported that several states have cracked down on payday lending practices, and legislation has been brought forward to limit how much these businesses can charge military personnel. A study of 15,000 payday lenders in over 13,000 zip codes in 20 states revealed that most were located near the military installations (Lukach, 2005a). About 9% of all enlisted personnel and as many as 12% of midlevel noncommissioned officers use payday loans. Lukach (2005a) quoted a DoD official who said, "The potential for detrimental impact on mission accomplishment is very real" (p. 5).

The Marine Corps (*Financial Problems*, n.d.) Web site pointed out that there are a number of demographic groups who are at a higher risk for financial problems. These include the junior enlisted rank, single parents, newly divorced or separated members, service members with a family member who has physical or emotional challenges, newlyweds, new parents, recently relocated service members, service members recently recalled to active duty from reserve status, and service members going through the cycle of deployment and reunion. Financial strain causes behavioral changes and has been linked to depression, which can affect duty performance, mission readiness, and interpersonal relationships. "If a [service member] is at risk for personal problems, marital problems, or suicide, that risk is exacerbated in times of financial stress" (*Financial Problems,* n.d., ¶ 1).

A major portion of military support organizations such as Military OneSource and military publications such as *Military Spouse* focuses on the financial issues and concerns of the military. The military has realized that these financial problems can and do cause considerable difficulties for the service members and their family. All services are attempting to find remedies in the form of education and counseling for these financial concerns by hosting fairs at military installations and educating military members about the dangers of payday loans as well as helping those at risk get their finances on sound footing (Lukach, 2005a). The Marine Corps article (*Financial Problems*, n.d.) made the point that most service members are hesitant to seek help because of a possible negative impact on their career, so even in career matters they may be reluctant to bring up the topic until it becomes too overwhelming. As with civilian couples and families, financial issues need to be addressed in counseling, as they obviously add to the stressors within the family. They might not be initiated by the military family without encouragement by the mental health professional.

CHAPTER **8**

The Transition Journey

Change, Grief, and Loss

In an article for the *Voice for Military Families* (2007), Raezer said that survivors of the fallen have asked for bereavement counseling, which is not a benefit covered by TRICARE, to ensure that families who have made the greatest sacrifice obtain appropriate care at the time they need it. In a statement before the Department of Defense Task Force on Mental Health in December 2006, representatives from the National Military Family Association requested specific training in bereavement and other counseling for family readiness group leaders and volunteers.

It is clear that more efforts need to be placed at the command level on supporting the long-term emotional needs of survivors and of communities affected by loss. Because TRICARE does not cover grief counseling, families who cannot access military hospitals are often left with no care because either they do not know what to ask for or they are not getting the assistance in obtaining services. Receiving grief counseling when a service member first expresses a need could prevent more serious issues from developing. Also important is understanding the effects of trauma in dealing with ongoing challenges involved in the care of service members. Mental health professionals must have a greater understanding of the effects of mild traumatic brain injury and polytrauma or post-traumatic stress disorder in combination with multiple physical injuries (National Military Family Association, 2006).

I included this chapter because of the overwhelming and constant issue of change and transitions, as well as grief and loss, experienced by virtually all military families. It is my intention to provide in this book the resources and expertise of others in the field, but the information shared in this chapter is actually the foundation I used in working with military kids and their families. After almost 10 years in Department of Defense schools, I believe that the greatest gift I left most of my students was a better understanding of the process and benefit of grieving and of the importance of understanding transitions. Regardless of the therapeutic approach or theory we work from (see chapter 9), to me counseling must include a psychoeducational component, which is the value of the information shared in this chapter.

Families do not have to be faced with what Raezer called the "greatest sacrifice" to need help dealing with loss. The reality is that the typical military family is faced with transitions in which they experience change, accompanied by the sense of loss and grief, on such a consistent basis that many don't even realize they have not grieved the previous transition before planning for the next. Wakefield (2007) reminded us that for the military family, loss includes the loss of a parent, spouse, or child and the "adjustments necessary to deal with the physical or emotional scars incurred during conflict. They need to be understood and supported, for this is a very stressful lifestyle" (p. 23).

A Framework for Healing: The Transition Journey

The Transition Journey is a model of healing not previously published but one I helped develop and used extensively during more than 25 years of my professional career. I was able to make sense out of what was happening to the students I worked with at both the middle and high school levels when I realized that their whole life was about transitions and about making change and dealing with loss. It was only then that I was able to make a difference in the lives of the children of the military families I worked with. It was also helpful as a high school counselor in a civilian public school where, in 3 years nine of our students died, in all but one case, accidentally. By using this model, both individually and in groups, the students could make sense of what often seemed like constant turmoil in their lives. Understanding each phase of the journey helped them, as well as parents and school staff, understand their constant level of confusion as they realized that they were always in the midst of a multitude of transitions. The Transition Journey is also extremely helpful in working with anyone going through issues of divorce and remarriage—both new transitions in people's lives and all other large and small transitions.

During the many workshops I presented on this journey, I found people saying that this simple framework helps them understand almost any difficult time in their lives. One of the most frustrating things for me as a counselor educator is that there is no requirement for students to take a grief and loss class. How can that be? To me, all of counseling is about change and loss; the reason people come to counseling is so that something will change in their lives, and that always demands they deal with loss. I remember when I was in graduate school, one of my mentors made the statement that "all counseling is dealing with unfinished grief." That has stayed with me for decades, and over and over, in whatever environment I find myself working, it seems to be continually true. The defining word for the military family is *change*; change is what their lives are about. The most useful tool any counselor or therapist can have is to understand transitions and change, which includes the process of grief and loss. Virtually all writers, authors, and authorities in the field of grief and loss (Freeman, 2005; Harvey, 2002; Kubler-Ross, 1975; Moore, 2004; Worden, 2002) have accurately stated that all people experience grief in individual ways and that helping professionals must acknowledge and honor those processes. What makes the field difficult to write and teach about is, indeed, the uniqueness of each person's grief.

Many years ago during the formation of the Divorce Recovery (http://www.divorcerecovery.net) project in Tucson, Arizona, those of us who created the program also created a model of transitions, loosely based on the three stages named by William Bridges (1995). This model continues to be used in the training of the Divorce Recovery group leaders almost 30 years later. I have continued to adapt and modify this journey, as it continues to hold true through many years of work with many different populations. This framework for healing that I call the Transition Journey worked particularly well for me with military families because of its simplicity and usefulness with all ages. When people make change, when they suffer loss, and when they face grief, they can find themselves somewhere along the "healing journey" and then can imagine how they can make their way through to the other end. In this way, it is viewed not as pathological, an illness, or craziness, but as a normal process of healing.

New Understandings of Grief and Loss

Whether we follow Kubler-Ross's five stages of grief (1975), William Worden's (2002) tasks of mourning, the phases of passage outlined by Moore (2004), the pattern ascribed to the hero's journey by Joseph Campbell (Moore, 2004), or the work by Parkes and Weiss, Bowlby, or Lindemann (Freeman, 2005), we can incorporate almost any approach to grief work into the framework of the Transition Journey. Doka (2005) provided a valuable overview of the "new perspectives on grief" in his review of current work on the topic of grief. He helps us understand that we need to extend the definition of grief from just thinking of death to viewing grief as a reaction to any loss and to go beyond affect when defining and working with grief. We also need to include the cognitive, physical, emotional, behavioral, and spiritual reactions and needs of clients. Doka also emphasized the need to continue the bond with that which was lost and understand that attachment may be beneficial in some way throughout life, instead of relying on the older concept of "getting over the loss."

Another new understanding of grief is that we must recognize that it is more than just coping and that the bereaved have choices in grief, including the choice to significantly grow through that experience. The last "new understanding" Doka pointed out is that we need to move away from the concept of stages and instead focus more on the necessary tasks that could be accomplished as the bereaved choose to work on their grief. In so doing, we move away from the assumption of linearity and instead stress the individuality of grief. Although I am very supportive of this last point, I believe the framework presented here will be a helpful one in which to view loss, even though it is roughly divided into three experiences, while focusing on the tasks that need to be accomplished. The framework also helps counselors assess the progress of their clients and, I hope, can help them determine the type of intervention that will be most appropriate and therapeutic with each experience.

The Constants of Loss and Change

Transitions happen to each of us on a daily basis. The transitions or changes that affect all of us occur often without our being involved in the decisions that create the change. This is particularly true for the military service member and, ultimately, for the military family. Other transitions, however, occur after we have made significant, and sometimes difficult, decisions to make changes in our lives. These also happen for the military family—changes they choose based on choices military members have available to them. In other words, there really are only two kinds of transitions:

- Those that are planned, in which some amount of forethought, decision making, and choice has gone into the creation of the transition; and
- Those that are unplanned, in which some unplanned or unexpected event has occurred that demands our attention as we face a new transition.

In both cases, the two constants are loss and change. What is clearly true of all transitions is that when one suffers a loss, he or she is forced to change, and when one chooses to change, he or she is faced with loss. For example, when someone chooses to join the military, he or she makes a decision to choose a way of life very different from civilian life and perhaps very different from the life experienced up until that time. Although the decision is made for many reasons, these reasons certainly include that person's wanting something positive in life. But consider the losses that person must deal with, everything from the loss of the chance to make many crucial decisions about life for a certain period of time, where that person might want to live, the family he or she left behind, the possibility of being put in harm's way—the list can go on and on. In another example, when a person is faced with a crisis that ends with perhaps the loss of a relationship, that person must make changes in his or her life to continue to live productively. The positive changes we make in life also demand loss; we all have had to give something up upon entering marriage, having a child, returning to school, or starting a new job. So the overarching reality is that all transitions require both loss and change.

Transitions are a part of everyone's life. Life is a series of changes made both naturally or through interruptions in our lives. Thomas Moore (2004) said, "We need to be born again and again further into our own humanity, discovering in increasingly sophisticated ways what it means to be a person in a community of persons" (p. 24). Sometimes the natural developmental transitions seem to be the hardest. Life-span theorists such as Erikson and Piaget have built their theories on these natural transitions. The Transition Journey can begin with events such as going to high school, graduating from high school, getting the first job, breaking up with the first love, having a friend move away, changing schools, getting married, or having children. Along the way, however, while facing these developmental transitions, life presents often more interesting and sometimes more painful transitions, such as a new baby brother or sister arriving, an older sibling graduating and leaving home, parents divorcing, grandparents dying, best friends moving away, or a parents dying. These crisis-oriented transitions take people to the depth and sometimes the limit of what they perceive is endurable. If, however, we add to the normal, and sometimes difficult, developmental transitions the constancy of change, of the unknown and sometimes impending crisis in the military family, the individuals in that family are almost always somewhere along the Transition Journey.

The question many members of the military family often ask is, "Will there ever be an end … does the healing ever actually happen?" In my experience of using this framework in both teaching and counseling, the Transition Journey seems to resonate for virtually everyone; it is flexible enough to include the unique perspective and attitudes about crisis and change that people develop, as well as their individual stories and background that affect their personal transition process. Transitions seem to be a part of the human condition, and because we are all more similar than different, most people go through a similar process—even though it certainly feels unique to each of us. Transitions can be a time of growth and learning or a time of utter despair and upheaval. Once counselors understand the process and how to help clients assess their progress through their individual journeys, they can assist their clients through the journey to find that they can complete the process in a much healthier place.

Perhaps the most important concept is that any change or loss requires the client, or family, to travel through the Transition Journey. During that journey, the members of the family will experience the effects and the consequences of that loss and change, even though they more than likely will face individual challenges along the way. An unknown author wrote, "The transition process is really a loop in one's life, a journey, a going out and away from the main flow for a time and then coming back around." But when the human being is constantly in transition, how does one learn from the journey and use it to process the next transition?

The framework for this Transition Journey is explained in three experiences, named after Bridges's (1995) work—the Endings, the Neutral Zone, and the New Beginnings—not because people neatly follow these three experiences linearly but because it gives us a framework that is teachable and understandable as a normal process, instead of something to be ignored or feared, and can be part of the counseling or therapeutic process. To better explain the three phases, I included a diagram that I have used, and modified, over the years with hundreds of people (see Figure 8.1).

Endings: The Impact

The Greek poet Euripides (480–406 BC) said, "There is something in the pang of change. More than the heart can bear. Unhappiness remembering happiness." The first experience of the healing journey is called, ironically, the Endings. Something has come to an end. Whether clients have chosen to make a change and now have to face a loss or a loss has occurred in their life that demands change, the journey has begun. For members of military families, these Endings are regular experiences in their lives: a new school, a new town, a new country, new friends, a new community. But add the obvious, as well as the natural, developmental transitions that families cannot ignore: the deployment of the military parent or spouse, the fear of uncertainty, the wonder and concern for the future.

The Endings begin when the change actually occurs: the day of the move, the withdrawal from school, the military spouse leaves home on

Healing Journey for the Military Family

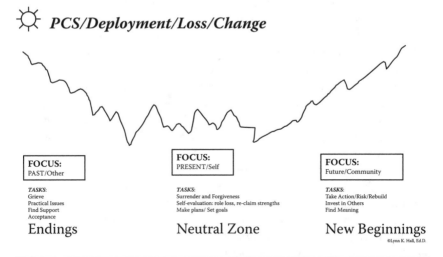

Figure 8.1 The Transition Journey

temporary duty orders. We know, however, for those changes that are planned or expected, there is often a significant portion of the transition made prior to any actual physical change. The planning, organizing, training, and communicating about the upcoming event, often called anticipatory grief, could be described much like the predeployment stage described in chapter 7. This can be a time when a lot of healthy grief work can be done, or it can be a time when emotions are denied and the family members believe they have to maintain their stoicism and deny their feelings.

When it comes, whether through a forced crisis or a planned change, the actual Endings usually start with a physical change: some thing or person or place is lost or has changed. It is a time of intense emotion, of confusion, and of what seems like never-ending painful days. As with the deployment stage, the initial experience in this journey is filled with uncertainly, heightened emotions, and often contradictory thoughts. Military families often hide behind their mask of stoicism to live up to the model of the strong military family instead of allowing each member to experience the emotions, confront the confusion, and feel the pain. Those who have been through many moves or many other transitions, and have recognized that planning for these times needs to include the expression of loss, fears, and hope, and have had support and the courage to experience the Endings can move on in a healthy way. Those who hide often suffer greatly, but no one can make changes in their life without some consequence—negative or positive.

Focus   One way to understand this phase of the journey and also to facilitate the grief of others is to understand what we might describe as psychic
energy (energy of the soul), will initially be focused on the past. A person's
dreams, thoughts, and stories seem to all be about what used to be. Clients
talk about dreaming of what was and constantly tell stories of how things
used to be. Children in my schools would repeatedly talk about how their
former school was better, the teachers were nicer, and there were more
things to do in their former community, forgetting they felt the same way
when they made the last move. Parents talk about the services that were
available at their last installation, how much more helpful the people were
at the former base or post, and how the former school was more open to
meeting the needs of their children.

It is only when people begin to see the present situation for what it is,
without comparing it to the past, and can evaluate the past from both positive and negative perspectives that they seem ready to move on. This is a
normal part of a healthy transition; if we attempt to persuade them otherwise, or if we try too early to get them to be realistic about the present,
we are only encouraging the mask of denial. The feelings and thoughts get
stifled only to reoccur later in more harmful and destructive ways. One
young airman shared that he and his wife gave birth to their third child,
Emma, when his son, Jimmy, was in first grade. It was over the winter
break from school, and after being home with the new baby, Jimmy had
to return to school. At the end of the first week back to school, the teacher
mentioned to Jimmy's dad that Jimmy was not finishing his work; he was
daydreaming all day and seemed to have lost interest in school. On the way
home, he asked Jimmy what was up, why wasn't he finishing his work at
school. Jimmy's reply was, "My head is too full of Emma." Young Jimmy
had just experienced a change in his life, obviously a positive one, but his
thoughts and emotions were all centered on this new young baby girl, and
he simply wasn't ready to get back to the normal routine of school. So not
all change has to be negative; even the positive experiences we have in life
demand change and therefore demand the experience of loss.

During the fall of the 2000–2001 school year, I began to get phone calls
from parents concerned about their senior daughters. In the course of a
week or two, I must have had four or five phone calls about different girls.
In addition, I had a number of teachers express concern about a number
of senior girls, all within the same time frame. This caused me some concern, until I looked at the records of the incoming seniors that year and
discovered that of the 96 seniors, there were 16 senior girls who were new
to the school. Even though we were certainly used to up to a 30% turnover
of students each year, this was extraordinarily high, especially for seniors
who were, more than any other class, less likely to have such a high turn-

over. Instead of contacting each one of them individually, I sent out for pizza and invited them to have lunch with me. Thirteen of the 16 girls came to lunch that day, which, in and of itself, told me a lot. I explained that I knew they were all new to our school that year and asked them simply to introduce themselves and talk about what it felt like to move to a new school (and, in most cases, a new country) in their senior year. Interesting enough, almost half of them had decided to view this year as a positive adventure, and because it was for only 1 year, they were planning to go back to the United States after graduation, they were looking forward to the adventure.

These stories were almost the complete opposite of those of the other half of the girls, who were angry that their parents had forced them to move during their senior year, and, even though they had made many moves before this one, they hated the new school, the new environment, and everything about the move, mostly because of the belief that this was just asking too much of them. There were even two girls who were in their early months of pregnancy who had been sent to live with relatives to get their lives in order. A short explanation: sometimes civilian families will send a problem child, or a child with a problem, to live with a military relative, thinking that the student will be attending a military school, which will straighten them out! What a shock when they discover that the school is not so different from any other civilian school in the United States and certainly not what most people think of when they think of a military school.

So the girls introduced themselves and began to see the world from a different perspective in two ways: there might be something positive about this experience, and they were not alone. As they began to talk, they realized that, in most cases, they shared at least one class with another girl in the room, so they started to make plans to study together, have lunch together, or meet on the weekend. As the bell rang for them to return to class, I interrupted their talk to ask when they would want to have lunch again—and one rather precocious girl stated, "Why would we want to have lunch with you again?" Obviously my work was done, and I was thanked by most of the girls. Oh, if school counseling could always be so easy!

As Robertson (n.d.) wrote, reassurance for young people who often feel such a loss of control and stability when they experience a major change that they could do nothing to prevent from occurring is so essential. And although it is essentially the parents' job to let these young people know that they will always love them and that they will survive this latest move together, it is also imperative that those in the schools, as well as other support services, validate everyone going through a transition, allowing them to express their pain and fears and helping them move forward in healthy and productive ways.

Tasks During the Endings stage, there are four tasks that are usually necessary to accomplish before one moves on. These tasks are the need to grieve, to find support, to deal with practical issues, and to come to an acceptance that the loss has occurred. The first is simply the need to grieve or experience all the emotions of grief, whatever those are for that person. This is where the work of Kubler-Ross (1975) is so important. It is working with the clients to go through the five emotions of grief, including denial, bargaining, depression, anger, and acceptance. Dass-Brailsford (2007) said that denial protects the individual from the intense emotions and allows the mind to exclude the pain. Denial is usually accompanied by numbness and shock, which are normal reactions and should not be viewed as a lack of feelings or a lack of care. As clients begin to acknowledge the impact and the accompanying feelings, the denial and disbelief begin to diminish. Bargaining seems to be necessary for individuals to evaluate the past and perhaps find ways that they could have responded differently or perhaps have prevented the loss; sometimes clients can get caught up in imagining all kinds of things that will never and could never have happened. This can sometimes lead to intense feelings of remorse that may hinder the healing.

As the numbness begins to wear off, individuals start to realize the extent of the loss and may experience depressive symptoms, including sleep and appetite disturbances, changes in energy and concentration, and frequent crying and tearfulness. Sometimes loneliness, emptiness, and self-pity are prevalent, but, for most, this is a necessary part of the process before they can begin to rebuild their lives. These depressive symptoms need to be assessed differently from true clinical depression, and, in most cases, medication or other intrusive procedures only prolong these feelings, as they seem to be necessary for individuals to heal.

When anger begins to surface, clients can feel helpless and powerless to the frequency and intensity of the rage and anger they feel. These feelings often are the secondary emotions to feelings of abandonment, hurt, frustration, resentment, and guilt, which may result from feelings of relief and hope as burdens are sometimes lifted by the loss. Finally, enough of the feelings are expressed, and individuals can begin to integrate the loss into their lives, so there is a sense of acceptance that the loss has occurred.

This hardly means that the transition is over; in fact, the hard work has just begun. Although Kubler-Ross defined these emotions in terms of stages, we know that most people don't go through the stages in a sequential or linear manner and that these stages are better understood as important emotions to be experienced. This first task corresponds to Worden's (2002) second task of mourning, which is to work through the pain of grief. We have all experienced or have worked with clients who have experienced all of these emotions, sometimes at the same time and often in a different sequence than outlined by Kubler-Ross.

The second task is the need for support, which is often provided by family, friends, or a religious or military community. When a military family moves to a new community, the support services, including counseling, need to be available and easy to access. It is through the support of others, provided either personally or professionally, that the first and third tasks seem to be accomplished with the least amount of pain and agony. When families in transition have a sense of isolation, they often remain in this early stage of the healing journey for much longer than necessary. Also, if the family tradition or traditional military culture promotes the stigma against asking for help, the family may be left to sink further in its pain and sorrow, with little hope for healing.

The third task is to take care of all the practical problems and needs of everyone involved in the family. These problems and concerns often come when people have little capacity to make these decisions that may have long-term or lifelong consequences. With an impending move, a new school, and a multitude of decisions to be made, all members in the family are forced to make choices at a time when they need to be grieving, when they need support, and when they might, ideally, want to be taking time to say good-bye. With all the work that has to be done, no wonder military kids learn early how to say good-bye easily, as was mentioned in an earlier chapter. Most people going through a transition don't have that luxury. When the loss is more of a traumatic nature, for instance, the death of a loved one or a divorce, the decisions become that much more difficult for everyone in the family. In these cases, the military support system also has much to do with the decisions that are required. After Kate Blaise (2006) lost her husband, she lamented that post housing was available only to married couples, and in the eyes of the world, she was no longer married. Yet she wrote, "In my heart I still was. How did I make that feeling stop? When would I feel no longer married? I took those vows with forever in mind; marriage had always been more than a ring and a new last name. I had embraced the idea of being half of a complete whole. What did I do now that my other half was gone?" (p. 311).

The fourth task is the ability to say good-bye and to come to an acceptance of the loss, accepting another change that may be perceived as being forced on them rather than chosen—but accepting nonetheless. This fourth task corresponds to Worden's (2002) first task of mourning, which is to accept the reality of the loss. How do we get to this point as we experience any loss? As I noted previously when defining Kubler-Ross's emotional stages, when some of the other difficult emotions are expressed and worked through, acceptance can be the natural next step in the process. When reflecting on difficult transitions, people often share that there is a sense that this acceptance "just happened." Many people have told me that it was like they woke up one morning and the world seemed different, or a dream they had was particularly significant, or a comment made by another person helped them consider the world in a different way. Then, unexpectedly, they realized that the sun was shining, that there was indeed a future, and that the past was, in fact, the past. Thomas Moore (2004) said, "You must have a similar story of a decisive moment, perhaps ... a turning point that made all the difference in your life" (p. 24). It was time to move on—not without sorrow, not without memories, and not without fear, but it was time to move on. It truly is not time that heals loss but what one does with the time that leads to the healing, and it appears, for most people, that the work they do in accomplishing these tasks and in living through the emotions of grief prepares them for the next step.

Therapeutic Assessment and Support I have been describing a process known as normal or uncomplicated grief (Worden, 2002). For people who are starting one of the many Transition Journeys of their life, the appropriate kinds of interventions will be of a more client-centered nature. Providing unconditional positive regard, empathic understanding, and narrative work and simply being present as they work through the pain are the primary therapeutic interventions. Worden suggested that using evocative language, for instance, "your son died" versus "you lost your son" (2002, p. 68); using symbols such as pictures or letters; writing journals or letters; creating art if it is a comfortable medium; role-playing; using cognitive restructuring; using a memory book or directed imagery; and using metaphors are often useful intervention techniques.

In addition, particularly in helping someone deal with the practical issues, it is also necessary to help families and individuals set very short-term and practical goals, defining the needs of everyone concerned and making sure assistance is available in solving problems and finding practical solutions. It is also of primary importance that people have a plan to take care of their physical, emotional, and spiritual needs so they have the energy to accomplish what they must and, when necessary, take care of those who depend on them.

On the other hand, not all people so neatly go through this process, and it is imperative that families, family support personnel, primary care physicians, and mental health professionals have the ability to assess the process made by someone who is experiencing a loss or traveling through the healing journey. If the grief is significantly affecting a client's, a family's, or a child's ability to function; if the typical symptoms of the Endings are still being experienced after a reasonable amount of time; or if one gets stuck in a single exaggerated emotion, such as depression, anger, or fear, then we are no longer talking about the normal grief process and have to look at some of the possible antecedents or causes for what Worden defined as complicated grief.

The mediators of mourning (Worden, 2002) are those aspects of the loss that can help us determine the extent of the grief, to some extent the length of the process, and the intensity of the grief. Understanding and assessing these mediators can help determine strategies and interventions that are appropriate. These mediators include the following:

1. Who or what is lost? Losing a close friend is usually very different from losing a job.
2. What is the nature of the attachment? For instance, a parent's death is very different from a friend moving away.
3. What is the mode of death or loss? For example, the ambiguous loss of a person missing in action is different from the murder of a close friend or the passing away of an 80-year-old neighbor in his or her sleep.
4. Historical antecedents might include a child who had a fight with the parent the day before the parent was killed or the loss of someone who was in a close, personal, and open relationship.
5. Personality variables might include a survivor who is unexpressive, closed and angry or one who is open, expressive, and thoughtful.
6. What are the social variables—for instance, a suicide, HIV, an abortion, or a military training accident—and what is the acceptability within cultural or religious contexts of the person grieving?
7. Concurrent stresses can include a military move after a divorce or parents being transferred to Germany after their daughter goes off to college.

These mediators are very similar, with a few exceptions, to Dass-Brailsford's (2007) factors that influence the recovery from trauma, which are intensity, chronicity, preexisting conditions, personality and cognitive style of the survivor, the relationship to the victim or the perpetrator, social support, continued exposure, and the possibility of physical injury.

Complicated grief (Worden, 2002) is most often defined as the failure to grieve. In addition to considering the previous mediators of mourning, one or more of the following factors may be present when people are either unable to grieve or have failed to complete their mourning. The first factors to consider are the relational factors, in which old wounds might be reopened, unfinished business is present, or the relationship was of an ambiguous, hostile, or highly dependent nature. The second group includes the circumstantial factors, such as the ambiguous loss of a missing person and the difficulty of multiple losses, from the perspective of both numerous people suffering the loss and one person suffering multiple losses. The third group includes the historical factors, including the unfinished previous losses, particularly those losses suffered early in life, leaving the bereaved with an insecurity in their childhood attachments. The fourth group includes the personality factors, including those personalities that do not tolerate dependency feelings or those that are unable to tolerate extremes of emotional distress. The last group includes the social factors, including those losses that might be culturally unspeakable such as HIV, suicide, or abortion. The presence of any of these factors may be cause for concern and, upon assessment, require more intense or long-term interventions. The choice of interventions would then depend on the underlying concern and may include medication, long-term therapy, hospitalization, or a combination of these.

Neutral Zone: Turbulent Adjustment

Sam Keen (1975) called this time the "empty center" and said that this empty center is the time "between who you were and might yet be ... a vacuum, nothing at all except a chance to begin again" (p. 54). The Neutral Zone begins when people accept that the loss or change has occurred. This in no way suggests that they are happy or glad that they have had to go through the turmoil. The agony, obviously, does not immediately disappear, and the confusion often returns, but slowly people realize there are also times when living in the present seems the right thing to do. One of the misconceptions about grief is a belief that once the intense feelings of the endings subside, then the grief, the transition, is over. What most people don't understand is that following the agony of the Endings, there must be a quiet time, a centering time, a time in which people need to reconstruct their identities, as well as their psyches.

Thomas Moore (2004) said that this part of the journey may "put you in touch with an unfamiliar realm, perhaps a new kind of existence altogether, and it may make you feel you are living in-between two places, the known and the unknown" (p. 39). Those who take the time to become aware of who they are, in their new reality, and make the necessary adjustments in their definition of who they are will be able to finish the journey with a high degree of self-confidence. Those who either skip or are encouraged to bypass this essential part of the journey by moving on too soon may have to return at some point to be prepared for the next loss. The difficulty for most military family members is that they are constantly in multiple transitions;

they are expected to deal with it, and they often simply don't have the time, the necessary resources, or the awareness of the need to plow through this difficult valley. This is also a time that requires a great deal of introspection that may be foreign in the warrior society of stoicism and denial. As with the sustainment stage of the deployment process, this is the time for people to find their own strengths, to grow individually and as a family, and to put in practice those new skills that they discover about themselves.

A major tragedy occurred during a break in the school year while I was a high school counselor in Germany. While on a nonschool, well-planned, and organized nondenominational religious trip to another country, attended by around 50 students, a freak accident occurred and 1 of our students was killed in the presence of 5 or 6 other students. Immediately upon returning to school, the counselors, parents, and chaplains on base spent a considerable amount of time working with those students who seemed to be most at risk. Then a few weeks later, I started hearing concerns from teachers and parents that many of the students who witnessed the tragedy just were not coming around. There were reports of increased absences, a lack of interest in school, and an overall change in behavior and attitude. I knew that those adults who had accompanied the students on this trip had done a terrific job with the students after the accident, and prior to coming home, so I consulted some of them to find that they also had concerns about many of the students.

As there were only 7 or 8 weeks of school left, I was concerned about these students making bad decisions in the midst of their grief that would have long-lasting consequences. So I got those together who I knew were struggling and, with their help, found a few more who were identified by their friends, and we started meeting weekly. Rather than calling this a counseling group, I let them know that I understood this was a difficult time, and if by getting together weekly until the end of school would help them meet their academic goals, we would continue to meet. With little intervention during the first few meetings, I began to steer their interactions toward understanding the process of grief, what it felt like, how important it was to acknowledge and process, and that, over time and with work, the intensity could begin to subside. What I tried mostly to do was help them change the focus of their interactions from reliving the tragic event by describing it over and over to each other in graphic detail, which only continued to retraumatize them, to talking about the impact the experience had on them personally.

As we moved through the weeks, I was also able to explain the Transition Journey as a way of teaching the students that this is what happens to everyone when they experience grief and loss, and it is a normal part of living. As they began to identify each week where they were on a scale of 1 to 10, 1 being as bad as it felt at the time of the tragedy and 10 being a time when they thought their life could go on and not be constantly interrupted with the overwhelming feelings and thoughts related to the tragedy, they began to see a change in themselves and in each other. And although I did not attempt to force them through the process and continued to point out that this would be with them forever, it was what they did with the thoughts and feelings, rather than the thoughts and feelings themselves, that eventually helped them heal.

During the last session before school was out in June, they did an art project on a huge sheet of paper in which they illustrated the Transition Journey with words, symbols, and pictures. It was powerful, not because they had completed the journey but because they could imagine it being possible and could begin to imagine what the end of the journey might feel like. In addition, they had gained some understanding and skills that they could use in future difficult situations.

Focus   The focus or the energy of the Neutral Zone moves from the past to the present, away from what is lost and back to the present and the self. It is during this time that a new kind of grief occurs, the grief over the loss of a part of oneself that no longer exists. If a relationship has ended, the role of girlfriend, boyfriend, or best friend is gone. If a marriage has ended, the role of a wife, friend, or partner no longer exists. For the students I described who lost a friend to a tragic accident, they had to face the loss of their innocence, the loss of the belief that "nothing bad will happen to us," and the loss of the role of being a friend. I remember after I had lost both of my parents that someone called me an "orphan." It seemed so silly to be called an orphan when I was in my 50s, but it did describe that lost sense that I was feeling of not having parents and of no longer being someone's daughter.

This is the time of role loss, even if the transition was the result of a choice, as in the case of a divorce or change of career. Whereas the Endings is a time to focus on the loss, this is the time to begin focusing on the internal change that must occur in oneself, rediscovering what is personally important, discovering our inner strengths, and perhaps re-creating our identity. People in this phase tend to need time alone, but they realize it doesn't necessarily feel lonely, as they had experienced during the Endings. Often people start writing journals, making plans, and wondering what the future will bring. It can be a very productive time of chosen solitude. This is when people begin to find new associations and new relationships, and they begin to be excited about new ideas and the chance to make a commitment to and identification with something new, even though this is somewhat frightening to begin with.

New students to the school, after the first few weeks, began to ask for ways they could get involved in school activities. They began asking about joining the athletic teams or the drama club or writing for the school newspaper. I noticed a change in their language from "this school" to "our school" as they began to feel a sense of belonging with each risk they took in their attempts to get involved or ask for information. One of the unique phenomena that counselors in the Department of Defense system frequently talked about was that it didn't seem to matter when students enrolled in school; they didn't feel like they belonged until school started the following year when they returned with the rest of the students and no longer felt they were the "newby." It is this sense of belonging, of ownership, of risking to be a part of a new reality that means the students were moving through the process.

Tasks   There is a kind of a surrender to this new reality, not in the sense that one is out of control but rather a belief in one's ability to take on the new challenge and the realization that denying the change will only make it worse. In this sense, there is also a need for forgiveness, whether it is forgiving the parents who forced them to move, the military who is always in charge, or God who allowed the tragedy to happen. Joan Borysenko (2003) said, "Forgiveness is not the misguided act of condoning irresponsible hurtful behavior. Nor is it the superficial turning of the other cheek that leaves us feeling victimized and martyred. Rather it is the finishing of old business that allows us to experience the present, free of contamination from the past" (¶ 5).

In addition to the tasks of surrender and forgiveness, there is also a need for self-evaluation and reconnection with our inner self through the grief work one does in the loss of the roles that no longer exist and the beginning of making plans and setting goals for the future. Moore (2004) said that our dark night forces us to consider alternatives and offers us our own approach to life, where we can sit with it and consider who we are and what we want to be. We can be born again not into an ideology but "into yourself, your uniqueness ... the life destined for you" (p. 20). This gives the bereaved the chance to make the necessary external, internal, and spiritual adjustments to the new environment, which is Worden's (2002) third task of mourning. This often misunderstood experience is perhaps the most important, as it is the time when internal adjustments can be made, healthy attitudes can be developed, and new patterns of living can be established that will carry people into the last experience of the journey.

Those people in military families who remain angry, frustrated, and hurt by their experiences and find themselves stuck in the secrecy, stoicism, or denial of the Fortress may find it very difficult to do the work necessary to get through the journey. This time is also one where interventions through individual or group work can be both productive and exciting. While in the midst of her grief after the loss of her military husband, Kate Blaise (2006) wrote, "It was the small, unpredictable moments that got to me the most.... Part of the gift of knowing and loving him was finding the confidence to go on.... He would have demanded that I find the strength and purpose to navigate my new life" (p. 330).

Years before becoming a school counselor, I worked with displaced homemakers who were making major changes in their lives after facing the death of a spouse or loss of a marriage through divorce. These women had given their lives to raising their children and being a spouse, believing that they were doing what was expected of them, only to discover that they would now be required to become a wage earner to protect themselves and, many times, their children. Those women who found the courage to grieve the loss of the role of wife and homemaker, evaluate their beliefs about who they were, and investigate their inherent strengths and interests made amazing progress as they explored returning to school or learning skills to join the labor force, in some cases for the first time in their lives. The same thing happened with the military families who, after struggling through yet another transition, take the time and considerable effort to find the courage to discover new strengths, new interests, and new cultures as they move forward into their next adventure.

Therapeutic Assessment and Support   Although this time of the healing journey often has a happy ending, it takes a lot of courage to risk looking at oneself, forgiving others, and learning new skills to move on. This part of the journey does not feel comfortable but instead a little like shedding old comfortable skin and growing new. Knowing when people are beginning to reach this experience is usually pretty easy; they find themselves bored with feeling bad, wanting something to change, and realizing that they have to move on, but they often just don't know how to change. If people have spent a considerable amount of time in the Endings, counselors may want to nudge them forward and begin to suggest that there are other possibilities. If it appears the client or student is stuck in the anger or depression and appears unwilling to take any steps, we have to reconsider whether this is what we call complicated or uncomplicated grief, and, as stated in the Endings section, more in-depth evaluation and interventions would be necessary.

Sometimes people who get through the first part of the journey only to arrive in a place of what feels like nothingness start believing they need therapy. Everyone knows that the first few months after a loss is full of tears, uncertainty, and confusion, but most don't understand that there is a time of fallowness that follows. For mental health professionals, chaplains, school counselors, or others attempting to assist someone through this time, focusing on small growth steps and on self-awareness is the key.

Coming from a cognitive-behavior, narrative, solution-focused, or Adlerian approach where the focus is on building strengths, identifying new ways of being, and moving forward seem to work the best. Sometimes all people need is a little encouragement to take things one step at a time and not get discouraged when things don't happen immediately. Those people who work in the addiction field will recognize that this is the time that relapse often happens, because to many former users the world begins to seem terribly boring. One young man in his early 30s, after being clean and sober for about 8 months and finally holding down a job for the first time in years, asked, "Is this all there is? You just go to work every morning and come home every evening; surely there is more to life than this?" Without new associates and someone to help him evaluate who he was and where he wanted to go, this man was ripe for a relapse. The same thing happens with military families when they get through the chaos of the Endings only to find that the new environment looks frightening or boring. They might need the military support people, the school counselor, or a civilian counselor to help them reevaluate who they are and what they want to accomplish in this new environment and help them make the plans to meet those goals.

New Beginnings: Rebuilding

As the crisis ends, I emerge into a new world of possibility and action. Time is a gift, no longer something to resent, or grasp, or dread. I remember the past with gratitude because it brought me to this moment. I look to the future with excitement because it allows me an open space in which I am free to become. I take pleasure in the present moment because it is the meeting point of all that has been and might yet be. Healing restores memory, hope, and the capacity for joy. (Keen, 1975, p. 123)

Although the future may be still unknown, most people get to a point where they begin to find the courage to give it a try, even if the steps are small and the movement is slight. The pain may still be just under the surface, and memories of the past may still fill us with agony, but the agony and the pain seem less intense and less frequent. Laughter occurs, and it feels good; making plans and carrying them out may cause people to remember that only a few weeks or months in the past they couldn't have accomplished that. Those who risk taking baby steps and who make short-term decisions to see how they work eventually find themselves right with the world again. Those who hang on to a lot of anger and try to push forward without doing the necessary work find themselves constantly resenting their new life.

One of the new understandings of grief outlined earlier by Doka (2005) challenges the old notion of grief work of detaching from the past and reinvesting in the present and future. There seems to be a need instead for the bereaved to often maintain some kind of contact with that which was lost, as long as this process does not delay their ability to function. Worden's (2002) fourth task of mourning is to relocate and memorialize the loved one; this change in perspective is often much more comforting for the bereaved than the often expressed comment to "get over it and move on." Finding ways for mourners to remain connected in a way that does not preclude them from going on in life is a significant goal. With the advent of e-mail and the Internet, this is becoming increasingly more possible, as military, students, and families can stay in contact with their extended family and former friends even though they physically move.

Focus   The focus of the New Beginnings turns to the future, where some of the planning and setting goals during the Neutral Zone turn into action. A sure sign that someone has moved into the New Beginnings is when they start reaching out and taking responsibility for this new life. Maybe they reach out to a new person, maybe they search out a support group, perhaps a student asks to join a club, or maybe they just risk talking to a stranger in class. Events start looking fun, or at least tolerable.

When people find themselves in this last experience of the journey, their focus also often turns to the community. People who have gone through major life transitions or traumas often decide to find ways to help others who have gone through similar experiences. This attempt to help others is actually part of the healing; one pastor called it a time of being a "stretcher bearer." The people who began Mothers Against Drunk Driving, America's Most Wanted, Divorce Recovery, and many other important programs came through this process, and part of their healing was to help others. As a former member of a dual military marriage, Blaise (2006) decided to write the story of her marriage, only because she believed that her husband, who died in Iraq the day before he was to return to the United States, would have said, "This is your chance to share a story that many soldiers in your combat boots will never get a chance to tell.... This story is for all of the spouses, parents, and children who have a million tales about the loved ones who sacrificed so much for this country, tales that will never be heard" (p. 336).

Tasks The tasks during the New Beginnings perhaps seem obvious; the first is a willingness to risk taking action to reach some of the goals established during the Neutral Zone. In a way it is also a willingness to stop making preparations and to start acting. Obviously the risks they take need to be appropriate and healthy, otherwise they have probably not reached the New Beginnings. The second task is an interest in making an investment in others, in the new surroundings, or in the community. This may simply start with people becoming connected with the community by joining a new church, getting involved in community events, or meeting new people. The last task, but probably the most important, is that people need to be able to make some kind of meaning out of the experience they have just gone through.

Is it possible to ever accept a major loss or an early trauma in one's life, such as losing a close friend, moving 10 times in 12 years, or having a spouse deployed two or three times in a period of 5 years? Most people, if they have the support and encouragement to do so, will not forget these losses but find meaning and growth that gives them the courage to face a new world. Perhaps they gained skills they never thought they could, or they find themselves helping others who may need their support, or they are stronger than they ever thought possible, or their spiritual life has been deepened. Whatever it is, helping people with this last task of finding meaning can become a spiritual journey as long as the time is right and the assistance is within the cultural context that makes sense for them. Thomas Moore (2004) wrote that the "dark night of the soul is dark because it doesn't give us any assurance that what is happening makes sense and will ultimately be beneficial" (p. 28). He said that we can find meaning in these times but only if we are willing to think differently about our lives by being less psychological and more philosophical and spiritual.

Therapeutic Assessment and Support We may not find too many people coming to counseling once they reach this part of the journey. Sometimes, however, we may be asked to provide the resources and support for those who have come through a tragedy and are interested in both continuing their healing and assisting in the healing of others. Sometimes people just need a chance to talk through the experience so it makes more sense and to have someone encourage them to move on during the hard days. Telling one's story and having someone validate that experience is extremely therapeutic. When people reach this point, our best approach is to be encouraging, to listen, and to help them create meaning out of their experience.

There may, however, be times when people make changes in their lives only to be confronted by friends and family who are not supportive of the choices and decisions they have made in this journey. Thomas Moore (2004) warned that when people go through a rite of passage, their family and friends have to adjust also. People may need assistance in knowing how to address those who see their adjustment as negative. For example, families who witness a daughter marrying into the military culture or the extended family who has to adjust to grandchildren moving a great distance away as a result of a remarriage may not react in the way that the new couple hoped. This is an important step in the process of transformation, but it may be an uncomfortable step when one expects the support and encouragement of family and friends. These are the times when a systems approach, perhaps even working with the extended family, can help someone find this final experience of the journey a positive one.

So the journey ends, but not without an additional word of caution: no one experiences this journey in just this way. We are not linear creatures; our emotions and thoughts are not always rational, and most people will go back and forth throughout the journey to reexperience the Endings for a while, then find themselves working in the Neutral Zone, and eventually see that more and more of their days are spent in the New Beginnings. In an attempt to get away from the "stage" concept, we need to see this framework as experiences and tasks to be lived and accomplished rather than as a systematic, linear, or rigid pattern. It can be a teaching and counseling tool that is descriptive, not proscriptive. Additional trauma, change, and loss will exacerbate the journey and make it that much more difficult. As the mediators of mourning tell us, numerous losses or losses that cause us to go back and complete unfinished losses grief will demand more time and more intervention.

Children and Grief

So much of our work with military families includes working with children within the context of either family counseling or the schools, so we have to acknowledge that children may need our support in different ways. Our interventions (National Association of School Psychologists [NASP], 2001) must be geared not only to the cultural diversity of the people we work with but also to the students' developmental level and capacity to understand the facts. Children will be aware of the reactions of adults and will often interpret and react to those reactions themselves. The range of reactions may include everything from emotional shock to an apparent lack of feelings. Behavior may become regressive or immature or very overt and belligerent; emotions may be explosive or withdrawn. Particularly young children will often ask the same questions over and over, obviously needing to hear the answers enough to make some sense out of them.

We can help children cope by allowing them to be the teachers about their grief experiences, letting them know that we want to understand what they are feeling and what they need, giving them the time and encouragement to sort out their feelings, and not assuming every child of a certain age group understands loss in the same way or with the same feelings as others. After one of the tragic deaths occurred during the 3 years I worked as a counselor in a civilian high school, we had grief groups going on for numerous days until I walked into a room with a group of boys, and one of them said, "Oh, no; we don't want to talk about feelings anymore." Understanding that grieving is a process, as outlined previously, instead of an event means that the grief may come back again for a considerable period of time in the child's life, and pressing children to resume normal activities without a chance to deal with pain may prompt more problems.

As adults, we need to be honest and not tell half-truths to help children, regardless of age, understand loss and death. We also need to understand that grief is complicated, sometimes because of a felt need for vengeance or justice and sometimes as a result of the lack of resolution or control one has in any given transition. A powerful line spoken in a recent movie is "Vengeance is a lazy form of grief." I am convinced that when vengeance or revenge is apparent, we still have grief work to do! I mentioned earlier my frustration with not having a required grief and loss class in the master's-level counselor education program, and I am also bewildered about why we don't teach children, as part of the required elementary school curriculum, about the experience of grief and loss, which will be perhaps the most consistent experience they will encounter in life.

As with all kinds of work with children, what we do must depend on their developmental level, cognitive skills, personality characteristics, religious or spiritual beliefs, and teachings by parents and significant others (NASP, 2001). Often infants and toddlers will perceive that adults are sad, but they have no real understanding of the meaning or significance of the loss. Preschoolers may deny the loss and see it as reversible, interpreting it instead as temporary separation or linking it with magical thinking. Early elementary students can start to comprehend the finality of death or a loss and may understand that certain circumstances cause death or loss, but they may overgeneralize or believe that it happens to others, not to them.

Middle school students have the cognitive understanding to comprehend that death is final and loss may be permanent, but they may not fully grasp other abstract concepts discussed by adults. They often experience a variety of feelings, and their expressions of grief may result in acting out or self-injurious behaviors as a means of coping with anger, vengeance, and despair. High school students can fully grasp the meaning of loss and will usually seek out either friends and, hopefully, family for comfort, or they may withdraw to deal with grief. Teens with a history of depression, suicidal behavior, and chemical dependency are at particular risk for prolonged and complicated grief reactions.

These are just a few thoughts and indicators of what children may experience, depending on their developmental levels. A very impressive Web site from the National Institute for Trauma and Loss in Children is a good place to begin to learn more about the impact and process of children's grief (http://www.tlcinst.org). There is much to learn in working with children, particularly about the appropriate interventions at each level. I hope anyone whose primary responsibility is with children will spend considerable time and energy learning about and being trained to work in appropriate settings with both the children and the family members who have experienced a loss.

CHAPTER 9

Effective Interventions

A Military OneSource article (*Choosing a Counselor or Therapist,* n.d.) helps military families find a counselor. In describing counseling, the article stated that counseling, therapy, and psychotherapy are often used to describe a process that usually involves a series of discussions with a trained professional who can help people identify their feelings or problems, talk about them, and find ways to cope with them or solve them. "During the counseling process, you may discover patterns of thinking and behaving that you want to keep or change. You are really retaining the time and expertise of a specialist who can help you understand more about who you are and how you can make changes in yourself or your life" (¶ 2).

Regardless what we call our work, civilian counselors are needed to work with military families; the Military OneSource article encourages families to engage in the process of counseling to accomplish all of the mentioned possibilities. In the first chapter of the book, I discussed the need to be a culturally competent counselor and addressed the first two competencies of understanding our own behavior, values, and biases and understanding the worldview of the populations we work with. It is in this chapter that we will address the third competency of developing and practicing appropriate, relevant, and sensitive strategies for working with this population. Although military families are now making the news regularly, there is little written regarding the forms of therapy that are the most effective when working with military families. In reviewing a half dozen currently popular marriage and family textbooks, I found one that included two pages about military families and one that included one paragraph. None of the others mentioned the military.

The following is a summary of the literature, as well as interviews I have conducted, that point to the most common approaches used, with, I hope, some insight as to why they are or could be effective. I have not attempted to address whether these different approaches would best be carried out through individual or group counseling, as I believe that is beyond the scope of this book. For experienced therapists this decision would be made based on experience, circumstances, and obviously the best interest of individual clients and families.

A therapist near a major Army base in Arizona shared that through counseling, one Vietnam veteran began to see that the only way he could heal and the only way his spouse could really understand him was to tell her what went on in his head, but "the last thing he wanted was for her to know what went on in his head." Sometimes the actual process of counseling becomes the therapeutic intervention, in and of itself, because family members learn to talk to each other and find new ways of coping. Of course, as with all therapy, it is often the therapeutic alliance that becomes the most powerful part of any intervention. This chapter is an attempt not to explain a specific theory or approach that works for all military families but rather to share a number of approaches that seem to be the most commonly used by therapists currently working with military families. I have also included hints and suggestions on ways to work with significant issues found while working with different subgroups of military families, including the concerns faced by the family following deployment, the unique concerns of stepfamilies, the issues found when working with post-traumatic stress disorder (PTSD) survivors and their families, and perspectives on working with military men.

I hope that with the knowledge and information gained from the previous chapters, experienced civilian therapists can find ways to effectively work with military families, using their own theoretical orientation and years of experience. It is often important to bring a psychoeducational dimension to working with military families, and the materials and information included in previous chapters will benefit both the counselor and the client while working in either a school or a mental health setting.

The majority of therapists interviewed for this book believe they were most successful when they came from a strength-based approach in which they were able, early in therapy, to engage the parents, family, or couple in finding solutions that made sense, to help empower each member of the family, and to use goal-oriented techniques so therapy would be a reasonably short process. Obviously there will be issues, concerns, and circumstances that arise when following these guidelines is not possible, and more long-term interventions, possibly even hospitalization or medication therapy, must be considered. These more in-depth and long-term interventions and treatments have not been the focus of my work, however.

Cognitive-Behavior Therapy

Throughout the literature, the most consistent approach to therapy when working with the military is some variation of cognitive-behavior therapy (CBT). Virtually all of the therapists interviewed for this book used either a cognitive approach or a cognitive-behavioral approach, even though at times it was used in conjunction with other approaches or techniques. A therapist in Tucson, Arizona, usually comes from a solution-oriented approach that is cognitively based, because the majority of his military clients are what he called "thinkers" rather than "feelers." At the same time, this therapist also encourages and finds many military service members open to more existential questions about life, about what is meaningful in their world, and about their personal mission, beliefs, and values as they confront the reality of living in the military world.

Another therapist who works from a CBT perspective also shared that helping her clients become aware of their spiritual or religious background was important, as this greatly influences much of their thinking and attitudes as well as their possible adjustment to the possibility of military combat stress. Figley and Nash (2007) said, "The experience of veterans of prior wars indicates that war-zone trauma frequently impacts the spirituality of survivors" (p. 7), so using spirituality as a healing resource is important for a full recovery. A therapist in San Diego, who starts from a CBT or solution-focused perspective, finds that adding narrative techniques can also be effective, as many couples and service members gain insight from reflecting on who they are and their unique stories that brought them to where they are in life.

Although the most well-researched therapy, particularly for trauma victims, is CBT (Dass-Brailsford, 2007), consideration must always also include the clients' cultural and social background. It is important to remember that trauma work may come well into the therapeutic process, as this material may not surface until considerable work is done and a very trusting relationship is built. In CBT both cognitive and behavioral approaches are combined, so clients learn how to weaken the connection between thoughts and their habitual reactions to them and how their thinking patterns cause difficulties by giving them distorted mental images leading to anxious, depressed, or angry feelings. Dass-Brailsford (2007) outlined a number of useful CBT approaches, especially when treating trauma, including exposure therapy, systematic desensitization, anxiety management, relaxation techniques, and stress inoculation therapy.

Fenell and Fenell (2003) suggested the use of rational emotive behavior therapy (REBT) when working with individual service members, as clients can recognize the activating event that may be creating the problem, acknowledge their self-defeating beliefs about that event, recognize the consequences of those beliefs, and, finally, learn how to dispute the self-defeating beliefs while observing the effects of replacing the beliefs with more rational ones. Some of the more common thinking mistakes are black-and-white thinking, "yes, but" thinking, mind reading, telling the future, emotional reasoning, labeling, "should" statements, overgeneralizing, and catastrophizing. Watching for these irrational beliefs can be helpful in assessing whether the use of REBT would be an effective intervention strategy.

Even in schools I found that students were open to learning and understanding REBT. Jonathan was upset about moving to a new school at the end of his junior year, and he continued to tell himself that his parents weren't considering what was important to him and were not concerned about his wish to play college basketball. The new school was much smaller, and he would be far less likely to get the exposure and develop the kinds of skills needed to be recruited. He began slacking off in school, because he decided it wasn't worth even considering college if he couldn't play ball. Through the use of REBT, Jonathan began to understand that he was defeating himself through his beliefs and actions rather than getting back at his parents, who had little control over which school he could attend during their military relocations. The intervention also included the necessary grief work (see chapter 8) regarding his losses, his ability to forgive, and a realization that his need for vengeance doesn't do harm to anyone but himself.

Solution-Focused Brief Therapy

Solution-focused brief therapy (SFBT) is also one of the most used therapies for many counselors working with military families, and it is particularly useful when working in the school setting. Sklare (2005) gave results of research done by a number of authors that show that as many as 78% of children 12 years old and younger and 89% of children between the ages of 13 and 18 made progress toward their goals in counseling after 7 to 9 months of using SFBT. He stated that this "model of counseling … can have tremendous impact in school settings" (p. 4), and it certainly has been found to be effective with adults as well. The basic assumptions (Sklare, 2005) of SFBT are as follows:

1. If we concentrate on successes, changes can take place, so the focus should be on what is right and working rather than on what is wrong and troublesome.
2. Every problem has identifiable exceptions that can be transformed into solutions, so it is important for counselors to listen for hints as to when, where, and how exceptions occur to help clients develop solutions.
3. Small changes have a ripple effect, and as clients begin to adjust to a minor change, the chain reaction expands into major changes.
4. All clients have what it takes to resolve their difficulties, so focusing on the clients' expertise and strengths rather than on deficits is important.
5. The clients' goals are seen as positive, pointing toward what the clients want to do, rather than as negative or reflecting on the absence of something.

In addition to these assumptions, a few additional concepts important for the therapists to practice are (a) avoiding problem analysis; (b) being efficient with interventions; (c) focusing on the present and future; and (d) focusing on actions rather than on insights (Sklare, 2005). By removing the need for in-depth exploration of the antecedents of the clients' problems and taking the investigation of the causes and origins of problems out of the process, therapists can dramatically shorten the time needed for counseling. Simply because the focus is on solutions, counseling becomes brief, and actions become of primary importance. Both of these reasons are why this model works well both in schools and with military families who may have a very limited number of counseling sessions available and also have a need to make changes quickly, as the changes in their lives occur so frequently.

I had many occasions to work from a SFBT perspective as a school counselor with parents who were concerned about troubling behavior of their children. Although we were not in a therapeutic setting where we could do long-term counseling, the parents and children were very open to focusing on possible solutions and short-term interventions. Often these simply included finding more time for the family to spend together or learning either new parenting skills or new communication skills so the students felt more acknowledged and cared for. As both parents and their children made small changes, they realized these changes had a major impact on their relationship.

Darren, a 10th-grade boy in my high school in Germany, began having problems in school, and teachers were reporting a major mood change. Upon consulting with Darren's parents, I learned that they were considering getting divorced, and because that wouldn't happen while they were stationed in Germany, they were basically just avoiding each other at home. In essence they had become, although perhaps only temporarily, a parent-focused family. What they had not done was discuss any of this with their son, and as negative school reports started to arrive home, they were taking their frustration and anger out on Darren. Simply helping the parents understand that they needed to keep the anger and frustration they were feeling toward each other separate from their relationship with their son and that Darren still needed their support and time, the family was able to find stability that allowed Darren to focus on school. Although we did not solve the parents' problems, we were able to come to a few solutions, in only a few meetings, that allowed Darren to return to being successful in school.

The characteristics of a solution-focused approach make it "an ideal counseling approach with diverse populations" (Sklare, 2005, p. 8), as the sessions focus on the clients' experiences within their own frames of reference. In addition, solution-focused counseling "uses the clients' terms and phrases rather than the counselor's, recognizes that clients are the best experts on themselves, and focuses on strengths rather than weaknesses" (p. 8). This is particularly important when working within the military culture, because therapists must help military families find solutions that work within the military context.

Sherman, Zanotti, and Jones (2005) stated that brief psychotherapy that focuses on the emotional conflicts caused by traumatic events can be very healing. By retelling the traumatic event to a calm, empathic, compassionate, and nonjudgmental therapist, the survivor achieves a greater sense of self-esteem and can develop ways of thinking about, coping with, and dealing more successfully with intense emotions.

A husband and wife were seen in counseling after he returned from combat, because he had completely withdrawn from his wife. His perspective was that he did not want to alarm her with the images in his mind, and her perspective was that he had stopped caring for her because he didn't want to be with her. As he told his stories in counseling, she could see how difficult it was for him to be with her but not tell her about what was going on in his mind. The therapist asked them to schedule 2 hours a week in a safe, comfortable place for him to share his stories and helped her learn the best way of responding to the stories. In a short time they could see the value of his sharing, and the connection between the two was reaffirmed. This was not someone whom we would diagnose with full-blown PTSD but someone who needed the compassion and understanding of a caring person and a short intervention to help the couple get back on track.

Obviously there is not enough material presented here for a therapist to begin using SFBT without more training. The work of Berg and Steiner (2003), deShazer (1985), Sklare (2005), and others should be used to learn more about the approach and gain skills necessary to work from a SFBT perspective, either in family counseling or in a school setting.

Family Systems Therapy

Wakefield (2007) wrote, "The responsibility of the profession is to address things systemically and recognize the family and community dynamics of military service" (p. 23). She believes that it is not unpatriotic to acknowledge and "understand the depth of trauma to soldiers, their children and their loved ones. It's neglectful not to" (p. 23). Many therapists interviewed for this book mentioned that having a systems approach was effective, and they referred to work by Jay Framo and John Gottman when working with couples and families. Having parents do their family-of-origin work from a systems perspective incorporates some of the cognitive-behavioral approaches with understanding the influence of their childhood, as well as their reasons for joining and their commitment to the military. However, because of the emphasis in the military on personal accountability, a systemic family-based approach may meet with initial resistance (Fenell & Fenell, 2003). "The counselor should be prepared for this response and begin to introduce the systemic paradigm that identifies dysfunctional relationship patterns as the focus of the problem rather than dysfunctional individuals" (p. 11).

Ridenour (1984) wrote that when mental health professionals first see families in the military setting, the families are often in conflict with the military or with each other over a matter related to the demands of military life. "Couples in the service may use the military as the third party in their dealing with one another. ... Therapists dealing with these families in such times of upheaval must not allow themselves to become allied with such maneuvers" (p. 5). Alfred Adler was probably the first systems theorist, even though he didn't use those words. Most theorists and practitioners who come from a systemic, developmental, and strength-based approach usually have some grounding in Adlerian psychology, so "it is not surprising to find the Adlerian model very much compatible with most currently popular systems-based models of marriage and family therapy" (Nicoll, 1989, p. 5). The Adlerian model focuses on the healthy development of the family, including parent education programs. The work by McKay and Maybell (2004), discussed in chapter 5, that helps parents learn new parenting styles and understand the democratic world children live in is an important source of information when working from a systemic base with military families.

The assumptions of the systems orientation (Nicoll, 1989) are based on seven major principles, including (a) circular causality, in which behavior is understood to be circular in nature instead of existing in a linear, unidirectional manner; (b) nonsummativity, in which the family is viewed as a whole that is greater than the sum of its parts, which was Adler's reason for calling his theory individual, or indivisible, psychology; (c) equi-finality, which is the idea that the meaning one attaches to events is far more important than the event itself, or seeing the world from a phenomenological approach; (d) communication, which is seen as the foundation of all behavior, and all behavior is understood in terms of its purposive and interpersonal context, or social interest; and (e) family and marital rules, which are a series of repetitive patterns based on explicit and implicit assumptions, or what Adlerians might also call a cognitive framework that creates each person's lifestyle. Two additional principles from a basic systems model are homeostasis, or the ways in which the family maintains stability within the system, and morphogenesis, which are the mechanisms that enable changes to occur when needed within the system (Nicoll, 1989).

Ridenour (1984) wrote that family systems theory and therapy as a "conceptual system and therapeutic methodology has a great deal to contribute in enabling helping professionals, especially mental health professionals, to understand and intervene more effectively in treating military personnel and their families" (p. 3). A therapist shared a story of working with a military officer and his daughter. The dad was furious with the acting-out behavior of his daughter and declared in the first session, "If she doesn't stop screwing around with older men, she'll end up. ..." One can readily imagine the rest of the sentence. Through the course of family counseling, it became clear that the acting-out behavior was the daughter's way of reaching her goal of getting her father's attention, and the repetitive patterns of his finding fault was his way of trying to force her to change and follow the family rules. Although this interactive communication pattern was driving them farther apart, it wasn't until the therapist took the time to teach the dad how to use "I" messages and he could see the negative consequences of his actions that he was willing to change. He had, of course, assumed that it was the daughter who would have to change. When he was asked to share his fears and concerns for his daughter in a new way, the large gruff military dad was able to say, "When you date older men, like the guy you saw last week, who is 27, I feel sad, lonely, afraid. ... Like you are going to leave me like your mother did." What a difference for this 16-year-old to hear the fears of her father rather than the condemnation of her actions. What became clear to him was that he was attempting to treat his daughter in ways that might be appropriate when he was addressing his command but were inappropriate when speaking to his daughter.

Keith and Whitaker (1984) pointed out that one of the discouraging ways military men reduce family tension is by leaving the family circle, and the military father can, all too easily and even in therapy, become a scapegoat, so it is frequently the mother who expresses the symptoms for the family. As the bond of the military takes precedence over the bonds of the family, it is essential to work with the whole system to eliminate some of these inherent tendencies. They stated, "The gulf that develops between the military man and his children is one of the most hopeless troubles in family therapy" (p. 151). Early in therapy the rank structure must be clarified and an agreement made that in the family both parents have equal rank. The manner in which the military member is handled early is often critical, and if the service member feels ignored, little work can be accomplished.

Often using metaphors of the military is valuable, and Carl Whitaker, as he was so well-known to have done, gave examples of using metaphors, such as asking a parentified child, "Did your mother court martial your father when he was gone and then promote [you] to General?" (Keith & Whitaker, 1984, p. 161). The authors also cautioned, "With rigid families the amount of intimacy possible correlates with what the most paranoid member can tolerate. The military is the paranoid edge of the culture ... [and] the paranoid component is difficult to disrupt because ... it is validated by his profession" (p. 150). Family therapy can, however, help the military service member discriminate between the military reality outside the home and the family reality inside the home.

Many of the factors that Donaldson-Pressman and Pressman (1994) looked for in their work with families that I defined as parent-focused families (see chapter 3) may also be important to watch for when working with highly traditional military families, including the need to do the following:

1. Watch for indirect communication in the family, in which the expression of feelings and concerns may be denied or not expressed in a timely or appropriate manner.
2. Watch for triangularization that often happens when the military parent is out of the picture and the other parent tends to confide in the children about inappropriate or more adults issues, building a coalition that will be either in the way or resented when the military parent returns.
3. Pay attention to parent inaccessibility, which often is part of the structure of the military family but may also include emotional

inaccessibility, as the parent who is left to run the household may be inaccessible because of the stress level or duties that are being required.

4. Watch for unclear boundaries between the subsystems, where the children may feel entitled to certain privileges when the military parent is gone but not when he or she returns; the children are parentified by the responsibilities they are expected to carry out, or the children have no right to privacy, as the parents feel it is their right to intrude into the children's private space, possessions, or thoughts to maintain a certain family image.

5. Watch for children who believe that love and affection are like moving targets because their relationship with their at-home parent totally changes when the military parent returns.

6. Watch for children who seem to have few ego boundaries, perhaps resulting from a belief that they do not have the right to express their feelings or ask for their needs to be met.

7. Watch for children who are hypervigilant and appear to be good at mind reading, as they feel a need to always be prepared for disaster or be ready to meet someone else's needs, only to discover that it almost never works.

Limitations of a Systems Approach

Even though one of the techniques common in a systems approach is to meet with the families of origin, this is often impossible when working with military families. Other issues that may be unique to military families are rigid time limitations due to work, training requirements, or impending moves; the short time frame in which the family is available; and the pervading sense of fear over what impact going to therapy may have on the service member's career (Ridenour, 1984). Civilian therapists must understand and respect the value of the military system, so that the family is not inadvertently triangulated against the military. The goals of family therapy should be to help the family's organization be more powerful and to develop boundaries between the rigid outside world and the interior world of the family, "where joy and human warmth can be part of living in any world" (Keith & Whitaker, 1984, p. 166).

The reality of the military world is that it is a balancing act between duty and family and that there will be times when duty requirements take priority, but it is possible to help families find that balance by learning to use time wisely, enhancing family resiliency, and sustaining personal and family networks (Martin & McClure, 2000). Family therapy is a valuable method of working with military personnel as long as we understand that it may be "more feeble than usual because of the power the military system has over its members [and because] the military family is separated from its family of origin" (Keith & Whitaker, 1984, p. 165).

Family Assessment

An important aspect of working with families is the understanding that often the crises that bring families to counseling are somehow related to marker events or transitional periods within a family's normal life cycle. Often these transitional periods, when combined with the normal events or transitions of military life, can lead to what looks like and feels like crisis. It is important for the therapist to focus the attention of the family "upon itself and its part in the unfolding drama and to facilitate [the family's] developing strategies for easing these passages and making them worthwhile individuation growth experiences" (Ridenour, 1984, p. 5). Some questions Ridenour suggested that we ask in the assessment phase of counseling include the following:

1. Where is the family in terms of its own stages of development?
2. Where is each member in his or her own individuation?
3. Where is the family in terms of its relationship with the military?
4. What style has it developed to deal with periodic separation and reunion phenomenon?
5. Is there any impact on the family caused by its particular branch of the military?
6. Does the changing role of women have any effect on the family's current situation, such as spouse employment concerns?
7. Is the family's current crisis being influenced by the service member's rank?
8. What is the family's concept of how the military sees that family?

Ridenour also suggested that we pay attention to factors that may have an impact on the crisis, including cultural, ethnic, or racial backgrounds; the presence of adopted or foster children (and I would add stepchildren); the issue of spouse or child abuse; the presence of alcoholism or drug use; and any significant physical or mental illness or financial difficulties.

Another form of family assessment is through the use of a genogram. Families may discover that patterns they are experienced and attributing to living in the military culture may, in fact, have been present in earlier generations and not a factor of military living at all. Obviously the ability to shift the blame away from the military structure may help in resolving issues that may be more family-of-origin or generational issues. In addition, the use of the Isolation Matrix (O'Beirne, 1983), discussed in chapter 3, can assist counselors in assessing families regarding the impact of isolation on their life and how they might begin to involve these external systems to contribute to their well-being.

Addressing PTSD in Family Therapy

PTSD and the Family

The National Center for PTSD Web site (http://www.ncptsd.va.gov) is an exceptionally valuable resource for understanding, assessing, and treating PTSD. "Trauma survivors with PTSD often experience problems in their intimate and family relationships or close friends. PTSD involves symptoms that interfere with trust, emotional closeness, communication, responsible assertiveness, and effective problem solving" (NCPTSD, n.d.-a, ¶ 1). Survivors often experience a loss of interest in social or sexual activities, feeling an emotional distance from others, as well as a sense of emotional numbness. Their partners, friends, or family members often feel hurt, alienated, or discouraged because the survivor has not overcome the effects of the trauma, and they eventually become angry or distant. There is usually a feeling of being irritable, on guard, easily startled, worried, or anxious, which will naturally lead the survivors to be unable to relax, socialize, or be intimate. Significant others then begin to feel pressured, tense, and controlled. Difficulty falling or staying asleep and having severe nightmares may prevent both the survivor and his or her partner from sleeping restfully. The trauma memories, trauma reminders, or flashbacks and the ways in which the survivor attempts to avoid such memories or reminders can make living with a survivor "feel like living in a war zone or like living with the constant threat of vague but terrible danger" (NCPTSD, n.d.-a, ¶ 7).

Living with an individual who has PTSD does not automatically cause PTSD, but it can produce vicarious or secondary traumatization, which is similar to having PTSD. Because the trauma memories, the attempts at avoiding the trauma reminders, and the struggles with fear and anger greatly interfere with a survivor's ability to concentrate, listen carefully, or make cooperative decisions, problems often go unresolved for long periods of time. Survivors of childhood sexual and physical abuse and survivors of rape, domestic violence, combat, terrorism, genocide, torture, kidnapping, and being a prisoner of war often report a lasting sense of terror, vulnerability, and betrayal when they begin to feel close or start to trust.

Becoming emotionally or sexually intimate may bring back feeling of letting down their guard, which can be perceived as dangerous. Sometimes survivors avoid closeness by expressing criticism toward or dissatisfaction with loved ones and friends, leading to intimate relationships that actually have episodes of verbal or physical violence. In addition, alcohol and drugs are often used in an attempt to cope with PTSD and obviously can destroy intimacy and friendships. In other cases, survivors may be overly dependent on or overprotective of their partners, family members, friends, or support persons (NCPTSD, n.d.-a).

In the first weeks or months after a traumatic event, survivors often feel an unexpected sense of anger, detachment, or anxiety in their intimate, family, and friend relationships. Although most are able to resume their prior level of intimacy and involvement in relationships, it has been found that up to 10% will develop PTSD with lasting problems in their relationships. Often it is only through therapy in a safe and caring environment that people with PTSD can learn to create and maintain successful intimate relationships, by establishing a personal support network to help them cope and rebuild relationships. By learning how to share feelings honestly and openly with an attitude of respect and compassion, by continually strengthening cooperative problem-solving and communication skills, and by including playfulness, spontaneity, relaxation, and mutual enjoyment in their relationships, clients can return to their former level of productivity.

As noted in chapter 7, I did not attempt in this book to write extensively about the issues, assessment, or treatment of PTSD. I did, however, devote a short section in this chapter to possible interventions for PTSD, including a section on working with PTSD from a systems or couples approach and a section on working with PTSD from a cognitive-behavioral perspective. As I noted earlier, it is extremely important that therapists have specific training in working with trauma and PTSD survivors.

Using a Systems Approach With PTSD

The NCPTSD fact sheet titled *PTSD and Relationships* (n.d.-a) points out that intimate, family, and friend relationships are extremely beneficial to the survivors of PTSD, as these provide (a) companionship and a sense of belonging that can act as an antidote to isolation; (b) a growing level of self-esteem that can help overcome depression and guilt; (c) opportunities to make positive contributions to others that can reduce feelings of failure or alienation; and (d) practical and emotional support when coping with life stressors. Survivors of PTSD find a number of different professional treatments helpful for dealing with relationship issues, including individual and group psychotherapy, anger and stress management, assertiveness training, couples communication classes, family education classes, and family therapy.

Families have long been known to be affected by the physical and emotional stress of war, and for services to be effective, they must be "built on a solid understanding of 21st century warfare, warrior culture, and stress injury science" (Figley & Nash, 2007, p. 2). Including the partner in working with PTSD survivors is essential to treatment, as this is the only framework available to conceptualize both the relationship issues and the potential treatment plans (Sherman et al., 2005). Couples therapy can be either a powerful adjunct or the primary treatment modality. "In contrast to its state after previous wars, the field of psychology is now better prepared to treat individuals dealing with the aftermath of trauma, including PTSD. ... Common sense and clinical intuition tell us that families are dramatically affected and are instrumental in the veterans' recovery" (Sherman et al., 2005, p. 626).

Well-designed couples therapy has the potential to help veterans cope more effectively with trauma related distress, to assist partners in understanding and empathizing the confusing behavior, and to strengthen intimate relationships. Although marital therapies focusing on communication and problem-solving skills have been developed as adjunctive treatments for PTSD, a systemic examination of their efficacy is generally lacking, and few families receive such services, at least partially because of the fact that marriage or couples counseling is often not available on military installations and is not covered through TRICARE (Department of Defense Task Force on Mental Health, 2007b). Given the large number of service members currently returning from Iraq and Afghanistan who are dealing with PTSD, additional and immediate attention to effective treatment modalities is critical (Sherman et al., 2005).

Research Findings

Research has clearly documented the adverse effects of PTSD on intimate relationships. Combat veterans experience a high rate of marital instability, and veterans with PTSD and their spouses describe their marital problems in more severe terms than do veterans without PTSD. Furthermore, Vietnam veterans with PTSD are twice as likely as those without PTSD to have been divorced and three times as likely to experience multiple divorces. Female partners of patients with PTSD are often unhappy and quite distressed with their relationships and report lower overall satisfaction, more caregiver burden, and poorer psychological adjustment. "Over three quarters of partners ... rate getting couples or family therapy as very important in coping with the stress of PTSD in the family" (Sherman et al., 2005, p. 627). In their recent book *Combat Stress Injury,* Figley and Nash (2007) shared the results of a study that concludes "a husband's impairment and a wife's sense of burden predicted both of the latter's emotional distress and the overall marital adjustment" (p. 5).

Sherman et al. (2005) pointed out that two findings in research highlight the need to intervene to help partners manage their stress level and experience greater relationship satisfaction. The first is that high levels of expressed emotion in the family has been shown to impede improvement in PTSD clients, and the second is that family members who are hurt by the veteran's behavior are often reticent to provide the necessary support during treatment and recovery. High levels of support have been associated with decreased intensity of PTSD symptoms, and increased social withdrawal has been associated with PTSD intensity. "In addition to withdrawing support, some partners become critical and hurtful; the survivors' interactions with unsupportive partners is associated with worsened mental health outcomes for the survivors" (p. 627).

It is clear that inclusion of family members in treatment increases the likelihood of creating positive, enduring change. Without helping service members address the individual's trauma-related issues and simultaneously altering the family's expectation of and ways of interacting with him or her, families will continue to engage in familiar, dysfunctional patterns. Treatment aimed at the interpersonal context does the double duty of addressing the PTSD symptoms within the context of strengthening the family's cohesiveness and supportiveness as well as dealing with family problems that arise as a result of PTSD. The family experience of PTSD can become one sided if the family expends considerable energy helping the veteran; although this may be functional at the time of the diagnosis, it could reinforce the role of the service member as the client and ignore the partner's or family's needs.

Goals of Couples Therapy

Couples therapy strives to move beyond the conceptualization of an identified patient and balance the needs of both partners by assisting both to recognize and empathize with each other's needs and a healthier balance in the relationship. A challenge for therapists is to help couples move beyond a focus on the veterans' diagnosis as an explanation or a rationalization for the confusing and uncomfortable behavior. If PTSD victims begin to identify themselves with the diagnosis, and partners also adopt this disability-based view, the unwanted behavior is often tolerated and excused, and the chance for making positive relationship changes is reduced dramatically (Sherman et al., 2005). Therapy can help couples move toward a new paradigm in which the service member is viewed as having challenges related to wartime experiences that need to be addressed, but the service member is not the problem. These challenges are similar to those faced when working with any couple in which one of the partners brings a chronic condition to the relationship, such as diabetes, heart disease, a bipolar diagnosis, or chronic depression. It is always unhealthy and an impediment to treatment to identify the person with the disorder; for instance, "she is bipolar" instead of "she has bipolar disorder." As a conference presenter who had bipolar disorder once stated, "We are not our disorder; how often do we identify someone with a broken leg as their medical condition, so why should we define a person with a mental disorder by that disorder?"

Sherman et al. (2005) noted that the therapists' attention might be focused more on symptom management than on helping couples communicate their wishes for how to cope with specific phenomena, such as flashbacks. Focusing solely on managing symptoms superficially tends to reinforce a pathology perspective and fails to address the couple dynamics. On the other hand, a sole focus on the couple's struggles would also be one-sided. Couples therapy can and should address issues in all three domains of PTSD treatment that were defined in more detail in chapter 7. Therapy must, however, always start with an assessment and determination that neither partner is abusing substances, that remaining in the relationship is physically safe, and that working together will promote acceptance by helping the partner learn to tolerate and respect relational differences rather than attempt to eliminate what seems like unsolvable problems.

The following short overview of the three domains and suggested interventions are based on the work of Sherman et al. (2005).

Interventions for Reexperiencing the Symptoms　Interventions for the first domain of reexperiencing the symptoms include the following:

1. Assist PTSD survivors in educating their partners about what it is like to reexperience the symptoms, framing the veterans as the experts, and supporting them in sharing their symptoms.
2. Help the survivors teach their partners how to be supportive by articulating their needs, and, if necessary, educate the partners about grounding techniques to help the couple stay in the present. If violence is possible, partners need to develop an escape plan and a means of securing assistance.
3. Teach couples a debriefing process to help deescalate difficult situations and promote learning by helping them master a structured dialogue to facilitate awkward discussions and promote interpersonal learning and closeness.
4. Help couples cope with upsetting reminders of the trauma that trigger symptoms by teaching them how to predict difficult times and plan in advance how to cope.

Interventions for Avoidance Symptoms　The second domain of PTSD are the avoidance symptoms, which often lead to social isolation, with the partner feeling embarrassed by the veteran's absence from social events or a desire for early or rapid departure from socializing events.

The couple then often becomes isolated, leading to emotional distance rather than emotional intimacy. Couples often have problems expressing caring, self-disclosure, and emotional expressiveness and problems with sexual disinterest, leading couples to describe themselves as cohabiting. This lack of connectedness can often lead to infidelity as a means of seeking connections but still avoiding true intimacy. Service members may experience survivor guilt and associate emotional connection with loss, often spending a great deal of solitary time in unfulfilling activities. If, through their military experience, they gained a strong sense of identity with the military, they may even be overcome with depression because of how meaningless civilian life seems. Positive intervention and treatment for this domain include the following:

1. Engage the couple in assessing its readiness and commitment to the difficult work involved in strengthening its emotional bond.
2. Empower the couple to risk trust and openness with each other, use cognitive interventions that may help the PTSD survivor realize that the military approach of keeping others at bay may not be useful or necessary, and help the partner avoid personalizing the distancing behavior.
3. Empower the couple to negotiate the degree of the trauma that is shared, as it is critical that the survivor has control over how often, when, and how to share these experiences, and help the partner respect these choices. Sometimes the partner may need assistance in coping with the veteran's decision to share more with his fellow veterans than with her. It is also crucial to help survivors explain what meaning the trauma holds and then process what meaning it may have for the couple.
4. Encourage the pursuit of enjoyable activities, both individually and together, so that, at least initially, there is a high chance of success, and help the couple to cope with solitude to create and use its own support networks. Help veterans be aware of the consequences of isolative behavior, and help their partners overcome feelings of guilt for enjoying themselves when the veterans choose to stay home.

Interventions for Increased Arousal   The third domain of PTSD includes increased arousal symptoms, including sleep disturbance and consequent fatigue that will exacerbate social withdrawal, hypervigilance, and startle responses. This constant low-grade irritability adds to tension and stress in intimate relationships, eroding positive feelings and often resulting in partners becoming critical or emotionally disengaged. Studies (Sherman et al., 2005) have shown that the risk of violence is elevated, with as many as 42% of men who are PTSD survivors engaging in physical aggression against partners, more than 90% becoming verbally aggressive, and virtually 100% reporting the use of psychological aggression. Interventions might include the following:

1. Assist the couple in giving each other feedback about their needs and setting limits on their emotional involvement. Understand that the hyperarousal phenomenon, known as flooding, where the veteran is emotionally overwhelmed and physiologically aroused, will render the vet less effective in communicating. Veterans say they are often unable to remain emotionally present at these times, so couples need to implement nonjudgmental means of setting limits by letting each other know when their personal boundaries are being invaded.

2. Assess the possibility of domestic violence, and if that possibility exists, referrals to appropriate additional services are essential. Couples therapy is usually contraindicated in the presence of domestic violence, but therapists specially trained in treating domestic violence may assist couples with lower levels of aggression by teaching nonviolent means of conflict resolution.

3. Assist couples in coping effectively with irritability and the expression of anger by exploring the triggers and learning effective ways of coping. Help survivors identify times when they may displace anger onto their partners, and assist the partners in providing feedback about the behavior, which opens avenues of communication and builds skills.

4. Teach conflict disengagement strategies or time-out processes to prevent escalation and create emotional safety.

5. Educate couples about anxiety management strategies and other healthy lifestyle changes, such as the need for exercise, healthy nutrition, sleep, and hygiene, that are necessary to maintain any changes they attempt to make.

The authors (Sherman et al., 2005) summarized their findings by stating, "The extent to which this proposed conceptual framework applies to noncombatant trauma is uncertain [but their belief and findings are that] adjunctive couples therapy can foster interdependent, balanced intimate relationships and can be an important element in the comprehensive treatment of PTSD" (p. 632).

PTSD and CBT

Friedman (n.d.) and Foa, Davidson, Frances, and Ross (1999) pointed out that many therapeutic approaches are available for working with clients diagnosed with PTSD but that the most effective interventions have been anxiety management, cognitive therapy, and exposure therapy, whereas play therapy is often useful with children who have been exposed to trauma. Results have been good when combining CBT, exposure therapy, and cognitive restructuring, especially with female victims of childhood or adult sexual trauma (Friedman, n.d.). Anxiety management includes relaxation training, breathing, positive thinking and self-talk, assertiveness training, and thought stopping. Exposure therapy can be done with imaginative exposure or exposure in reality.

Medication (Friedman, 2006), particularly selective serotonin reuptake inhibitors, were the first medications to receive FDA approval for PTSD and are still being used to reduce anxiety, depression, and insomnia. Antidepressant drugs have contributed to improvement in some trials, and other classes of drugs have shown promise. Medication is often useful for symptom relief, which makes it possible to participate in psychotherapy. "While pharmacotherapy cannot be considered a cure for operational stress injuries, the benefits of medications are often substantial, and they should always be considered in a management program" (Figley & Nash, 2007, p. 6). Medications are usually recommended (a) if the symptoms are severe or have lasted for an extended period of time; (b) if there are other psychiatric problems; (c) if there are thoughts of suicide; (d) if a lot of stress exists; (e) if a client has a hard time functioning; and (f) if psychotherapy alone is not making an impact on the symptoms (Foa et al., 1999).

Friedman (n.d.) and Foa et al. (1999) also reported success with eye movement desensitization and reprocessing (EMDR). One of the therapists I interviewed also mentioned that EMDR has been successful in working with trauma clients. Although relatively new, EMDR, particularly in combination with CBT, has been effective in accessing and processing the trauma. Numerous studies have been conducted regarding the success rate of work with EMDR, and this is certainly an area one might want to investigate further (Allen, Keller, & Console, 1999).

Perhaps the best option for mildly to moderately affected clients has been group therapy, where the discussion of memories, symptoms, and functional deficits can be brought out in the open with others who obviously can relate on an emotional and experiential level. A therapist in Arizona has been very successful with group work with war veterans, particularly for those older vets who were reexperiencing symptoms of trauma. In a group setting, through sharing the trauma in a cohesive and empathic setting, clients can achieve understanding and resolution, as well as move toward feeling more confident and trusting.

A fact sheet on *The Treatment of PTSD* (NCPTSD, n.d.-b) outlines the following common components of treatment from a cognitive-behavioral approach:

1. Evaluation and development of a treatment plan that meets the needs of the survivor should be started after the survivor has been safely removed from the crisis situation. If the client is still exposed to trauma, is severely depressed or suicidal, is experiencing extreme panic or disorganized thinking, or is in need of drug or alcohol detoxification, addressing these crisis problems is important as part of the first phase of treatment.
2. Educate trauma survivors and their families about how and why PTSD develops and how it affects survivors and their loved ones.
3. It is necessary to help the survivor examine and resolve strong feelings such as anger, shame, or guilt during the first phase of treatment while teaching them ways to cope with the memories, reminders, reactions, and feelings without becoming overwhelmed or emotionally numb. Realize and understand that trauma memories can become manageable but usually do not entirely disappear as a result of therapy.
4. Exposure to the event with the use of imagery will allow the survivor to reexperience the event in a safe and controlled environment.

Addressing Deployment in Family Therapy

A considerable amount of information is shared in chapter 7 regarding the psychological processes that families go through during a deployment, but often the most difficult time in the process is the return of the service members.

> Most of the returning wounded are amputees; most of them are under 25; most of them earn less than $30,000 a year; most of them suffer from multiple problems—including post traumatic stress syndrome; most of them jump when they go over railroad tracks (or hear a car backfire or a balloon pop) and most of them find their marriages are a new battleground. (Houppert, 2005b, p. 194)

When military parents come home, they often want to make up for the time they were gone, sometimes by sacrificing their own needs or the needs of the couple to be with the kids and often going overboard, only to undermine the structure, rules, and rituals set up by the spouse. "Feelings of not belonging anymore are common in soldiers returning from war, even in the absence of more serious problems such as combat stress" (Alaimo, 2006a, ¶ 18). Each time the service member leaves and returns, the couple has to make the kinds of adjustments new couples face, and often it is tough on everyone; the returning military member finds it hard to fit into the new structure created by the family and often feels that by returning home the family has been turned upside down. This is indeed another transition journey the entire family must endure.

For some, the reintegration may be slow and painful (Brothers, 2006). War changes everyone, the warriors and their families. Spouses who have set their hopes on getting back the same person they sent to war the year before have a rude awakening when they find themselves next to a virtual stranger for weeks after their return. And kids who sent their daddy all those loving cards and drawings can be found crying, "Why don't you go back to Iraq!" when their idea of their dad doesn't match the angry, depressed, or withdrawn man lying on the couch when they get home from school (Brothers, 2006, p. 5).

Returning home can be fraught with more complications than just readjusting to the family. "One fifth of the soldiers returning from Iraq suffer from major depression, anxiety or trauma" (Brothers, 2006, p. 4). In a survey (Lyons, 2007) conducted to determine the level of involvement of the families of veterans in treatment for PTSD, spouses reported that they had a very active role in the treatment and care, including getting military members to appointments, reminding them about medication, orchestrating family life around the symptoms to minimize relapses, and taking on many of the roles that the veterans can no longer fulfill.

Obviously these additional duties create a great deal of difficulty if the spouse is working outside home, perhaps now in the role of the primary breadwinner, and inside the home as the primary caretaker for children and the veteran. Many of the spouses in the survey expressed an interest in therapy for themselves to improve their relationships or to reduce stress. They added that they did not need more information to understand the problems their returning spouse was going through but that they needed therapy that would focus on their needs and additional social activities to offset the isolation they felt. A therapist in Tucson who works primarily with military wives understands how the trauma of living with military veterans affects the spouses and families. She does family and group counseling with the women, teaching anger management, self-regulation, identification of perceived threat, and resolution of their own PTSD-like symptoms that they were often attempting to resolve through pain medication and other addictions.

Joyce Brothers (2006) believes that counselors are greatly needed to help families adjust following deployment. She believes that giving the returning military member time and letting him or her know that it is not necessary to talk about the experience immediately can be powerful. It then becomes important to teach family members, especially the spouse, how to listen and realize that the recollections may come out over the course of weeks or months. In addition, helping family members realize that things will be different, some jealousy over what has been missed may be present, and they may have to renegotiate family routines. It is also important to help family members understand that returning service members need to spend time with their war buddies and that this lifeline to their peers often makes the difference between coping and a withdrawal into isolation.

It often takes 6 to 8 weeks, a typical period of adjustment, for life to approach anything close to normal and for the individual, couple, or family to realize that if problems persist for more than 3 months, they more than likely need help. Helping families through the healing journey outlined in chapter 8 will be helpful. Rotter and Boveja (1999) recommended that intervention strategies always approach the issues of anticipation, separation, and reunion from a systems orientation; these recommendations include (a) clarifying boundary issues, so spouses can maintain separate identities and privacy is allowed and acceptable; (b) being aware of contextual issues, so that desires and expectations are handled through open and consistent communication; (c) approaching power issues from an egalitarian and mutually supportive point of view where equity, individuality, and happiness are valued more than being right or maintaining control; (d) assisting with affective issues, where a wide range of emotions, including anger, optimism, good-natured teasing, and even a sense of the absurdity of life, is allowed; (e) teaching negotiation skills to provide for the possibility of a win–win solution rather than compromises that may be experienced as a loss by at least one member of the family; and (f) addressing spiritual or value issues to promote discussions of shared beliefs, a kinship with the world, a belief that the family members matter, and an abiding sense of meaning and purpose.

Working with Military Stepfamilies

For many years I have focused much of my attention on working with stepfamilies by forming stepfamily groups, training counselors to work with stepfamilies, going to stepfamily conferences, and writing about stepfamilies. This experience was vital in my later work as a counselor in the Department of Defense schools working with military dependent children. In working with military stepfamilies, counselors have to consider certain issues in addition to the concerns and characteristics outlined in chapter 6. During the formation of stepfamilies, stepfamilies face a number of tasks that they may need help in accomplishing before they can have a sense of wholeness and integration. These tasks can also be viewed as goals for counseling (Carter & McGoldrick, 1999; Gladding, 2007; Visher & Visher, 1996). They are not chronological, as they should begin immediately and continue throughout counseling and, it is hoped, the life of the family. If a family attempts to become a stepfamily without working on these tasks, the members may be overcome with difficulties. It becomes clear in working with stepfamilies that if they are finding life difficult, they probably have not completed these tasks successfully.

Mourn the Previous Losses

The first task is for all family members to mourn their own personal losses. Chapter 8 of this book is dedicated to the importance of working through transitions, and this is a major transition in the life of a family. The time and place of this mourning will differ for everyone. Often children will delay and deny the loss felt from a divorce of a parent for a great deal of time. They may continue to believe that somehow the parents will magically get back together. Remarriage may remove that final veil, forcing the children to accept the previous loss of the parents' divorce. To them all of a sudden life changes when, for example, their mom begins to express her affection for another adult and may have less time for the children, and the children may perceive this loss of a special place of significance in the family structure. Adults also must mourn both their previous spouse and the loss of their previous relationship. If that has not been done adequately, the residual baggage from the former marriage too easily gets mixed in with the present one. The divorce rate for those who marry again within 1 year after divorce is almost double the average divorce rate of first marriages, again illustrating that it takes time and work to move through life's transitions.

In the middle school where I first worked in Germany, a young middle school girl by the name of Summer came to see me, crying about the loss of her mother; when she was finally calm enough to talk, she explained that she had not seen her mother since she was 3 years old and hardly remembered her. However, that morning her father, who had long since remarried, told Summer that he had just learned that her biological mother had recently died. He then walked away, saying it probably wasn't important because she more than likely didn't remember her mother anyway. What her dad did not know was that, even though this young seventh grader was quite happy in her current stepfamily and successful in school, she had held on to a belief since she was very young that when she graduated from high school, she would find her "real" mother and be reunited with her. She was inconsolable for a considerable amount of time because her long-held dream would never come to pass and because her father had not allowed her to know her mother while she was growing up.

Counselor interventions for this first task are often to teach and model the open expression of feelings, hopes, and wishes to relieve the possible past reluctance or denial of grief. With children this can be done through telling stories, drawing pictures, or engaging in play or sand therapy. We can also encourage acceptance and respect of each person by giving them permission to express any and all feelings. Acting on feelings is quite different from having feelings, and families can learn early the difference. In addition, we can encourage movement through the grief process, as outlined in chapter 8.

Establish New Traditions

This task means addressing the obvious holidays, birthdays, and vacations but also includes the not-so-obvious things, such as language patterns, ways of expressing affection, humor, decision-making and conflict styles, role adjustments, and the ongoing everyday activities of the home. While expressing some of the fears of upsetting a new relationship, one newly remarried mom said,

> I was so determined to make this marriage work, for the sake of myself as well as the children, that I would do anything to avoid conflict. For months after we were married, my new husband would get up early, read the newspaper, and when my alarm went off, immediately appear by my bedside with coffee, ready to talk and share his daily agenda. It took me months to get up the nerve to share that I hated mornings and that the last thing I wanted in the morning was a bright shining face eager to talk about the day. (O'Hern-Hall & Williams, 2004, p. 72)

Because it takes at least 1 year to live through all the holidays, vacations, and birthdays and at least 1 more year to begin to develop patterns, in most cases a minimum of 2 or 3 years is required for the establishment of new traditions and rituals. Gladding (2007) stated that on average it takes anywhere from 2 to 5 years for stepparents to form in-depth relationships with their stepchildren. For the military family, life can be unstable to begin with; for a newly remarried couple who is also in the midst of a move, deciding whether the children will make the move or stay with the other parent and making all the difficult decisions this entails, these rituals and traditions get put on the back burner until things settle down. But do they ever? A 2- to 5-year time period may be adequate for those families who realize ahead of time what the concerns, differences, and values are; who have some stability in their lives; and who are willing to negotiate and plan ahead. For the majority of military families, the first few years may go by with little negotiation and a lot of resentment over what seems like minimal issues, such as who cleans toilets and when Christmas presents are opened. When people come into a marriage believing their way is the right way, negotiations break down before ever having begun, with resentment and misunderstanding being the norm. Most of the students who enrolled in the schools where I worked in Germany who were in stepfamilies were angry, not just about the move but about living in the stepfamily. As time went by and we worked through some of their grief, they usually were able to understand that the stepparent was the focus of their anger not because that person was so bad but because they were angry at other issues in their life and that person was the most obvious target.

For this second task, counselors can teach and model negotiation and decision-making skills through encouraging the use of the family council or family meetings to plan ahead, negotiate requests and expectations, and share upcoming schedules or plans. Teaching communication skills may be necessary so all family members believe they have a right to express their feelings and needs. It is also important to encourage the adults to jointly make major parenting and visitation decisions rather than force the children to choose between in-home parents and out-of-home parents. Also the ability of the entire system to work together, including ex-spouses, grandparents, or any significant others, when possible, on issues that concern the welfare of the children goes a long way in avoiding loyalty problems.

An article from the Military OneSource Web site (*Couples: Building a Strong Marriage When You're in a Stepfamily,* 2006) suggested that there are four ways to keep a remarriage strong; the first two apply to this task of establishing and negotiating new traditions and rituals. The first is the ability to adjust one's expectations, which may include forgiving the partner for what one considers his or her less-than-perfect parenting skills, accepting each other for who each is, and seeing each other as equal partners. The second suggestion is to resolve conflicts fairly by keeping disagreements private, avoiding saying mean or hurtful things, being respectful, using "I" statements, keeping the focus on the issue at hand, and later finding a way to talk about what happened. These are skills that may be difficult to learn for some parent-focused military families, so looking at parenting styles may also be necessary.

Form New Relationships

The third task of the family is the formation of new relationships while continuing to maintain the old. This is a particularly important task for children who have a stepparent in the military and who are more than likely a great distance away from their out-of-home parent, as well as their extended family. The skills gained by children in forming new relationships will be a skill that will serve them well throughout their lives. Children need to feel that they have a right to continue their feelings for and attachments to both parents while beginning to share experiences and interests with the new stepparent. If the biological parents and remarried parents encourage these new interactions, the children will not be faced with the ugly feelings of disloyalty to one or guilt about caring for another. If, on the other hand, the new couple's relationship is threatened by prior claims or there is ongoing animosity between ex-spouses, the children quickly learn that they are supposed to take sides—usually against their will.

Counselors can encourage and actively work with the new couple for them to see that their primary long-term relationship is the key (Gladding, 2007) to the success of the new family. They will need to build strong, intimate ties by spending time together when possible without the children, exploring goals and a shared meaning for their relationship. The focus on strengthening the couple's relationship is extremely important for the success of the military stepfamily, as they will be tested repeatedly just because of the military culture they have brought the children into.

Counselors might work with different combinations of dyads at different times and encourage the dyads to spend time together; for example, the stepfather with each stepchild, stepmother with child, biological parent with biological child. Too many times parents force entire family functions on all the children, in an attempt to build a family when what is also needed is the building of one-on-one relationships. This becomes extremely important at the time of deployment. If a stepmom has never had a chance to build a one-on-one relationship with the stepchild and the service member father is deployed, the stepmom will find it very difficult to become the sole parent in the home. If possible, prior to deployment and early in the remarriage, the biological parent should spend some time away from the family for the stepparent to start building one-on-one relationships with the children. This is often done if the biological parent is the military parent but is less likely if the biological parent is the spouse who doesn't work outside the home. Both parents, step and biological, should be encouraged to interact with the children on a regular basis in a parental role.

Counselors will also want to explore what the family members want to be called, how they want to be introduced, and how they want to be talked about. For example, one of my students said she was uncomfortable because her mom insisted that she introduce her new stepfather as "dad." I suggested to the parents that Jenny be allowed to introduce her stepfather by saying either "This is my mom's husband" or "This is my stepdad," as it is often best to allow children to decide which is most comfortable for them.

Almost a year later, Jenny's stepdad shared that she was now introducing him as her stepdad instead of introducing him as her mom's husband. He felt this was a major step toward them having their own relationship, instead of the sense that he was important only because he had married her mom. When parents insist that the stepchildren call the new stepparent mom or dad, they can be very conflicted, and this can be avoided simply by asking what the children's preference is, then giving them permission by saying "You can call me Susan or you can call me mom." Negotiating the issue of names so everyone feels comfortable can be a very empowering process, and it is one that is often overlooked.

Restructure the New Family

The fourth task is the integration and restructuring of this new family form. "Remarried families have structural characteristics that make them unique" (Gladding, 2007, p. 293). Part of this is the result of task number two, which includes the patterns the family develops over time. However, this task goes beyond that to a belief that this new family form has value, can be successful, and is worth the commitment needed from every member. This family will be structured with permeable boundaries for the give-and-take of people and ideas to come in and out of the traditional household boundaries. Carter and McGoldrick (1999) stated that many of the difficulties in life and in therapy for stepfamilies "can be attributed to attempts by the family or therapist to use the roles and rules of first marriage families as a guideline" (p. 417). For the children and often the spouse who is entering a military family for the first time, this lifestyle is also a culture shock. While adjusting to the concept and structure of a stepfamily, they also have to learn the military lifestyle. This has created animosity for more than just a few stepchildren. It also creates difficult feelings for military stepparents who might believe that this new lifestyle will bring positive experiences for the new spouse and stepchildren but who may not understand the need to make the difficult emotional and physical adjustments first.

Gladding (2007) said that by "understanding the nature of remarried families, family therapists can assess areas of distinction and commonness" (p. 288). Possible interventions for this task include educating all members and helping them understand the complexities and confusions of stepfamilies, the length of time it takes, and the tasks that are necessary to accomplish it. Helping parents understand the many levels of transitions, which include the loss and grief issues that need to be addressed, is particularly important in stepfamilies when children are new to the military culture. As Gladding noted, helping the family members assess themselves according to stepfamily norms rather than biological family norms is important, and encouraging them to express their own expectations of the relationships by exploring the unrealistic myths about stepfamilies can be valuable.

It is obvious that continuing to teach negotiation and conflict management skills is vital so that planning and movement within and outside the boundaries can be done with less chaos. While creating this new family form, it is important to pay attention to actively maintaining the relationships (*Couples: Building a Strong Marriage When You're in a Stepfamily*, 2006) by respecting each parent–child relationship, staying out of conflicts between the biological parent and his or her children, sharing household chores, being flexible, and giving everyone their own space. An additional structural difference is that stepfamilies may need to change their concepts of traditional gender roles. "This model overturns completely the notion that the stepmother, just because she is a woman, should be in charge of the home, the children or the emotional relationships throughout the system" (Carter & McGoldrick, 1999, p. 418), because, at least initially, the parent with the longest relationship with the children will need to take on the primary parenting tasks.

These suggestions are sometimes difficult in military families, particularly when the military parent is gone for significant periods of time and because many military families are structured after very traditional models. If the nonmilitary parent is the stepparent, the typical household and parenting chores become overwhelming challenges and require a great deal more patience, so working with this parent on his or her issues around self-esteem, confidence, and independence might be valuable.

Individuate Each Family Member

The fifth task is to focus on each individual member of the household, particularly as it relates to basic developmental needs. Each member of the stepfamily must begin a process of individuation and autonomy apart from, but within, the ambiguous boundaries of this family. Biological families, whether civilian or military, often are able to function with dogmatic, autocratic structures. Biological families may even be able to function in a permissive home, but stepfamilies do not function well under either of these parenting styles. A stepparent cannot come into a home demanding, ruling, and controlling without the tradition, bonding, or trust having been established. On the other hand, if a stepparent uses a permissive parenting style, the lack of attachment and respect will only prevent future commitment to the family and to the stepparent. In most cases, the most encouraging and healthy parenting style is a respectful leadership style, described in chapter 5, by McKay and Maybell (2004). This parenting style encourages respect for each person's worth, while maintaining the hierarchy and control by the parents. It also includes the encouragement of opinions, thoughts, beliefs, and actions; the setting of legitimate limits with logical and natural consequences; and the belief in the worth of each person as a valuable, significant human being.

It is in this kind of protective environment that family members will be encouraged to begin the process of autonomy or individuation, while learning the necessary skills of decision making, conflict management, communication, and respect for others. In the rather complicated system of a stepfamily that includes ambiguous boundaries, undefined structure, countless relationships, and confusing feelings, the respectful leadership system appears to be the most viable and workable structure, particularly in the military environment.

Possible intervention for this fifth task includes educating and modeling the principles of respectful leadership, including respect, natural and logical consequences, encouragement, responsibility for self, and communication and negotiation skills. Also, if children are living in more than one residence, setting aside a special place for each child, even if it is just a special drawer for personal things, gives the children a sense of belonging whenever they are in that home. Gladding (2007) called these the "boundary difficulties," which include who are the real members of the household, what space belongs to each person, who is in charge, and how to negotiate time. Encouraging the use of language that suggests stability needs to begin early, such as "living" in two homes, even if only occasionally, rather than "visiting."

Although I mentioned earlier that parents need to make the major parenting decisions for the children, as children grow older, the adults can begin to back away from making all arrangements, from settling disputes, or from requesting favors from the out-of-home parent. Instead, parents can begin to encourage and teach the children to take responsibility for resolving these issues with the out-of-home parent. This is more than difficult in a military family, where the out-of-home parent may be half a continent away, but as children enter high school, and certainly as they plan college, they need to be given the chance to negotiate issues with both parents rather than be forced to comply with one parent's demands. Families can be "encouraged to set up an open system with permeable boundaries between current and former spouses and their children" (Gladding, 2007, p. 301).

Build a Solid Couple Bond

The sixth task relates to the newly remarried adults in the stepfamily, who must be supported and encouraged to form a strong couple bond. Developing this strong relationship is essential not only for their survival as a couple but also so the couple can be a role model for the children. The Military OneSource article mentioned previously (*Couples: Building a Strong Marriage When You're in a Stepfamily*, 2006) suggested that the couple must continue to actively build intimacy in their relationship by scheduling regular time alone, taking up a sport or hobby, enjoying activities that allow and encourage touch, giving each other praise, staying in touch, and creating rituals that are unique to them as a couple. This focus on the couple is particularly important in the military family when the strength of the couple is mandatory to get through the numerous other stresses they face. "Because parent–child bonds predate the marital bond ... stepparents tend to compete inappropriately with their stepchildren for primacy with their spouse" (Carter & McGoldrick, 1999, p. 418).

All adults must attempt to work to develop a civil relationship with the ex-spouses for the benefit of the children and make sure that discussions about the ex-spouses are not always negative. Parents need to understand that when they talk disparagingly about the other parent, the children hear them talking about half of themselves. The out-of-home parent–child relationships continue even after a divorce, and effective communication is the key to the children's adjustment. A functional stepfamily will allow for the ambiguity of these relationships and the different ties that are present because of historical connections (Carter & McGoldrick, 1999).

Suggestions for working on this task include helping the new couple build their relationship by seeing them alone at least after some of the chaos of the family has been reduced through family counseling. It is important for the new couple to get to know each other within this military environment and take the time to be alone on a regular basis without feeling guilty. It is helpful to work with the older children so they understand the need for their parent and stepparent to build their relationship, and it is vital that the adults learn how to make necessary arrangements, particularly given the distances often involved, with the out-of-home parent in a businesslike manner without old resentments and guilt getting in the way. Also, it is important to help the adults understand the harm that can be done to the children and eventually to the new couple by keeping children in the middle, maintaining power struggles, or speaking negatively of a former spouse.

These tasks have been presented as a reference for a stepfamily's growth and as suggestions that counselors can use in working with stepfamilies. Gladding (2007) suggested that structural family therapy, experiential family therapy, and transgenerational work are usually effective in working with stepfamilies. I always found it very helpful to take an extensive history and, as Gladding suggested, come from a systems perspective to pay attention to the larger systems outside the family that have influence on how the family functions. In military stepfamilies, there is simply more history to take, often full of loss, change, and ambiguity.

Often the first step in working with military stepfamilies is to help the family lessen some of the chaos that is presently bringing them to counseling. It may be a conflict between two family members, a child's behavior problem, chaos as a result of the stress of being in the military, or just overall ambiguity and uncertainty. As stated earlier, the norms of a stepfamily are very different from those of a biological family, but the norms of a military family are also different from the norms of a civilian stepfamily. Any assessment must be done in the context of the diverse cultures that the members of the family come from and live in. A child moving back and forth is a norm in a stepfamily; a child coming and going would not be the norm in a biological family. A child changing schools every 2 to 3 years is the norm in a military family; it may not be the norm in a civilian family.

As in all work from a systems perspective, even though one child may be in crisis when counseling begins, the focus will shift to the family as a whole and away from the possible scapegoated child as soon as possible. Some initial work with the child may be appropriate, but too much emphasis on the child or the child's problems might cover up the source of the concern, which is often the family organization or the struggles of the new couple. Also, early emphasis on grief work and moving through loss is essential. The complexity of the family structure demands a therapist's creativity in keeping people organized and at the same time perceiving the situation from each person's point of view.

Working with Military Men

There is general agreement that men seek help from mental health professionals less often than women; that generalization is also true in the military. As noted in chapter 1, there is an inherent stigma against seeking help in the military culture, so one wonders if the stigma is because of the military or because the military is traditionally a male environment and if the increased numbers of women joining the military will have an impact on that stigma. Regardless of the reason for the stigma, the concern regarding men's reluctance to seek counseling is real and has to be addressed and understood for counselors who will be working with the military.

Ryan McKelley (2007) stated that although there have been a number of reasons offered for men's aversion to seeking professional help, the general conclusion points to the lack of fit between the culture of masculinity and the therapeutic process. In other words, the socialization of men has promoted the avoidance of emotional expression, the absence of admitting weaknesses or vulnerabilities, and the need to solve problems without the help of others. "Research indicates that masculine gender role conflict is consistently inversely related to men's willingness to seek psychological help" (McKelley, 2007, p. 52). Studies have shown that the more men adhere to traditional male role norms, the more they report underusing mental health services and having negative help-seeking attitudes. Research also "indicates that traditional men are less attracted to feeling-oriented therapy and instead favor strategic problem-solving therapies" (p. 52).

In an article focusing on working with adult male survivors of trauma, Mejia (2005) discussed the influences of gender roles on the lives of men and how men cope with trauma. Mejia stated that the essential features of the masculine ideology of toughness, fearlessness, and the denial of vulnerability have made it difficult for both men and society as a whole to acknowledge that men can indeed be victimized and that, like all victims, they can suffer. "It is therefore very difficult for people to be cognizant of the contradictory view of men as tough and invulnerable on the one hand and hurt and suffering on the other" (p. 31).

It is imperative, then, within the context of therapy to address male gender role socialization for effective intervention. With this in mind, McKelley (2007) suggested that individual psychology, or an Adlerian approach to working with men, could address many of the characteristics of the traditional male role socialization. These characteristics include (a) an achievement and goal orientation; (b) the restriction of emotional expression; (c) a focus on independence and self-reliance; and (d) active problem solving. These characteristics are at the heart of the military training and tradition and could be translated into the values of honor and sacrifice in the military context. We might have a tendency to challenge these characteristics in working with military couples and families, but Dr. Butler, who has worked for years with military men, maintained that direct confrontation of the commitments to honor, tradition, and sacrifice will usually result in a premature termination of therapy.

Although a basic premise of psychotherapy might be that everything is open to examination, Dr. Butler stated that these concepts of honor, tradition, and sacrifice are so integrated into the character structure of the career military male, especially those in the officer corps, that to question these values is to attack the very core of the person. Therapists can find themselves in a double bind with the male military client who may need to evaluate how these gender roles create a barrier in his family but who only respects a therapist who can match his aggressiveness and lay it on the line. As mentioned earlier regarding men's reluctance to seek therapy, military men often see it as a form of weakness, and the uncovering of inner fears and insecurities would be seen by many as evidence of their inadequacy as a person. The potential for shaming such individuals is quite high, and any hint of this will result in extreme anger and almost always immediate termination of therapy, especially for those men who experienced a great deal of shaming as part of their childhood expectations of what being a boy was all about (Mejia, 2005).

Making Therapy Fit

Most men come to counseling because of some external pressure, often as a result of a crisis in the family, at work, or with their health. Therefore counselors must be aware of their own biases when working with men and realize that emphasizing the release of emotions early in counseling will more than likely turn off most male clients and reinforce the notion that counseling is strictly for the purpose of dealing with feelings (Mejia, 2005). Given this caution, McKelley (2005) proposed that some of the corner-stones of Adlerian psychology could address these characteristics, including the beliefs that all human beings are purposely moving toward goals, that individuals are responsible for their own lives and can make decisions to change, and that each individual must take responsibility for problem solving. This nicely fits with Mejia's (2005) suggestion that using gender role analysis can be effective in developing appropriate strategies in working with men. He stated, "Counseling can help men develop insights and options, but it is necessary to consider issues of control, fear of dependency and fear of vulnerability" (p. 34). While addressing these issues, it is also valuable to incorporate the concept of social interest, or interdependence, rather than allow the primary focus to be independence or moving away from others, and to focus on the ability to solve problems in cooperation with others rather than to solve problems as a means of striving for superiority over others (McKelley, 2007). By reframing therapy, the counselor can explore how resistance to therapy is part of gender role stereotyping and that often the rules one lives by are indeed "gendered prescriptions for behavior that are social constructions that fit a particularly historical time frame" (Mejia, 2005, p. 34) and, within the military, a particular culture.

It is also, of course, imperative to consider other issues and influences, including ethnicity, socioeconomic status, race, cultural heritage, family of origin, sexuality, physical capabilities, and genetics, in addition to gender role socialization (Mejia, 2005). So it is possible, particularly in the context of couples and family counseling, that masculine concepts such as honor and sacrifice can be reframed into what could be called relationship competence, to move these concepts from a sense of weakness to strength. As with nonmilitary clients, it will be valuable for the male military client to see "that emotional understanding and openness are part of masculinity and that to convey one's inner life and understand the inner lives of one's family is to acquire an additional honor, the honor of wisdom" (Butler, personal communication, October 6, 2006).

Male Survivors of Trauma

Mejia (2005) stated that male survivors of trauma have actually experienced two interacting traumas: they have been socialized into an ideology of masculinity that often has limited the resources with which they live their lives, and they have had a traumatic experience that usually complicates the legacy of their masculine socialization. To work with men, counselors must proceed both on the level of redefining masculinity and its legacies and on the level of confronting the trauma and its legacies. "Virtually all men feel to some degree that they do not measure up to the standards of masculine ideology, because the standards literally defy men's basic humanity" (Mejia, 2005, p. 38), therefore counseling with male trauma survivors must also incorporate an effort to treat the legacies of masculine socialization.

Considering issues of control, fear of dependency, and fear of vulnerability during the therapeutic process is crucial because these are the things that masculine socialization has so rigidly taught men not to do. Male military clients have very distinct scripts and socialization histories, often from both their childhood and the military. As referenced earlier in the book, working with the military requires a multicultural perspective, and working with men also requires another multicultural perspective. Mejia (2005) wrote that it is important for all therapists to be aware of the cultural, racial, political, historical, and economic context that influence male socialization; to recognize the interface between the male client's socialization and his beliefs and feelings about seeking help; to incorporate a gender role analysis into their work with men; and to be aware of their own values and biases related to male socialization.

Steps in Therapy

Mahalik et al. (2003) suggested that the first step in the therapeutic relationship is to determine the salient masculinity scripts (tough guy, "give 'em hell," playboy, homophobic, winner, or independent) for a particular client, then identify the positive functions that the individual script serves the client and how often "conforming to traditional masculinity scripts also offers clear guidance about how one is supposed to act in society" (p. 127). After exploring how the specific script or scripts have been of value to the client, the therapist can help the client examine the costs of living out those scripts, in relation to the presenting concerns; these may include the costs to his emotional or physical health, his work, and his family or other relationships. Last, the therapist can help the client find more flexible ways for him to enact the masculine scripts that are causing him distress. By going through this process, therapists and clients are "more likely to understand what changes need to be made, and clients are more likely to be motivated to make those changes" (Mahalik et al., 2003, p. 127).

It is important for the client to understand that our goal in therapy is not to change a client's script or somehow shame him because he has bought into the script. Instead, the goal is to recognize and acknowledge that men with traditional conceptions of masculinity have a great deal of strengths that are beneficial and absolutely essential for success in the military. The goal is also not to eliminate the client's definition of masculinity but to teach him how to survive within that definition. "Research on masculinity and therapy has identified an important irony associated with how elements of masculinity contribute to men's psychological distress as well as to their reluctance to seek help for psychological problems" (Mahalik et al., 2003, p. 129), so it is imperative that clinicians who work with military families understand masculine socialization and make efforts to find ways to make the therapeutic experience more comfortable, effective, and acceptable within the military culture.

CHAPTER 10

Military Family Case Studies

This chapter begins with the rest of the story that I started in chapter 1, which is a case study provided by Dr. Michael Hand, a therapist in El Paso, Texas. As a counselor educator, I believe it is important to be able to conceptualize and collaborate on cases that give us concern. The family situation that follows is not atypical of the issues and concerns that counselors will face when working with military families. The second part of the chapter is an additional case study from my personal experience in working with a military stepfamily.

Following the case studies are a number of questions that might stir further investigation and thoughts regarding what the therapist would need to know to work with each family, how the therapeutic relationship would begin, what methods and strategies might be used, and what the hoped-for outcomes are. To make these studies most effective, one might read the history and presenting problems initially, then refer to the questions prior to reading the therapeutic process and outcomes. Obviously there is never one right way to proceed in counseling, so there may be many approaches, depending on the training and experience of the counselor and the setting and time frame one has to work with the client.

Case Study 1: The Rest of the Story

Presenting Problem

A staff sergeant (SSgt), John, and his wife, Paula, presented as self-referrals for problems of acute marital strife following the sergeant's return from his second tour in Iraq. At the time of the first session, they were living together, but the SSgt had filed for divorce. The counseling setting is a community center, not on a military installation.

Background

This couple had been married for 10 years, have two daughters, ages 8 and 4. The couple had some discord in their relationship prior to his having enlisted in the service 8 years ago, mostly about finances—particularly the way Paula spent money and what she spent it on—and the amount and frequency of his drinking. These sources of conflict had abated somewhat until after John's first deployment, and they have escalated over the past 3 years. They separated briefly after his first deployment following an argument that became physically aggressive on both their parts, but they reconciled after a month apart. The relationship was somewhat better, until he was deployed again. During the second deployment, Paula had an affair with an officer in the medical corps. The SSgt discovered e-mail between his wife and the officer, filed for divorce, and brought charges against the officer in question. The SSgt had been married previously and was divorced after he was discovered having had an affair himself, as well as having problems with excessive drinking and anger management. John has one son, age 12, from his previous marriage who lives with his ex-wife. Paula had been married once before but did not have children in her first marriage. John and Paula married only a few months after he was divorced from his first wife, but Paula had been single for a number of years and has always worked in the retail industry.

Upon initial exploration, it seemed clear that, although the SSgt was very angry with his wife, he continued to love her and did not want to lose her or break up the family. Paula was feeling very guilty and sorry for the affair but also angry with him for what she saw as his long-standing emotional distance, anger, and drinking pattern and for the loneliness and hardship involved in his being deployed for so long on two occasions. The SSgt had experienced intense combat, having survived two improvised explosive devise attacks where others under his command were killed and he was slightly wounded. He downplayed any lingering emotional or physical symptoms from these experiences, but his wife reported that he had frequent nightmares, had been drinking more and more often, was emotionally distant and socially detached (even before the discovery of her affair), and had volatile and unpredictable moods, frequently including anger and aggressiveness.

Paula had also been having difficulty sleeping, had gained weight from overeating for self-admitted self-comfort, had her own mood volatility, and generally felt hopeless, lethargic, and without energy or desire to do any of the things she had once enjoyed. She felt guilty, not only for her part in the affair but also because the officer she had had the affair with was now facing a court martial and likely the end of his career for his part in the affair.

Case Conceptualization

This couple had long-standing conflicts in their relationship that were at tolerable limits prior to the SSgt's initial deployment but got worse during and following his second. Both had dysfunctional concepts with regard to a husband's and wife's role and responsibilities, and both had habits that were antagonistic to the comfort of the other and the family as a whole. Both had poor models for successful and happy marriages, coming from markedly dysfunctional families themselves. Both were strong willed and considered compromise as a personal loss. Both had the strong tendency to bring up long-past transgressions of the other whenever a disagreement arose. Both tended to interrupt the other in discussions, and any difference of opinion on almost any subject resulted in anger and spiteful behavior in response. The SSgt's experiences in combat, though minimized by him, seemed to reflect at least a moderate post-traumatic stress disorder, which exacerbated his tendency to drink excessively, act aggressively, detach emotionally, and behave erratically. The wife's affair was an attempt to gain some emotional support, fill the loneliness of the long separations from her husband, and reassure herself that she was still desirable. Her rather compulsive spending also seemed to be a method of self-soothing and distraction from her troubles as well, perhaps, as a means for punishing her husband.

Therapeutic Approach and Process

A cognitive approach was used for therapy. This seemed a good fit for these individuals, as both were bright, educated at a college level, and responsive to logic—at least with the therapist, if not each other. The initial steps were to ask each individual the following two questions: "What are you willing to do to make this relationship work?" and "What are you *not* willing to do to make this relationship work?" The purpose of these questions is twofold: to identify at the onset whether each did, in fact, have a continuing investment in the relationship, and to clearly identify what, if any, deal breakers existed so far as each was concerned. Both were encouraged *not* to try to discuss their issues outside of the therapy sessions for the time being. Instead, they were to focus only on finding ways to enjoy each other's and their children's company and attempt to reinstate some of their previously enjoyed activities and interests. The hope in this was to remind them of why they had become a couple in the first place and to recapture some of their previous activities (and mind-set) that had worked for them in the past.

Both were encouraged to ramp up their stress management practices, including increased aerobic exercise, decreased alcohol consumption, and more focus on recreation. Because both were having significantly impaired sleep, as well as other anxiety and depression symptoms, both were encouraged to speak with their physicians regarding possible medication support for these problems. Both followed through with this recommendation, though John did so reluctantly because of concerns of the possible impact on his career. Both received prescriptions for Zoloft for depression and Ambien for sleep.

Both were introduced to the role of habit in the day-to-day conduct of everyone's lives. The point was made that formation of habit is one of the great strengths of the human mind, so as to free up awareness for other, less routine, actions. The example of arriving at a destination after having driven across some distance, with no real recollection of all the turns, stops, and actions required to get to the destination helped make the point that we often operate on automatic.

The next concept introduced in concert with the previous one is that we humans also form habits of thoughts, beliefs, and emotions, as well as behaviors. This is sometimes a harder sell, as most tend to think of thoughts, beliefs, and emotions as something more basic and immutable, as well as inaccessible to conscious change. However, this was overcome by highlighting the certainty that neither one *thought* exactly the same way about some things, *believed* exactly the same way about some things, *felt* exactly the same way about some things, or *behaved* exactly the same way as they had 10 years earlier. The point was then made that most of these *evolutions* of thoughts, beliefs, feelings, and behaviors had happened rather mindlessly. And if we can—and do—change these things mindlessly, then we certainly can do so mindfully and intentionally. These two concepts of habit and ability to mindfully change habits provided the couple with hope for both their own and the other's change with regard to key thoughts, beliefs, feelings, and behaviors. It is also very empowering to consider that no one is permanently stuck with any thought, belief, feeling, or behavior that is the source of pain and problems. The mechanics of changing habits were also described in a step-by-step fashion: first, becoming aware of a habit that is not serving your needs well—obviously if you are not aware that you have a habit, then you cannot mindfully change it; second, and perhaps most critical, deciding that changing the habit is important enough *to you* that you are willing to put whatever energy, effort, and time necessary to change it; and finally, engaging in the rather straightforward process of catching yourself doing whatever habit needs to be changed and substituting a more desirable or appropriate one (thought, belief, feeling, behavior) in its place—and doing so consistently enough and long enough until the substitution becomes the new habit.

In addition to teaching the couple these concepts, the counselor instructed and coached them in more effective communication (mostly listening) skills and techniques so as to enhance their ability to work through any subsequent (and past) issues with less likelihood of escalation to argument. They were also encouraged to make whatever effort necessary to abandon the issues and hurts that each had experienced from the other in the past—likened to "emotional baptism," where all is forgiven and only the present and future now count, thereby relieving each of the lingering hurt, anger, and recriminations from their present lives and relationship.

Therapeutic Outcome

The couple participated in roughly one weekly session for a total of 17 weeks, with 2- and then 3-week intervals toward the end. Both remained on their antidepressant medication, and over time decreased the use of their sleep medications. The SSgt decreased his alcohol consumption, though he did not stop entirely. The wife greatly decreased her compulsive spending, though the issue of any spending continued to be somewhat of an issue with her husband, because they had gotten into a rather serious financial situation that would take some time to resolve. Both improved significantly in their communication and problem-resolution techniques and ability to "seek first to understand" the other's point of view before objecting. Both worked to do activities together that they had previously enjoyed, and they began having date nights, which they had not had since the birth of their first child. Both continued with their enhanced exercise regimens, losing weight and feeling better in the process. Although neither was completely successful in the struggle to let go of the past, they both were able to at least resist using these as weapons or defenses in disagreements. The SSgt dropped the petition for divorce. Although they have no guarantee that their relationship will weather all possible future storms, they seemed to have embraced important concepts and developed new tools to use if and when needed.

Case Study 2: Not Quite the Brady Bunch

Susan, the mother of three children, called to ask if she could see the school counselor about her youngest son, Benjamin, who was 13 and in eighth grade. She explained that his teachers were having trouble with Benjamin, and she stated that ever since their move to Germany, Benjamin had been belligerent and withdrawn, both at school and at home. Kevin, her husband, was a career officer in the Army, and he didn't believe they needed counseling, so he was reluctant to have them see a social worker or psychologist on base. She explained that her daughters, Carolyn, age 15, and Kathryn, age 16, seemed to be adjusting to the move reasonably well.

Background Information

The couple, Susan and Kevin, had been married for 3 years, and this was their first tour overseas and away from the children's biological father and their extended family. The couple had married at Kevin's last duty station; Susan had grown up in that community and was excited about being able to travel and see the world with her new husband. Susan had been married to her first husband, the father of the three children, for 15 years and was divorced for 3 years prior to marrying Kevin. She reported that her first husband was very upset about her marriage to a military man and her taking the children with her overseas; however, he had not remarried, worked long hours, and felt unable to care for the children on his own. Kevin had been married previously also but did not have children in his previous marriage. His former wife was also a military service member, and they had been married for 10 years.

Before coming to Germany, the family had lived close to the school where the children had grown up, and the children had gone to school with the friends they had known since first grade. Susan shared that the first year or two they were married, the kids basically ignored Kevin, both because they had their friends and extended family and because Kevin was gone a lot. Upon arriving in Germany, they had all felt a great deal of isolation, but the girls seemed to have adjusted well, because they were involved in high school sports and drama. It was Benjamin who seemed to be suffering the most, as he complained about his school, about the loss of his friends, and about how much he missed his father.

Although Susan explained that she and Kevin were doing OK in this new marriage, she was beginning to feel some strain because of his insistence that they spend most of their spare time alone instead of with the children. She had tried to explain to Kevin that because this was a new lifestyle for all of them, the children needed to be included in everything they did so they wouldn't feel abandoned by her, like they had felt when she divorced and their father had moved out of the home. Kevin shared that he was quite uncomfortable with the children around all the time, and he just wanted to have some quiet, alone time with his wife. He thought things were fine before coming to Germany, but now he felt his wife was spending far too much time with the children and had not adjusted well to the military lifestyle. He also would get quite annoyed with Benjamin when he would ask him to do the slightest thing around the house and Benjamin would ignore him.

Case Conceptualization

This is clearly a couple that has come together without understanding or, perhaps, even considering the changes that were being demanded of the children and, to some extent, them. Although the focus is initially on the young boy who seems to be the one acting out, there are apparent strains on the new couple as well as family formation issues that have never been considered. It appears that the two older girls have a lot going for them, as they are close in age, they appear to have found a place to belong in the school and in their extracurricular activities, and they seem to be looking at this move as a source of adventure and new experiences. Susan and the children had 2 years prior to coming to Germany to learn about the military culture, but as they had continued to live off base in their hometown, the culture shock did not occur until they were required to move to a foreign country and live on a military installation. To deal with her initial sense of loneliness and confusion, Susan put all her energy into the children and into their activities through the school. It was also clear that Susan and Kevin were attempting to maintain traditional gender roles with the children, with Kevin coming on strong as the disciplinarian. This appeared to be a change from their attempts to discipline the children when they lived in the States, but for some reason Kevin had taken over this role once they moved to Germany.

The world of the military was not new, however, to Kevin, and because he had been in the military for many years and had previously been married to another military service member, it had not occurred to him that Susan and the children would struggle with this new lifestyle. It was obvious upon meeting both Kevin and Susan that they were, indeed, committed to their marriage. And although initially Kevin was somewhat reluctant, they eventually both believed that perhaps through counseling they might be able to help Benjamin feel better about the situation so that he could get back on track in school. School records showed that he was a bright child with average to above average grades in his former school.

Upon meeting Benjamin, the counselor was struck by a young man who was unwilling to make eye contact and seemed very uncomfortable being the center of attention. When asked why he thought the counselor might want to see him, he stated that he had no idea and thought it was a pretty dumb idea. He was willing to share that he also thought the school was pretty stupid, most of his teachers were uninteresting, and the idea of living in Germany basically "sucked."

Therapeutic Approach and Process

A basic family systems approach was used for counseling; however, stepfamilies often also benefit from a psychoeducational dynamic, both in terms of learning about living in stepfamilies and regarding the ever-present issues of grief and loss. Because the setting was in a school, it was not the norm to spend a great deal of time with an entire family, so a more solution-focused approach was also incorporated.

The initial work was gathering information about the history of the new stepfamily and how each member of the family, including the two daughters, viewed the family and his or her role in the family. The two daughters were asked to attend the first few sessions, because it was important for them to gain the knowledge about stepfamilies and also for them to be aware of their possible grief and loss issues resulting from the changes they were experiencing in their lives.

The first goal was to help the family members talk about and share their feelings of loss as a result of the changes they were going through. As Susan and even Kevin began to share some of their feelings of loneliness and sadness about leaving friends and family, about the difficulties of living in a foreign country, and about having less time together, the children began to understand that they were not the only ones with confusing feelings. The girls were able to share that they were also feeling a lot of the same feelings but were trying to ignore them and focus on the activities at school so they wouldn't worry their mom. They felt they had to be the model for their brother, and they discovered that by sharing their feelings, Benjamin was able to also admit how angry and sad he was about not being around his father and his friends from his former school.

During the first few sessions, the tasks necessary for healthy stepfamily formation were shared with the family and activities were developed around these tasks. For example, no one had ever asked the children what they felt comfortable calling their stepdad; instead Kevin had just insisted they call him Dad, so he wouldn't have to explain to everyone that they were not his children. This made the children uncomfortable, because, as they explained, they had a dad and Kevin was, at best, just their mom's husband. Benjamin was, also for the first time, allowed to express his anger toward his mom for marrying someone else and making his father leave the home. By helping him understand that no one was trying to take his father away from him and that he should always love and care for his father, his fears about losing his father were somewhat alleviated. It was also helpful for him to know that the family made the necessary plans for him to visit his father during the holidays. As so often happens during the initial stages of stepfamily formation, the children are left with a lot of unexplored and unexpressed feelings and thoughts; it is only when they are given permission to express their fears and hopes do they understand that they will not have to replace their biological parents with these new strangers in their lives.

A suggestion was made that the couple renegotiate their responsibilities at home, with Susan taking back the role of disciplinarian. It was explained, however, that this should be in consultation only with Kevin, so that the children, particularly Benjamin, learn that their mom was not going against Kevin's wishes but rather working together for the sake of the family. Another task was for Kevin to begin to spend time alone with Benjamin, and at Benjamin's request, Kevin began sharing what it was like for him to be in the military. They soon discovered they were interested in the same sports, and Benjamin was able to teach Kevin how to play his video games. Because Kevin had never had children, this was at first quite uncomfortable for him, but being the trooper that he was, he took it on as a challenge and eventually found he was enjoying the companionship.

It was also suggested, almost immediately, that the couple begin to experience some alone time again so not to lose the important feelings they had for each other. Susan soon discovered that she didn't have to spend all her time hauling the girls back and forth to school activities or helping Benjamin with his homework. She instead was able to find time to spend with Kevin but also became involved in the Family Support Program on base to work with other families. In so doing, she was able to learn more about the military lifestyle and the role of an officer's wife.

Because Kevin had not yet been deployed during their marriage, the couple was anxious about how Susan would handle the household and parenting tasks while living in a foreign country upon his first impending deployment. Again a psychoeducational component was incorporated in which Susan discovered the printed materials and Web sites created for families facing deployment. She felt that her knowledge helped her prepare for the upcoming separation.

Therapeutic Outcome

The family, in different combinations, saw the counselor 8 to 10 times over the course of 3 or 4 months. By relieving some of the anxieties Benjamin was feeling about living in the stepfamily and about his perceived loss of his relationship with his biological father, and then helping him express his sadness and loneliness, the counselor helped him begin to find some positive aspects in his new home. The school counselor was also able to help the teachers work with Benjamin to acknowledge his strengths and begin to find success in his schoolwork. He was persuaded by one teacher to sign up for the JROTC (Junior ROTC) program, and he was surprised by how much he enjoyed learning about and being part of a military program.

Susan and Kevin were able to reconnect as a couple, and most of the frustration and subtle competition Kevin felt with the children was slowly dissipating. His relationship with Benjamin grew, also, so that by the end of the school year, they were quite good friends, even though Benjamin still bristled when Kevin tried to discipline him. Kevin found he could enjoy being with the children and found that his affection for them as individuals was growing. Toward the end of the school year, Kevin was facing a long deployment, so Susan and the children were nervous about the upcoming separation, as well as a trip back to the States to visit family and the children's father. Susan felt she had gained a lot of knowledge and self-confidence, however, and believed that with the strengths the family gained through counseling, she could manage the upcoming changes.

Questions for Discussion

The following questions were designed to be used with both case studies. After reading the presenting problem and background information for each case, think through or discuss with colleagues the following questions. Then return to the case study and compare your thoughts with the therapist's case conceptualization and therapeutic approach and process and the outcome.

1. What would you need to know about military families *prior* to working with this family?
2. What would you need to know about stepfamilies?
3. What specific training or experience would be helpful for you to have to successfully work with this family?
4. What information gathered while reading the chapters of this book might help in your work with this family?
5. What information is not given that you would want to gather early in therapy?
6. What *might* be issues or concerns that could come up in working with this couple and family? In other words, what do you have to keep your ears open for or specifically ask questions about to both rule out issues that could get in the way of therapy and identify issues that you will want to engage the couple or family in working on?
7. How would you work with the children, if at all?
8. How might the fact that both partners had been married before affect counseling?

9. What external resources *might* you want to use or call on for your support and information or for additional support for this family?
10. What general theoretical framework would you want to come from in working with this family?
11. What specific strategies or tools might be effective in your work?
12. How do you see the process of therapy happening?
13. What would you hope for in terms of an outcome?
14. How would you know when therapy is complete or your work is over?

References

About the National Guard. (n.d.). Retrieved June 2, 2007, from http://www.ngb. army/mil/about/default/aspx

Adler-Baeder, F., & Pittman, J.F. (2005, March). *Marital transitions in military families: Their prevalence and their relevance for adaptation to the military.* Retrieved October 6, 2006, from Purdue University, Military Family Research Institute Web site: http://www.cfs.purdue.edu/mfri

Ahrons, C.R. (1980). Redefining the divorced family: A conceptual framework. *Social Work, 25*(6), 438.

Air Force Reserve Command "Fact Sheets." (n.d.). Retrieved May 10, 2007, from http://www.afrc.af.mil/library/factsheets/index.asp

Alaimo, C.A. (2006a, February 21). Army helps couples stressed by Iraq duty. *Arizona Daily Star.* Retrieved February 21, 2006, from http://www.azstarnet.com

Alaimo, C.A. (2006b, April 16). Reports of abuse rise at fort. *Arizona Daily Star,* pp. B1–B2.

Allen, J.G., Keller, M.W., & Console, D.A. (1999). *EMDR: A closer look* (Video and program manual). New York: Guilford.

Alpeter, D. (2007, May–June). Out of the mouths of babes. *Military Spouse, 3,* 30.

American Academy of Child and Adolescent Psychiatry. (2005, May). *Coming home: Adjustments for military families.* Retrieved August 24, 2006, from the American Academy of Child and Adolescent Psychiatry Web site: http://www.aacap.org

American Psychiatric Association. (2000). *Diagnostic and statistical manual of mental disorders* (4th ed.). Washington, DC: Author.

American School Counselor Association. (2003). *American School Counselor Association national model: A framework for school counseling programs.* Alexandria, VA: Author.

Ames, G., & Cunradi, C. (n.d.). *Alcohol use and preventing alcohol-related problems among young adults in the military.* Retrieved April 24, 2007, from the National Institute on Alcohol Abuse and Alcoholism Web site: http://pubs/ niaaa.nih.goc/publications/arh284/252-257.htm

Armitage, D.T. (1984). Legal issues encountered in treating the military family. In F.W. Kaslow & R.I. Ridenour (Eds.), *The military family: Dynamics and treatment* (pp. 18–45). New York: Guilford.

Army Reserve "Mission Statement. (n.d.). Retrieved May 10, 2007 from http://www.armyreserve.army.mil/ARWEB/MissionStatement.htm

Army: Suicide tally in '05 was highest in years. (2006, April 22). *Arizona Daily Star*, p. A11.

Baker, A. (2004). *The Viking.* New Jersey: John Wiley & Sons.

Baldor, L.C. (2007, May 17). Access to YouTube, MySpace cut for military. *Associated Press.* Retrieved June 16, 2007, from http://www.msnbc.msn.com/id/18659901/

Bannerman, S. (2007, March 5). *60,000 marriages broken by Iraq, including mine.* Retrieved March 5, 2007, from http://www.alternet.org/story/48788/

Barron, P.M. (2007). State initiatives ease burden on military children. *The Voice for Military Families, 18*(4), 1, 4.

Berg, I. K., & Steiner, T. (2003). *Children's solution work.* New York: Norton.

Blaise, K. (2006). *The heart of a soldier: A true story of love, war, and sacrifice.* New York: Gotham Books.

Borysenko, J. (2003, February). *Forgiveness.* Retrieved June 1, 2007, from http://www.heartquotes.net/monthly-Feb-203.html

Boss, P. (2006). *Loss, trauma and resilience: Therapeutic work with ambiguous losses.* New York: Norton.

Bowman, T. (2005, February 22). Part time soldiers also battling "pay-gap": Number of proposals could help ease financial pinch. *Baltimore Sun.* Retrieved February 23, 2005, from http://www.baltimoresun.com

Braver, S.L., Ellman, I.M., & Fabricius, W.V. (2003). Relocation of children after divorce and children's best interests: New evidence and legal considerations. *Journal of Family Psychology, 17*(2), 206–219.

Bray, R.M., Bae, K.H., Federman, E.B., & Wheeless, S.C. (2005, March). Regional differences in alcohol use among U.S. military personnel. *Journal of Studies on Alcohol, 66,* 229–238.

Bridges, W. (1995). *Transitions: Making sense of life's changes.* Reading, MA: Addison-Wesley.

Brothers, J. (2006, April 16). Can we get it right this time? When the troops come home. *Parade Magazine,* 4–5.

Carter, B., & McGoldrick, M. (1999). Remarried families. In B. Carter & M. McGoldrick (Eds.), *The expanded family life cycle: Individual, family and social perspectives* (3rd ed., pp. 417–435). Needham Heights, MA: Allyn and Bacon.

Center for Substance Abuse Research. (2007, April 30). *Young adults in the military report lower rates of illicit drug use than civilians; higher rates of cigarette and heavy alcohol use.* College Park: University of Maryland. Retrieved on June 10, 2007, from http://www.cesar.umd.edu/cesar/cesarfax/vol16/16-17/pdf

Ceridian Corporation. (2005, May). The susceptibility of military families to domestic violence, part II. *Military OneSource Update,* p. 2.

Choosing a counselor or therapist. (n.d.). Retrieved August 24, 2006, from the Military OneSource Web site: http://www.militaryonesource.com/skins/MOS/display_print.aspx

Clark, J. (2006, October). [Letter to the editor]. *Counseling Today, 49*(4), 4.

Collins, K. (2005, March). *Dealing with deployment.* Retrieved March 10, 2007, from the American School Counselor Association Web site: http://www.counseling.org/printarticle.asp?article=765

Conroy, P. (1976). *The great Santini.* New York: Houghton Mifflin.

Conroy, P. (1991). Introduction. In M. E. Wertsch, *Military brats: Legacies of childhood inside the fortress.* St. Louis, MO: Brightwell. http://www.brightwellpublishing.net. (Original work published by Harmony Books)

Contemporary debate on women's roles in the military. (n.d.). Retrieved February 20, 2007, from http://en.wikipedia.org/wiki/Women-in-the-military

Couples: Balancing work and life as a dual military couple. (2006). Retrieved August 24, 2006, from the Military OneSource Web site: http://www.militaryonesource.com/skins/MOS/display.aspx

Couples: Building a strong marriage when you're in a stepfamily. (2006). Retrieved February 22, 2007, from the Military OneSource Web site: http://www.militaryonesource.com/skins/MOS/display

Crary, D. (2007, March 4). Military faces tough test as ranks of bereaved grow. Retrieved from *Arizona Daily Star* Web site: http://www.azstarnet.com

Dass-Brailsford, P. (2007). *A practical approach to trauma: Empowering interventions.* Thousand Oaks, CA: Sage.

Decker, J.P. (2004, June 14). At home, budget heroics. *Christian Science Monitor.* Retrieved September 10, 2006, from http://www.csmonitor.com/2004/0614/p14s02-wmgn.html

Defense Task Force on Domestic Violence Reports. (2003). Retrieved March 14, 2007, from http://www.endabuse.org/programs/publicpolicy/files/DTFDVReports.pdf

Department of Defense. (1997, October 21). *RAND report: New opportunities for military women* [News release]. Retrieved February 16, 2007, from http://www.defenselink.mil/releases/release/aspx?releaseid=1451

Department of Defense. (2007, March 31). *Active duty military personnel by rank/grade.* Retrieved May 3, 2007, from http://siadapp.dmdc.osd.mil/personnel/MILITARY/rgo703.pdf

Department of Defense Education Activity. (2007, May 3). *Military parents in Iraq and Afghanistan to view graduations live via Webcasts* [News release]. Retrieved June 15, 2007, from http://www.dodea.edu/pressroom/releasesDisplay.cfm

Department of Defense Task Force on Mental Health. (2007a). *An achievable vision: Report of the Department of Defense Task Force on Mental Health.* Falls Church, VA: Defense Health Board. Retrieved June 16, 2007, from http://www.ha.osd.mil/dhb/mhtf/MHTF-Report-final.pdf

Department of Defense Task Force on Mental Health. (2007b, April 16). *Proceedings of the Task Force on Mental Health Care.* Falls Church, VA: Defense Health Board. Retrieved May 25, 2007, from http://www.ha.osd.mil/DHB/mhtf/meeting/mhtf-transcripts-070416.pdf

DeShazer, S. (1985). *Keys to solution in brief therapy.* New York: Norton.

Dickinson, D. (2007, February 27). *Female troops make task easy: Female soldiers help to uphold respect for local customs.* Retrieved May 20, 2007, from http://www.defendamerica.mil/articles/feb2007/a022707ms2.html

Doka, K.J. (2005, November). New perspectives on grief. *Counseling Today, 47*(5), 56–57.

Donaldson-Pressman, S., & Pressman, R.M. (1994). *The narcissistic family: Diagnosis and treatment.* San Francisco: Jossey-Bass.

Due to debt, some U.S. soldiers aren't being sent overseas. (2006, October 23). *Silver City Daily Press,* p. 2.

Durand, D. (2000). The role of the senior military wife—then and now. In J.A. Martin, L.N. Rosen, & L.R. Sparacino (Eds.), *The military family: A practice guide for human service providers* (pp. 73–86). Westport, CT: Praeger.

Einstein, E. (1982). *The stepfamily: Living, loving, and learning.* New York: Macmillan.

Engels, D.W. (2004). *The professional counselor: Portfolio, competencies, performance guidelines, and assessment* (3rd ed.). Alexandria, VA: American Counseling Association.

Ephron, D., & Childress, S. (2007, March 5). *How the U.S. is failing its war veterans.* Retrieved March 28, 2007, from the MSNBC Web site: http://http://www.msnbc.msn.com/id/17316437/site/newsweek/

Fenell, D.L., & Fenell, R.A. (2003). Counseling services for military personnel and their families. *Counseling and Human Development, 35*(9), 1–20.

Fenell, D.L., & Weinhold, B.K. (2003). *Counseling families: An introduction to marriage and family therapy* (3rd ed.). Denver, CO: Love Publishing.

Figley, C.R., & Nash, W.P. (Eds.). (2007). *Combat stress injury: Theory, research and management.* New York: Routledge: Taylor and Francis Group.

Financial problems: General information. (n.d.). Retrieved May 2, 2007, from the U.S. Marine Corps Web site: http://www.usmc-mccs.org/leaderguide/Personal/Financial/generalinfo.cfm

Fleck, C. (2007). In need of help for kin of fallen soldiers. *AARP Bulletin, 48*(4), 4.

Foa, E.B., Davidson, J.R.T., Frances, A., & Ross, M.A. (1999). Expert consensus treatment guidelines for posttraumatic stress disorder: A guide for patients and families. *Journal of Clinical Psychiatry, 60,* 69–96. Retrieved February 20, 2007, from the Expert Consensus Guidelines Web site: http://www.psychguides.com/ptsdhe.pdf

Freeman, S.J. (2005). *Grief and loss: Understanding the journey.* Belmont, CA: Thomson Brooks/Cole.

Friedman, M.J. (2006). Posttraumatic stress disorder among military returnees from Afghanistan and Iraq [Electronic version]. *American Journal of Psychiatry, 163*(4), 586–593.

Friedman, M.J. (n.d.). *Posttraumatic stress disorder: An overview.* Retrieved October 9, 2006, from the National Center for Post-traumatic Stress Disorder, Department of Veterans Affairs Web site: http://www.ncptsd.va.gov/facts/general/fs_overview.html

Furstenberg, F., Jr. (1979). Recycling the family: Perspectives for a neglected family form. *Marriage and Family Review, 2*(3), 1.

Garamone, J. (2005, November 27). *U.S. military recruiting demographics.* Retrieved February 23, 2007, from the American Forces Press Service Web site: http://usmilitary.about.com/od/joiningthemilitary/a/demographics.htm

Gegax, T.T., & Thomas, E. (2005, June 20). The family business. *Newsweek, 145*(25), 24–31.

Gilligan, J. (1996). *Violence: Reflections on a national epidemic.* New York: Random House.

Gladding, S. (2007). *Family therapy: History, theory and practice* (4th ed.). Upper Saddle River, NJ: Pearson Education.

Gottman, J.M., & Silver, N. (1999). *The seven principles for making marriage work.* New York: John Wiley & Sons.

Hallman, L. (2004, March 12). *Red Cross eases the transition for military families.* Retrieved August 24, 2006, from http://www.redcross.org/article/0,1072,0_485_2354,00.html

Harben, J. (2006, December 18). *Mental Health Advisory Team III findings released.* Retrieved February 23, 2007, from the U.S. Army Medical Command Public Affairs Web site: http://www.armymedicine.army.mil/news/releases/20061218mhat.cfm

Harben, J. (2007, May 4). *Mental Health Advisory Team IV findings released.* Retrieved June 4, 2007, from the U.S. Army Medical Command Public Affairs Web site: http://www.armymedicine.army.mil/news/releases/20070506mhat.cfm

Harvey, J.H. (2002). *Perspectives on loss and trauma: Assaults on the self.* Thousand Oaks, CA: Sage.

Henderson, K. (2006). *While they're at war: The true story of American families on the homefront.* New York: Houghton Mifflin.

Hoare, K.M. (2003). *Pastoral care with military families: An annotated bibliography.* Retrieved February 20, 2006, from http://www.visionlink.org

Hosek, J. (2006). *Iraq and beyond: Promoting reenlistments.* Retrieved February 28, 2007, from the RAND Corporation Web site: http://www.rand.org/publications/randreview/issues/spring2006/reenlist.html

Houppert, K. (2005a, July–August). *Base crimes: The military has a domestic violence problem.* Foundation for National Progress. Retrieved June 10, 2007, from http://www.motherjones.com/news/featurex/2005/07/base_crimes.html

Houppert, K. (2005b). *Home fires burning: Married to the military—for better or worse.* New York: Ballantine Books.

Huebner, A.J., & Mancini, J.A. (2005). *Adjustments among adolescents in military families when a parent is deployed* (Final report of the Military Family Research Institute and the Department of Defense: Quality of Life Office). Falls Church, VA: Department of Human Development, Virginia Polytechnic Institute and State University.

Hull, A., & Priest, D. (2007, June 17). *Walter Reed patients say mental care falls short for vets: Doctor shortage, unfocused methods leave Iraq combat vets frustrated.* Retrieved June 19, 2007, from the MSNBC Web site: http://www.msnbc.msn.com/id/19279863/

Jeffreys, D.J., & Leitzel, J.D. (2000). The strengths and vulnerabilities of adolescents in military families. In J.A. Martin, L.N. Rosen, & L.R. Sparacino (Eds.), *The military family: A practice guide for human service providers* (pp. 225–240). Westport, CT: Praeger.

Jumper, C., Evers, S., Cole, D., Raezer, J.W., Edgar, K., Joyner, M., & Pike, H. (2006). *Report on the cycles of deployment: An analysis of survey responses from April through September, 2005.* Alexandria, VA: National Military Family Association. Retrieved August 24, 2006, from http://www.nmfa.org/site/DocServer/NMFACyclesofDeployment9.pdf?docID=5401

Kaslow, F.W. (Ed.). (1993). *The military family in peace and war.* New York: Springer.

Kaslow, F.W., & Ridenour, R.I. (Eds.). (1984). *The military family: Dynamics and treatment.* New York: Guilford.

Keen, S. (1975). *Beginnings without end.* New York: Harper & Row.

Keen, S. (1983). *The passionate life: Stages of loving.* New York: Harper & Row.

Keen, S. (1991). *Fire in the belly: On being a man.* New York: Bantam Books.

Keith, D.V., & Whitaker, C.A. (1984). C'est la Guerre: Military families and family therapy. In F.W. Kaslow & R.I. Ridenour (Eds.), *The military family: Dynamics and treatment* (pp. 147–166). New York: Guilford.

Kennedy, A. (2004). Emotional cycle of deployment: Information for civilian counselors about the military family. *Counseling Today, 47*(1), 1, 12, 45.

Kozaryn, L.D. (2000, October 11). When violence happens. *American Forces Press Service.* Retrieved February 10, 2007, from http://usmilitary.about.com/library/milinfo/milarticles/bldomesticviolence.htm

Kozaryn, L.D. (2001, March 9). Task force calls for crackdown on domestic violence. *American Forces Press Service.* Retrieved March 10, 2007, from http://www.defenselink.mil/news/newsarticle/aspx?id=45791

Kubler-Ross, E. (1975). *Death: The final stage of growth.* New Jersey: Prentice Hall.

Lowe, C. (2007, March 14). *Mental illness plagues current vets.* Retrieved April 10, 2007, from http://www.military.com/newscenter/0,13319,128465,00.html

Lukach, T. (2005a, July 7). DoD cautions service members against "loan-shark" lenders. *Fort Sam Houston News Leader.* Retrieved May 15, 2007, from http://www.samhouston.army.mil/pao/pdf/07-07-06.pdf

Lukach, T. (2005b, February 18). Terror war highlights need for military medical transformation. *American Forces Press Service.* Retrieved February 18, 2005, from http://www.defenselink.mil/news/newsarticle.aspx?id=25851

Lyons, J.A. (2007). The returning warrior: Advice for families and friends. In C.R. Figley & W.P. Nash (Eds.), *Combats stress injury: Theory, research and management* (pp. 311–324). New York: Routledge: Taylor and Francis Group.

Mahalik, J.R., Good, G.E., & Englar-Carlson, M. (2003). Masculinity scripts, presenting concerns, and help seeking: Implications for practice and training. *Professional Psychology: Research and Practice, 34*(2), 123–131.

Marshall, J. (2006). Counseling on the front line: Providing a safe refuge for military personnel to discuss emotional wounds. *Counseling Today, 48*(8), 1, 32–33.

Martin, J.A. (2000). Afterword: The changing nature of military service and military family life. In J.A. Martin, L.N. Rosen, & L.R. Sparacino (Eds.), *The military family: A practice guide for human service providers* (pp. 257–269). Westport, CT: Praeger.

Martin, J.A., & McClure, P. (2000). Today's active duty military family: The evolving challenges of military family life. In J.A. Martin, L.N. Rosen, & L.R. Sparacino (Eds.), *The military family: A practice guide for human service providers* (pp. 3–24). Westport, CT: Praeger.

Martin, J.A., Rosen, L.N., & Sparacino, L.R. (Eds.). (2000). *The military family: A practice guide for human service providers.* Westport, CT: Praeger.

Martz, E. (2005). *The prediction of levels of posttraumatic stress levels by depression among veterans with disabilities.* Retrieved March 9, 2007, from http://findarticles.com/p/articles/mi_m0825/is_1_71/ai_n13592433/print

Matsakis, A. (2005). *In harm's way: Help for the wives of military men, police, EMTs and firefighters.* Oakland, CA: New Harbinger.

McKay, G.D., & Maybell, S.A. (2004). *Calming the family story: Anger management for moms, dads, and all the kids.* Atascadero, CA: Impact.

McKelley, R.A. (2007). Men's resistance to seeking help: Using individual psychology to understand counseling-reluctant men. *Journal of Individual Psychology, 63*(1), 48–58.

Mejia, Z.E. (2005). Gender matters: Working with adult male survivors of trauma. *Journal of Counseling and Development, 83*(2), 29–40.

Mental Health Advisory Team. (2006, May 29). *Operation Iraqi Freedom 04-05 report.* Office of the Surgeon Multinational Force-Iraq and Office of the Surgeon General United States Army Medical Command. Retrieved February 23, 2007, from http://www.armymedicine.army.mil/news/mhat/mhat_iii/MHATIII_Report_29May2006_redacted.pdf

Mercier, P.J., & Mercier, J.D. (2000). *Battle cries on the home front: Violence in the military family.* Springfield, IL: C.C. Thomas.

Military Child Education Coalition. (2001). *United States Army secondary education transition study.* Arlington, VA: Military Family Resource Center.

Military creates mental health hotline. (2007, January 30). Retrieved April 25, 2007, from http://www.military.com/newscenter/0,13319,123699,00.html

Military faces mental crisis. (2007, January 17). *USA Today.* Retrieved January 17, 2007, from http://www.military.com/newscenter/0,13319,122282,00.html

Military Family Research Institute. (2006). *2005 demographics report.* Retrieved March 8, 2007, from Purdue University Web site: http://www.cfs.purdue.edu/mfri

Military Family Research Institute. (n.d.). *Military families on the move: A guide for helping kids and their families during PCS moves.* Retrieved October 6, 2006, from Purdue University Web site: http://www.cfs.purdue.edu/mfri

Military of the United States. (n.d.). Retrieved October 9, 2006, from the Wikipedia Web site: http://www.wikipedia.com

Military women "firsts." (1996). Retrieved April 10, 2007, from http://userpages.aug.com/captbarb/firsts.html

Military Woman Organization. (2003, June 24). *Women in combat.* Retrieved May 3, 2007, from http://www.militarywoman.org/combat6.htm

Moore, T. (2004). *Dark night of the soul: A guide to finding your way through life's ordeals.* New York: Gotham Books.

Musil, D. (Producer). (2005). *Brats: Our journey home* [DVD]. Eatonton, GA: Brats Without Borders.

Napier, A. (1978). *The family crucible.* New York: Harper & Row.

Nash, W.P. (2007). The stressors of war. In C.R. Figley & W.P. Nash (Eds.), *Combat stress injury: Theory, research and management* (pp. 11–32). New York: Routledge: Taylor and Francis Group.

National Association of School Psychologists. (2001). *Helping children cope with loss, death and grief: Response to a national tragedy.* Retrieved September 10, 2003, from http://ericcass.uncg.edu/vrituallib/stresstrauma/1007.html

National Center on Domestic and Sexual Violence. (2006). *Executive summary: Second annual report on sexual assault prevention and response.* Department of Defense NCDSV. Retrieved November 15, 2007, from http://www.ncdsv.org/images/2ndAnnRepSexAssPrevRespPrgrmExSum.odf

National Center for Post-traumatic Stress Disorder. (n.d.-a). *PTSD and relationships: A National Center for PTSD fact sheet.* Retrieved August 24, 2006, from National Center for Post-traumatic Stress Disorder, Department of Veterans Affairs Web site: http://www.ncptsd.va.gov/facts/specific/fs_relationships. html

National Center for Post-traumatic Stress Disorder. (n.d.-b). *Treatment of PTSD: A National Center for PTSD fact sheet.* Retrieved October 9, 2006, from the National Center for Post-traumatic Stress Disorder, Department of Veterans Affairs Web site: http://www.ncptsd.va.gov/facts/treatment/fs_treatment.html

National Coalition Against Domestic Violence. (n.d.). *Domestic violence in the military.* Retrieved April 25, 2007, from http://www.sc.edu.healthycarolina. pdf/facstaffstu/safely/DomesticViolenceinthemilitary.pdf

National Institute for Trauma and Loss in Children. (n.d.). *Grief and trauma.* Retrieved May 13, 2007, from http://www.tlcinst.org/griefandtrauma.html

National Military Family Association. (2006, December 20). *Statement before the Department of Defense Task Force on Mental Health.* Arlington, VA: Author. Retrieved February 23, 2007, from http://www.nmfa.org/site/docserver/ NMFA_DoD_Mental_health_task_force_12-20-06.pdf?docID=7701

Nicoll, W. (1989). Adlerian marital therapy: History, theory and process. In R.M. Kern, E.C. Hawes, & O.C. Christensen (Eds.), *Couples therapy: An Adlerian perspective* (pp. 1–28). Minneapolis, MN: Educational Media Corporation.

O'Beirne, K.P. (1983). *Isolation matrix: A tool for discovery.* Paper presented at the Military Child Education Coalition conference, 2000, Tampa, FL.

O'Hern-Hall, L., & Williams, F. (2004). Stepfamilies. In O.C. Christensen (Ed.), *Adlerian family counseling* (3rd ed., pp. 59–94). Minneapolis, MN: Educational Media Corporation.

Operation Comfort. (n.d.). Retrieved August 24, 2006, from the Operation Comfort Web site: http://www.operationcomfort.com

Paulsen, G. (1998). *A soldier's heart.* New York: Random House.

Pavlicin, K. (2007). Surviving deployment: Making it through the deployment phase. *Military Spouse, 3*(3), 26–29.

Pavlicin, K. (n.d.). *Deployment extensions: Staying positive in the midst of disappointment.* Retrieved May 25, 2007, from http://www.survivingdeployment. com/DeploymentExtension.html

Peck, A.D. (2007). Career harmony: Balancing a traditional career with a transient military lifestyle. *Military Spouse, 3*(1), 38–42.

Pincus, S.H., House, R., Christenson, J., & Adler, L. (n.d.). *The emotional cycle of deployment: A military family perspective.* Retrieved October 19, 2006, from http://www.hooah4health.com/deployment/familymatters/emotionalcycle. htm

Pope, K. (n.d.). *Resources for working with military personnel and their families.* Retrieved October 5, 2006, from http://www.kspope.com/torvic/war.php

Powers, R. (n.d.). *United States military: Rank insignia charts.* Retrieved May 30, 2007, from http://military.about.com/ad/theservices/a/rankchart.htm

Pryce, J.G., Ogilvy-Lee, D., & Pryce, D.H. (2000). The "citizen-soldier" and reserve component families. In J.A. Martin, L.N. Rosen, & L.R. Sparacino (Eds.), *The military family: A practice guide for human service providers* (pp. 25–42). Westport, CT: Praeger.

Raezer, J.W. (2007). Ensuring quality mental health care for military families: A task for the new congress. *The Voice for Military Families, 18*(2), 1, 4.

RAND Corporation. (2003). *Domestic violence in the military: Implementing collaborative MOUs.* Retrieved March 14, 2007, from the RAND Corporation Web site: http://www.rand.prg/pubs/research-briefs/RB6016/RB6016.pdf

RAND Corporation. (2007, April 12). *RAND study finds divorce among soldiers has not spiked higher despite stress created by battlefield deployments.* Retrieved May 25, 2007, from the RAND Corporation Office of Media Relations Web site: http://www.rand.org/news/press.07/04/12d.html

Rentz, E.D., Martin, S.L., Gibbs, D.A., Clinton-Sherrod, M., Hardison, J., & Marshal, S.W. (2006). Family violence in the military: A review of the literature. *Trauma, Violence and Abuse, 7*(2), 93–108.

Ridenour, R.I. (1984). The military, service families, and the therapist. In F.W. Kaslow & R.I. Ridenour (Eds.), *The military family: Dynamics and treatment* (pp. 1–17). New York: Guilford.

Robertson, R. (n.d.). *Helping children handle deployments.* Retrieved August 24, 2006, from http://www.suvivingdeployment.com/helpchildrenhandle.html

Rodriguez, A.R. (1984). Special treatment needs of children of military families. In F.W. Kaslow & R.I. Ridenour (Eds.), *The military family: Dynamics and treatment* (pp. 46–72). New York: Guilford.

Rogers, J. (2006). Parents of military members—often in the shadows. *The Voice for Military Families, 17*(9), 8.

Rosen, L.N., & Durand, D.B. (2000). Marital adjustment following deployment. In J.A. Martin, L.N. Rosen, & L.R. Sparacino (Eds.), *The military family: A practice guide for human service providers* (pp. 153–167). Westport, CT: Praeger.

Rotter, J.C., & Boveja, M.E. (1999). Counseling military families. *Family Journal: Counseling and Therapy for Couples and Families, 7*(4), 379–382.

Russo, T.J., Dougherty, L.M., & Martin, J.A. (2000). Military spouse employment: Challenges and opportunities. In J.A. Martin, L.N. Rosen, & L.R. Sparacino (Eds.), *The military family: A practice guide for human service providers* (pp. 87–102). Westport, CT: Praeger.

Schouten, F. (2004, April 1). No soldier's child left behind: Defense Department school system gets results. *USA Today,* p. 7D.

Schwabe, M.R., & Kaslow, F.W. (1984). Violence in the military family. In F.W. Kaslow & R.I. Ridenour (Eds.), *The military family: Dynamics and treatment* (pp. 125–146). New York: Guilford.

Shay, J. (2007). Foreword. In C.R. Figley & W.P. Nash (Eds.), *Combat stress injury: Theory, research and management* (pp. xvii–xx). New York: Routledge: Taylor and Francis Group.

Shephard, B. (2001). *A war of nerves: Soldiers and psychiatrists in the twentieth century.* Cambridge, MA: Harvard University Press.

Sherman, M.D., Zanotti, D.K., & Jones, D.E. (2005). Key elements in couples therapy with veterans with combat-related posttraumatic stress disorder. *Professional Psychology: Research and Practice, 36*(6), 626–633.

Skipp, C. (2006). *It's tearing families apart.* Retrieved October 11, 2006, from the MSNBC Web site: http://www.msnbc.msn.com/id/15210279/site/newsweek/?GT1-8618

Sklare, G.B. (2005). *Brief counseling that works: A solution-focused approach for school counselors and administrators* (2nd ed.). Thousand Oaks, CA: Corwin.

Soldiers struggle to find therapists who will take their insurance. (2007, June 11). *Silver City Daily Press*, p. 3.

Spouse employment: Military spouse employment; Work that travels well. (n.d.). Retrieved March 24, 2007, from the Military OneSource Web site: http://www.militaryonesource.com/skins/MOS/display.aspx

Staub, A. (2007, January 26). *Breaking gender barriers in war: Female combat medics earn respect from Afghan Army.* Retrieved June 5, 2007, from http://www.ngb.army.mil/news/archives/2007/01/0122607-gender-barrier.aspx

Stern, S. (2001, October 16). New worry: Kids with both parents in combat. *Christian Science Monitor.* Retrieved September 10, 2006, from http://www.csmonitor.com/2110/1016/p1s4-usmi.html

Sue, D.W., Arredondo, P., & McDavis, R.J. (1992, March–April). Multicultural counseling competencies and standards: A call to the profession. *Journal of Counseling and Development, 70,* 477–486.

Sullivan, T. (2006). He's the spouse? The most neglected military spouses: Husbands. *Military Spouse, 2*(6), 52–56.

Survivors take action against abuse by military personnel (STAMP). (n.d.). Retrieved June 3, 2007, from the Military Woman Web site: http://www.militarywoman.org/stamp/htm

TRICARE beneficiaries may seek mental health care if they need it. (2005, January 18). Office of the Assistant Secretary of Defense and the TRICARE Management Activity, Falls Church, VA. Retrieved July 23, 2006, from http://www.tricare.osd.mil/pressrom/news.aspx?fid=13

TRICARE: Choices for the reserve component: An overview. (n.d.). Office of the Assistant Secretary of Defense and the TRICARE Management Activity, Falls Church, VA. Retrieved July 23, 2006, from http://www.tricare.osd.mil

U.S. Air Force fact sheet: Air Force Reserve Command. (n.d.). Retrieved May 30, 2007, from http://www.af.mil/factsheets.asp?fsID=151

Visher, J., & Visher, E. (1996). *Therapy with stepfamilies.* New York: Brunner/Mazel.

Wakefield, M. (2007). Guarding the military home front. *Counseling Today, 49*(8), 5, 23.

Welcome back to the United States. (n.d.). Retrieved August 24, 2006, from http://www.cnn.com/specials/2006/coming.home/resources

Wertsch, M.E. (1991). *Military brats: Legacies of childhood inside the fortress.* St. Louis, MO: Brightwell. http://www.brightwellpublishing.net. (Original work published by Harmony Books)

Whealin, J., & Pivar, I. (n.d.). *Coping when a family member has been called to war: A national center for PTSD fact sheet.* Retrieved March 9, 2007, from the National Center for Post-traumatic Stress Disorder, Department of Veterans Affairs Web site: http://www.ncptsd.va.gov/ncmain/ncdocs/fact_shts/familycoping.html?printable-template=factsheet

Williams, D.L. (2005). *Interviewing and counseling military service and family members in family law cases.* Retrieved August 30, 2006, from http://www.divorcenet.com/divorcenet_2/states/texas/interviewing_and_counseling_military_service_and_family_members_in_divorce

Wood, S. (2006, December 19). *Army releases results of third soldier mental health survey.* Retrieved February 23, 2007, from http://www.defenselink.mil/news/newsarticle.aspx?ID=2468

Worden, W. (2002). *Grief counseling and grief therapy: A handbook for the mental health practitioner* (3rd ed.). New York: Springer.

Appendix A
Organizations and Programs

Air Force Aid Society (AFAS): The mission of the AFAS is to help relieve financial distress of Air Force members and their families and to assist them in financing their higher education goals. http://www.afas.org

American Red Cross: Among its services is the latest in computer and telecommunications technology. The Red Cross allows military members stationed all over the world to send messages to loved ones back home during an emergency or other important events. These communications are delivered around the clock, 7 days a week, 365 days a year. http://www.redcross.org

Army Emergency Relief (AER): In partnership with the Department of the Army, the AER administers funds that provide financial assistance to Army soldiers and their families, as their needs require. This assistance is available to all active duty soldiers and Reserve component soldiers ordered to active duty for more than 30 consecutive days. http://www.aerhq.org

Battlemind Training: This new program by the Army for postdeployment training provides service members with scenarios they might face on their return home as well as show them how skills developed on the battlefield to keep them alive may make their readjustment more difficult. http://www.battlemind.org

Children of Fallen Soldiers Relief Fund: This organization provides college grants and financial assistance to surviving children and spouses of military service members who have lost their lives in the Iraq and Afghanistan wars. The financial assistance program assists disabled service member families as well. http://www.cfsrf.org

Family Advocacy Program: The Family Advocacy Program (FAP) provides services to troops and family members experiencing domestic abuse and child abuse through prevention efforts, early identification and intervention, support for victims, and treatment for abusers. http://www.defenselink.mil/fapmip

Federal Benefits for Veterans and Dependents: This online guide from the Department of Veteran Affairs informs veterans and their dependents of the variety of federal benefits available. http://www.va.gov/index/htm

Iraq Veterans Against the War: http://www.ivaw.net

Legal Information and Resources for Military Personnel and Their Families: The Judge Advocate General's Corps provides online legal information and resources in areas such as family matters, financial issues, insurance, immigration, housing, estates, the Soldiers and Sailors Civil Relief Act, and consumer and contract issues. http://www.jag.navy.mil, http://www.jaganet.army.mil, or http://www.airforce.com/jag

Members of the Military Working for Peace: http://www.veteransforpeace.org

Military Brats Registry: This is a registry brats can use to locate each other. http://www.militarybrat.com

Military Families Speak Out: This is an organization of people who are opposed to the war and who have relatives or loved ones currently in the military. http://www.mfso.org

Military HOMEFRONT: The official Department of Defense Web site for reliable quality-of-life information designed to help troops and their families, leaders, and service providers. http://www.militaryhomefront.dod.mil

Military OneSource: Military OneSource offers private counseling in the local community, including couple counseling, parenting information, and issues related to deployment and reunion, provided at no cost for active duty, Guardsmen, and Reservists (regardless of activation status) and their families. The number of visits is limited to six. http://www.militaryonesource.com

Military Sentinel: This joint project of the Federal Trade Commission and the Department of Defense provides information and resources for consumer protection issues that affect members of the U.S. Armed Forces and their families. The information from Military Sentinel can also be used by members of the JAG staff and others in the Department of Defense to help protect armed services members and their families from consumer-protection-related problems. http://www.military-homefront.dod.mil or http://www.consumer.gov/military

Military Woman Organization: This organization was started in 1996 so military women could exchange information unique to their military experience. http://www.militarywoman.org

National Center for PTSD: The mission of this program, which is within the Department of Veteran Affairs, is "to advance the clinical care and social welfare of America's veterans through research, education, and training in the science, diagnosis, and treatment of PTSD and stress-related disorders." http://www.ncptsd.va.gov.com

National Military Family Association: This organization's purpose is to educate military families concerning the rights, benefits, and services available to them and to inform them regarding the issues that affect their lives. It is the only national organization whose sole focus is the military family. Its goal is to influence the development and implementation of policies that will improve the lives of those family members. http://www.nmfa.org

National Personnel Records Center—Military Personnel Records (NPRC [MPR]): This site provides information regarding military personnel and health and medical records stored at the NPRC (MPR). Individuals who are a veteran or next-of-kin of a deceased veteran can now use http://www.vetrecs.archives.gov to order a copy of their military records. http://www.military.com/benefits/resources/military-records/getting-record-of-military-personnel

Navy–Marine Corps Relief Society: This private nonprofit charitable organization is sponsored by the Department of the Navy and provides financial, educational, and other assistance to members of the Naval Services of the United States, eligible family members, and survivors. http://www.nmcrs.org

Operation USO Care Package: This USO program enables individuals to financially support care packages that will be delivered to service members en route to overseas destinations. The care packages contain an assortment of items specifically requested by the military, such as prepaid international calling cards, disposable cameras, toiletries, and sunscreen. http://www.usocares.org

Standard Installation Topic Exchange Service: This service provides information on every Department of Defense installation. http://www.dmdc.osd.mil/sites/sites/html

Tragedy Assistance Program for Survivors (TAPS): The TAPS program is a national nonprofit organization made up of, and providing services to, all those who have lost a loved one while serving in the Armed Forces, including grief counseling referral, case worker assistance, and crisis information, all available to help families and military personnel cope and recover. http://www.taps.org

TRICARE: TRICARE is the official insurance carrier for military personnel. http://www.tricare.osd.mil; for reservists: http://www.tricare.osd.mil/reserve/reserveselect/index.cfm

Veterans for Peace: http://www.veteransforpeace.org

Women for Peace: http://www.codepink4peace.org

Appendix B
Resources for Kids and Families

Channing Bete Company: This company provides fun workbooks for kids, such as *We Get Ready for Deployment, The Deployment Issue, The Reunion Issues,* and *Reunions Are Special.* http://www.channing-bete.com

Children, Youth and Families Education and Resource Network (CYFERnet): http://www.cyfernet.org/hottopics

College Board: Its mission is to prepare, inspire, and connect students to colleges and universities. http://www.collegeboard.com

Coming Home: A Guide for Parents, Extended Family Members or Friends of Service Members Returning From Mobilization/Deployment. This is available from the American Red Cross. http://www.redcross.org

Cooperative Extension Services: This provides materials dealing with issues such as deployment, the Strengthening Relationships Family Program, and Guard and Reserves Family Readiness Programs. http://www.csrees. usda.gov/qlinks/partners/state_partners.html

Department of Defense Education Activity: This organization details information on all schools in the world run by the Department of Defense, including the Department of Defense Dependent Schools overseas and the Department of Defense Domestic Dependent Elementary and Secondary Schools in the United States. http://www.dodea.edu

Department of Defense Military Children and Youth Program: http://www. defenselink.mil/mapcenter/children.html

Kids Health: Kids Health provides up-to-date information on growth, food and fitness, childhood infections, immunizations, and medical conditions from the Nemours Foundation. http://www.kidshealth.org

Military Child Education Coalition: http://www.militarychild.org; including the School Transfer Checklist: http://www.militarychild.org/checklist. asp

Military Family Resource Center: http://www.mfrc.calib.com/policy.htm

Military Money: Magazine: http://www.militarymoney.com, published by InCharge Institute. http://www.incharge.org

Military Spouse: This magazine is published bimonthly. http://www. milspousemag.com

Military Student Web site: This site deals with issues facing military children. http://www.militarystudent.org

Myarmylife2.com: This site offers dad support groups for male civilian spouses of military members. http://www.myarmylife2.com

Operation: Military Kids: This is an Army partnership with 4-H to create support networks through schools. http://www.operationmilitarykids.org

Operation Purple: Operation Purple is a partnership between the Department of Defense and Johns Hopkins School of Public Health and the National Military Family Association that provides free summer camps that are held across the country for children whose parents are deployed. http://www.operationpurple.org or http://www.nmfa.org

Specialized Training of Military Parents (STOMP): STOMP was established to assist military families who have children with special education and health needs. http://www.washingtonpave.com

Talk, Listen, Connect: Helping Families During Military Deployment: This kit funded by Wal-Mart includes a Sesame Street DVD, a parent and caregiver magazine, and a children's activity poster. http://www. sesameworkshop.org/tlc/

Third Culture Kids: This site addresses the issues for those children who straddle more than one culture; the term refers to the fact that the parents may identify with one culture but the child may grow up at least partly in a second culture. http://www.tckworld.com

The Voice for Military Families: This is the newsletter of the National Military Family Association. http://www.nmfa.org

Appendix C
Resources for Mental Health Providers

American School Counselors Association (ASCA): http://www.schoolcounselor.org

Department of Defense Domestic Violence Report: http://www.defenselink.
mil/specials/domesticviolence/

Educational Testing Service: http://www.ets.org

Give an Hour: This organization asks mental health providers to donate 1 hour
per week for a year to assist service members or family members. http://
www.giveanhour.org

Ken Pope: This independent Web site has resources for those working with military personnel and their families. http://www.kspope.com/index.php

Miles Foundation: This foundation has information regarding domestic violence in the military. milesfdn@aol.com, milesfd@yahoo.com, or http://
www.militarywoman.org

Military Mental Health Self-Assessments Program: This program includes information and self-assessments for post-traumatic stress disorder, depression, bipolar disorder, alcohol use and abuse, and anxiety disorders. http://
www.militarymentalhealth.org

National Institute for Trauma and Loss in Children: http://www.tlcinst.org/
tlc/html

Operation Comfort: Operation Comfort is a nonprofit organization that has
been providing free psychotherapy to military families and returning soldiers since March 2003. It consists of a network of more than 450 (as of
April 2006) psychologists, marriage and family therapists, licensed professional counselors, and social workers, who donate their time and expertise
to provide meaning, understanding, and comfort to returning soldiers
and their loved ones. Operation Comfort is a nonpartisan organization,

independent of the military or Department of Defense, and can facilitate a partnership between licensed clinicians and military families in communities across the nation. http://www.operationcomfort.com

Appendix D
Military Service Web Sites

Air Force: http://www.af.mil
Air Force Reserve Command: http://www.afrc.af.mil
Air National Guard: http://www.ang.af.mil
Army: http://www.army.mil
Army National Guard: http://www.arng.army.mil
Army Reserve: http://www.armyreserve.army.mil
Coast Guard: http://www.uscg.mil
Marine Corps: http://www.usmc.mil
Marine Forces Reserve: http://www.marforres.usmc.mil
Navy: http://www.navy.mil
Navy Reserve: http://www.navyreserve.com

Appendix E
Glossary of Military Acronyms

The military is a massive organization of acronyms; in fact there is a joke in the military that it doesn't use acronyms, it uses TLAs (Three-Letter Acronyms). I included the most common acronyms and those used in this book.

ACS	Army Community Services
AER	Army Emergency Relief
AFB	Air Force Base
AG	Adjutant General
AIT	Advanced Initial Training (usually the school a recruit goes to after boot camp)
BAH	Basic Allowance for Housing
BAS	Basic Allowance for Subsistence
BCAC	Beneficiary and Counseling Assistance Coordinator
BH	Behavioral Health
CENTCOM	Central Command
CID	Criminal Investigation Division
CO	Commissioned Officer
COLA	Cost of Living Allowance
CONUS	Continental United States (does not include Hawaii)
DDESS	Department of Defense Domestic Dependent Elementary and Secondary Schools (stateside)

DHS	Department of Homeland Security
DoD or DOD	Department of Defense
DoDDS	Department of Defense Dependent Schools (outside the United States)
DoDDS-E	DoDDS–Europe
DoDDS-P	DoDDS–Pacific
DoDEA	Department of Defense Education Activity (includes DoDDS-E, DoDDS-P, and DDESS schools)
DROS	Date of Rotation From Station
FACS	Family Assistance Center
FCP	Family Care Plan
FRG	Family Readiness Group (Army); see FSG, KSP, KVN
FSG	Family Support Groups (Navy and Coast Guard); like the FRG in the Army
IED	Improvised Explosive Devices
JAG	Judge Advocate General (legal office)
KSP	Key Spouse Program (Air Force); like the FRG in the Army
KVN	Key Volunteer Network (Marines); like the FRG in the Army
LES	Leave and Earnings Statement
MEDCOM	U.S. Army Medical Command
MH	Mental Health
MI	Military Intelligence
MLFC	Military and Family Life Consultant
MOS	Military Occupational Specialty
MP	Military Police
MRE	Meals, Ready to Eat
MTF	Military Treatment Facility (can be a hospital, clinic, or mental health center)
NCO	Noncommissioned Officer, or noncom
NGFP	National Guard Family Programs
OCONUS	Outside Continental United States (includes Hawaii)
OEF	Operation Enduring Freedom, Afghanistan
OIF	Operation Iraqi Freedom
OT	Occupational Therapists

OTS	Officer Training School
PA	Physicians Assistant
PC	Primary Care
PCS	Permanent Change of Station (where the next assignment is)
PNOK	Primary Next of Kin
PSYOPS	Psychological Operations
ROTC	Reserved Officer's Training Corps
SOP	Standard Operating Procedures
TDY	Temporary Duty Assignment
UCMJ	Uniform Code of Military Justice
UMT	Unit Ministry Team
USAREUR	U.S. Army Europe
VFW	Veterans of Foreign Wars

Appendix F
Military Glossary of Terms

Note: **Most definitions were retrieved from http://www.militaryterms.info.**

Battalion: a unit smaller than a brigade but larger than a company; there are two to three battalions in a brigade

Brigade: a unit smaller than a division but larger than a battalion; there are usually two or more brigades in a division

Commissary: the grocery story on the military instillation

Company: a unit larger than a platoon but smaller than a battalion; there are usually three companies in a battalion

Corps: a unit larger than a division; there are only two corps in the Army

Deployment: a long-term assignment, usually to a combat or war zone

Division: a unit larger than a brigade and smaller than a corps; there are two to three divisions in a corps

Exchange: shopping area on the military instillation; can be called *post exchange* or *base exchange*

Home of record: the state where the service member came from

Installation: the military complex; *installation* is a generic word: *base* is used by the Army, *post* is used by the Air Force, *station* is used by the Navy

In theater: sometimes spelled *theatre*; the global areas of operations, that is, European or Asian theatre

Last four: the last four digits of the service members social security number; all dependents use this for identification

On the economy: living in the community rather than in a housing area within the military installation

Platoon: a unit larger than a squad but smaller than a company; there are usually four platoons in a company

Relocation: move to a new location or PCS

Rotation: how often one changes duty assignments, usually 3 to 4 years, depending on the branch of the service and the rank

Squad: the smallest unit; there are usually four squads in a platoon

Unaccompanied tour: an assignment in which the family is left behind, usually no longer than 1 year

Unit: an organization title of a subdivision of a group or any military element whose structure is prescribed by competent authority

U.S. military academies: only the following are operated by the federal government:

Air Force: U.S. Air Force Academy, Colorado Springs, Colorado
Army: U.S. Military Academy, West Point, New York
Coast Guard: U.S. Coast Guard Academy, New London, Connecticut
Merchant Marines: U.S. Merchant Marine Academy, Kings Point, New York
Navy: U.S. Naval Academy, Annapolis, Maryland
Virginia Military Institute: supported by the federal government but run by the state of Virginia, Lexington, Virginia

Appendix G
Rank and Pay Grade Charts

Commissioned Officers

	Army/Air Force/Marines	Navy/Coast Guard
O-1	Second Lieutenant (One gold stripe) Army – 2LT Air Force – 2d Lt USMC – 2dLt	Ensign (ENS) One stripe, one star
O-2	First Lieutenant (One silver stripe) Army – 1LT Air Force – 1st Lt USMC – 1Lt	Lieutenant Junior Grade (LTJG) One wide stripe, one thin stripe and one star
O-3	Captain (Two silver stripes) Army – CPT Air Force – Capt USMC – Capt	Lieutenant (LT) Two stripes and a star
O-4	Major (One gold leaf) Army – MAJ Air Force – Maj USMC – Maj	Lieutenant Commander (LCDR) Two wide stripes, one thin stripe and one star
O-5	Lieutenant Colonel (One silver leaf) Army – LTC Air Force – Lt Col USMC – LtCol	Commander (CDR) Three stripes and a star

Commissioned Officers (continued)

	Army/Air Force/Marines	Navy/Coast Guard
O-6	Colonel (Silver Eagle) Army – COL Air Force – Col USMC – Col	Captain (CAPT) Four stripes and a star
O-7	Brigadier General (Silver Star) Army – BG Air Force – Brig Gen USMC – BGen	Rear Admiral (lower half) (RDML) Gold lapel with one star and one anchor
O-8	Major General (Two silver stars) Army – MG Air Force – Maj Gen USMC – MGen	Rear Admiral (upper half) (RADM) Gold lapel with two stars and one anchor
O-9	Lieutenant General (Three silver stars) Army – LTG Air Force – Lt Gen USMC – LtGen	Vice Admiral (VADM) Gold lapel with three stars and one anchor
O-10	General (Four silver stars) Army – GEN Air Force – Gen USMC – Gen	Admiral (ADM) Gold lapel with four stars and one anchor

Note: Navy uses Air Force/Army/Marine style rank on the collar.

Enlisted Rank (I have not attempted to describe the insignia for each branch and rank)

	Army	Navy/Coast Guard	Air Force	Marine Corps
E-1	Private (PV1)	Seaman Recruit (SR)	Airman Basic (AB)	Private (PVT)
E-2	Private (PV2)	Seaman Apprentice (SA)	Airman (Amn)	Private First Class (PFC)
E-3	Private First Class (PFC)	Seaman (SN)	Airman First Class (A1C)	Lance Corporal (LCpl)
E-4	Corporal (CPL) 1 Specialist (SFC)	Petty Officer Third Class (PO3)	Senior Airman (SrA)	Corporal (Cpl)

	Army	Navy/Coast Guard	Air Force	Marine Corps
E-5	Sergeant (SGT)	Petty Officer Second Class (PO2)	Staff Sergeant (SSgt)	Sergeant (Sgt)
E-6	Staff Sergeant (SSG)	Petty Officer First Class (PO1)	Technical Sergeant (TSgt)	Staff Sergeant (SSgt)
E-7	Sergeant First Class (SFC)	Chief Petty Officer (CPO)	Master Sergeant (MSgt)	Gunnery Sergeant (GySgt)
E-8	Master Sergeant (MSG) First Sergeant (2SG)	Senior Chief Petty Officer (SCPO)	Senior Master Sergeant (SMSgt) First Senior Master Sergeant	Master Sergeant (MSgt) First Sergeant (1stSgt)
E-9	Sergeant Major (SGM) Command Sergeant Major (CSM)	Master Chief Petty Officer (MCPO)	Chief Master Sergeant (CMSgt) First Sergeant (Chief Master Sergeant) Command Chief Master Sergeant	Master Gunnery Sergeant (MGySgt) Sergeant Major (SgtMaj)
Special Pay Grades	Sgt. Major of the Army (SMA)	Master Chief Petty Officer of the Navy (MCPON)	Chief Master Sergeant of the Air Force (CMAF)	Sgt. Major of the Marine Corps (SgtMajMC)

Note: There are two types of E-4s in the Army: corporals and specialists; a corporal is a noncommissioned officer, a specialist is not.

Source: Information from Powers, R. (n.d.). Rank Insignia Charts. Retrieved June 1, 2007 from http://usmilitary.about.com/od/theservices/a/rankchart.htm

Index

DATE DUE